Intercultural Engagement Through Short-Term Faculty-Led Study Abroad

Intercultural Engagement Through Short-Term Faculty-Led Study Abroad

A Practitioner's Guide with Multidisciplinary Perspectives from a Public University

Edited by

Priya Ananth and Seok Jeng Jane Lim

Middle Tennessee State University

Intercultural Engagement Through Short-Term Faculty-Led Study Abroad: A Practitioner's Guide with Multidisciplinary Perspectives from a Public University

© 2023 the Authors

Published by the Lightning Series imprint of *MT Open Press* at Middle Tennessee State University · Murfreesboro

Each chapter has been editor and press reviewed. The entire book has also been externally reviewed by experts in the field as part of the quality review process. While the publisher and authors have used good faith efforts to ensure the quality of information in this work is accurate, the publisher and authors disclaim all responsibility for errors or omissions. Use of the information in this work is at your own risk. All URL links worked at the time of publication.

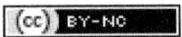 This work is licensed under a Creative Commons Attribution-NonCommercial 4.0 International License.

Identifiers
ISBN (paperback) 979-8-9871721-3-1
ISBN (digital PDF) 979-8-9871721-2-4
DOI: https://doi.org/10.56638/mtopb00223
Keywords: Faculty-led program, short-term study abroad, intercultural competence, global competence, intercultural engagement

Library of Congress Data
Library of Congress Control Number: 2023943895. Full LCCN record at https://lccn.loc.gov/2023943895.
Library of Congress Subject Headings: Foreign study—Administration—Handbooks, manuals, etc.

Press Operations
MT Open Press and Lightning Series are imprints of *Digital Scholarship Initiatives* at the James E. Walker Library, Middle Tennessee State University. https://openpress.mtsu.edu

Copyeditor: Emma Sullivan; Production editor and cover design: A.Miller with cover image adaptions from @corelens and Canva. Typeset in Baskerville, Roboto, and Rockwell.

Digital version (PDF) available at https://openpress.mtsu.edu
Print-on-demand version (paperback) available at https://www.lulu.com/spotlight/mtop

Suggested Citation
Ananth, P., & Lim, S. J. J. (Eds.). (2023). *Intercultural engagement through short-term faculty-led study abroad: A practitioner's guide with multidisciplinary perspectives from a public university*. MT Open Press, Middle Tennessee State University. https://doi.org/10.56638/mtopb00223.

 0823-2341 / Middle Tennessee State University does not discriminate against students, employees, or applicants for admission or employment on the basis of race, color, religion, creed, national origin, sex, sexual orientation, gender identity/expression, disability, age, status as a protected veteran, genetic information, or any other legally protected class with respect to all employment, programs, and activities sponsored by MTSU. More information is available at www.mtsu.edu/iec

Contents

Preface *i*
Acknowledgments *iii*

Section I Understanding the Framework of Faculty-Led Study Abroad Programs

Chapter 1
Introduction 1
Priya Ananth and Seok Jeng Jane Lim

Chapter 2
Supporting Intercultural Competence Through Education Abroad at a Public University: Thoughts from Two Administrators 13
Rehab (Rubie) Ghazal and Robert Summers

Chapter 3
Intercultural Competence and Theoretical Framework 29
Jason Lee Pettigrew and Priya Ananth

Section II Short-Term, Faculty-Led Study Abroad Programs Across Disciplines

Introduction of Case Study Chapters 55
Priya Ananth and Seok Jeng Jane Lim

Chapter 4
Traveling a Thousand Miles: The Role of Education Diplomacy through Study Abroad in Early Childhood Programs 57
Seok Jeng Jane Lim and Karen Nourse Reed

Chapter 5
Creating Intercultural Learning Opportunities in a Study Abroad Japanese Culture Course 77
Priya Ananth

Chapter 6
Developing Learner Autonomy Through a Three-Week Learning Trip in Japan 95
Mako Nozu

Chapter 7
This Isn't What I Expected in Cuba: Challenging the Imaginative Geographies of Students Through Study Abroad 113
James Chaney

Chapter 8
Cultural Immersion in France   129
Nancy Sloan Goldberg

Chapter 9
The Historic Preservation Approach: The Importance of Place and 'Boots on the Ground'   149
Stacey Graham

Chapter 10
From One Music City to Another: The History of Western Art Music in Vienna   167
Joseph E. Morgan

Chapter 11
Intercultural Competency Education Via Food   179
Tony V. Johnston

Chapter 12
International Management: Exploring Educational and Cultural Immersion in the Chinese Environment   195
Sesan Kim Sokoya

Chapter 13
Experiential Learning in London: Evaluation of Study Abroad Learning for Criminal Justice Students   209
Lee Miller Wade

Chapter 14
Covering the Anniversary of D-Day in France: A Journalism Study Abroad Experience   223
Christine C. Eschenfelder

Section III Moving Forward in Short-Term, Faculty-Led Study Abroad Programs

Chapter 15
Conclusion   245
Seok Jeng Jane Lim and Priya Ananth

About the Authors   261
Press Acknowledgements   263
Index   264

Preface

***

When I first took students to Japan in 2016, it was an eye-opening experience for me. Since I had never chaperoned a large group of people anywhere, I had not realized how many different hats I would need to wear during the 4-week program. Also, I had no idea how fulfilling the entire experience would eventually become both for my students and me alike. Even though it was fulfilling, there seemed to be a constant rush to the next deadline with not much time to reflect in between the programs. After taking students abroad for three consecutive years, I felt the need to pause and reflect on the program. Then COVID-19 happened…and the program had to be halted temporarily due to travel restrictions. Around that time, I saw a publication from our university's Office of International Affairs highlighting some of the faculty-led study abroad programs at Middle Tennessee State University (MTSU). I was fascinated to see the variety of programs offered across various academic colleges. While flipping through the pages, I was thinking about a common thread that could tie those programs together, and that is when the thought of intercultural competence dawned.

As research has shown, intercultural and global competencies are relevant to all fields regardless of discipline. Hence started the journey of this book project. After my co-editor Seok Jeng Jane Lim agreed to come on board, there was no looking back. I am forever grateful to Jane not only for being an outstanding collaborator but also for her warm friendship and generosity. Jane and I often joke, but it is true that we could not have completed this project without each other. I am also extremely indebted to all our chapter authors for their excellent contributions and for being highly professional and respectful of our requirements. For me, this was a writing project that I truly enjoyed from start to finish.

—Priya Ananth, co-editor

***

You often hear the saying it takes a village to raise a child; likewise, in this situation, it took a whole village of study abroad advocates to complete this book. When I read the call for chapter contributions for this book in fall 2021, I knew that I wanted to be a part of this book. Having led four study abroad trips to Singapore since 2013, I was excited to share what I know and what the students have gained because of being a part of study abroad. When Priya asked to meet in spring 2022 on a beautiful afternoon to further discuss the book, I had no idea she wanted me to be her co-editor for the book. I was truly honored and humbled by this invitation, and what an amazing journey it has been.

From our initial conversation that spring afternoon, we decided the contributing authors need to have a clear vision of this book. We wanted the authors not only to share their expertise but at the same time grow in the process and unite in this common vision of advocating for intercultural competencies in study abroad. First, we started with a Zoom meeting for interested authors who wanted to contribute, in which we presented the chapter template and timeline. Second, we had a writing day with lunch provided for contributing authors in summer 2022 to help them kickstart their chapter writing, feeding both soul and brain. Third, Priya and I met weekly to plan, coordinate, and write. We also invited any contributing authors to contact us via phone, Zoom, or email regarding any questions they had in the process. Finally, we had an arduous journey of reviewing each chapter numerous times, sending it back and forth to the authors before sending it out to external reviewers and the publisher for further review. This book is indeed a labor of love as each contributing author went above and beyond to give their best.

Of course, I could never imagine myself being a part of this amazing journey without Priya Ananth. I have known her since 2013 when I planned my first study abroad to Singapore, but it was only through the collaboration of this book that we affirmed and grew our friendship. Our weekly meetings became a time for emotional support in our ups and downs as we experienced health issues, work stress, and even death in our families. Priya was a solid rock throughout the whole process, and I am so thankful for having a friend like her.

As you embark on reading this book, we want to invite you to come alongside us as a friend, traveling the world through the book and starting your own journey of encouraging intercultural engagement in your course, class, and institution. We would love to hear about your journey and process, so please write to and share your story with us. (Priya.Ananth@mtsu.edu or Jane.Lim@mtsu.edu)

—Seok Jeng Jane Lim, co-editor

ACKNOWLEDGMENTS

We wish to express our deep gratitude to everyone who was a part of our book project. First, we thank the chapter authors for sharing their experiences, expertise, and course materials. We also thank Dr. Kathleen Burriss, Dr. Olaf Berwald, and Dr. Leah Tolbert Lyons for their valuable feedback on several chapters of the book. We are grateful to Middle Tennessee State University's (MTSU) Dr. Robert Summers (Vice Provost for International Affairs) and Dr. Rehab (Rubie) Ghazal (Associate Vice Provost for International Affairs) for their unrelenting support. We express thanks to our respective department chairs at MTSU, Dr. Olaf Berwald (World Languages, Literatures, and Cultures) and Dr. Eric Oslund (Elementary and Special Education), for their encouragement. We are thankful to our two student assistants, William "Wesley" Birdwell and Tabitha Brown for their conscientious work that helped us submit the manuscript on time. We are most grateful to the *MT Open Press* editorial team for their thorough professionalism and guidance throughout the process. We also want to thank the two external reviewers for their excellent feedback. Finally, we thank our families for their love and for believing in us.

We received funding support for this book project for which we are extremely grateful:

> *Digital Seed Grant* ($2000)
> James E. Walker Library, Middle Tennessee State University, 2022-2023.
>
> *OIA Internal Funding* ($2800)
> Office of International Affairs, Middle Tennessee State University, 2022-2023.

Priya Ananth and Seok Jeng Jane Lim

Section I
Understanding the Framework of Faculty-Led Study Abroad Programs

Chapter 1

Introduction

Priya Ananth and Seok Jeng Jane Lim

> *Twenty years from now you will be more disappointed,*
> *by the things you didn't do than by the ones you did do.*
> *So, throw off your bowlines.*
> *Sail away from the safe harbor.*
> *Catch the trade winds in your sails.*
> *Explore. Dream. Discover.*
> *--Jackson H. Brown--*

This quote by Jackson H. Brown, and commonly attributed to Mark Twain (Quote #571, n.d.), is likely to garner a nod from almost everyone, but especially from those who are engaged in studying abroad–students, faculty leaders, faculty scholars, education abroad administrators, and anyone with an interest in this area. Following the initial disruption of the COVID-19 pandemic, we are embarking on a new phase of rebound and recovery in the field of education abroad. As various study abroad programs in higher education begin a global restart, Jackson Brown's words remind us to not be afraid of taking risks or stepping outside of our comfort zone, but rather to once again boldly express our curiosity to explore and discover the world beyond the known.

This is the right time for study abroad faculty leaders to pause, reflect on, and rethink how they design and implement effective curricula, activities, tasks, and assignments to foster not only content knowledge but also students' critical intercultural and global competency skills and attitudes. This edited volume focuses on short-term, faculty-led study abroad programs in a variety of disciplines and describes the intercultural engagement nurtured by experienced faculty leaders in every aspect of their study abroad course curriculum. For the purposes of this study, the term "short-term, faculty-led study abroad program" is defined as two-to-eight weeks in duration and led by one or more faculty leaders from the home institution.

HISTORICAL CONTEXT

At the national level, the number of U.S. students studying abroad for academic credit has consistently increased in the last 30 years with few exceptions. According to the data collected in the Open Doors Report published by the Institute for International Education (IIE), the number of students studying abroad increased from 70,272 in 1989-90 to 347,099 in 2018-19 (Open Doors, 2022a). These increases were recorded across all durations of study abroad programs, namely long, mid-length, and short-term. In the past three years, however, these numbers have demonstrated a dramatic decrease due to travel restrictions imposed by the COVID-19 pandemic. Beginning in March 2020, study abroad participation came to a halt due to the pandemic. The Open Doors Report showed a seismic 53% decline in 2019-20 over the previous year. Also, in 2020-21, the percentage of students who traveled abroad declined by 91% over the previous year. To understand these figures in perspective, in the last 30 years, the only other year showing a drop in student participation was 2008-09 by a mere 0.8% over the previous year (Open Doors, 2022a). The year 2008-09 saw the Great Recession when the global economic downturn had a direct negative impact on students traveling abroad. Despite the complex challenges posed by the COVID-19 pandemic, the U.S. institutions of higher education have indicated resilience and cautious optimism as the in-person study abroad programs have begun to rebound since summer 2022 (Soler et al., 2022).

According to the Spring 2022 Snapshot on International Education Exchange survey published by IIE (Martel & Baer, 2022), in summer 2022, 58% of the responding institutions were offering in-person study abroad programs, and an additional 31% were offering hybrid programs. The percentage of in-person study abroad programs was reported to increase to 65% in fall 2022 and 64% in spring 2023. Additionally, 83% of the institutions noted an increase in study abroad numbers in 2022-23 compared to the previous year, thus signaling a definite rebound in traditional study abroad programs (Martel & Baer, 2022). While these aggregate percentages provide a general direction regarding national trending in study abroad participation (that is, upwards or downwards), a close-up view of participation by program types based on their duration can offer deeper insight into the rebounding phenomenon. In order to expedite this rebounding effect, this content becomes useful to study abroad faculty leaders and administrators in determining an efficient use of their limited time and finite resources. Toward this objective, a review of the data points for program types based on duration published in the 2022 Open Doors Report becomes relevant. According to this report, 14,549 students from the U.S. studied abroad for academic credit in the post-COVID lockdown year 2020-21. Especially noteworthy is that during that year 64% of the participants opted for short-term programs, as compared with 28% for mid-length (one or one and a half semesters) and only 8% for long-term (academic or calendar year) programs (Open Doors, 2022b). A direct comparison of these data points for the last three years is illustrated in Table 1.1 followed by a graphical representation in Figure 1.1.

Table 1.1. Study Abroad Participation in the U.S. 2018-2021

Category	2018-2019	2019-2020	2020-2021
Total participants on study abroad from U.S. for academic credits	347,099	162,633	14,549
Short-term programs [any semester: eight weeks or less]	65%	16.8%	64%
Short-term programs [summer: two-to-eight weeks]	29.6%	0.6%	40.3%
Mid-length programs [one to one-and-a-half semesters]	33%	32%	28%
Long-term programs	2%	3.7%	8%

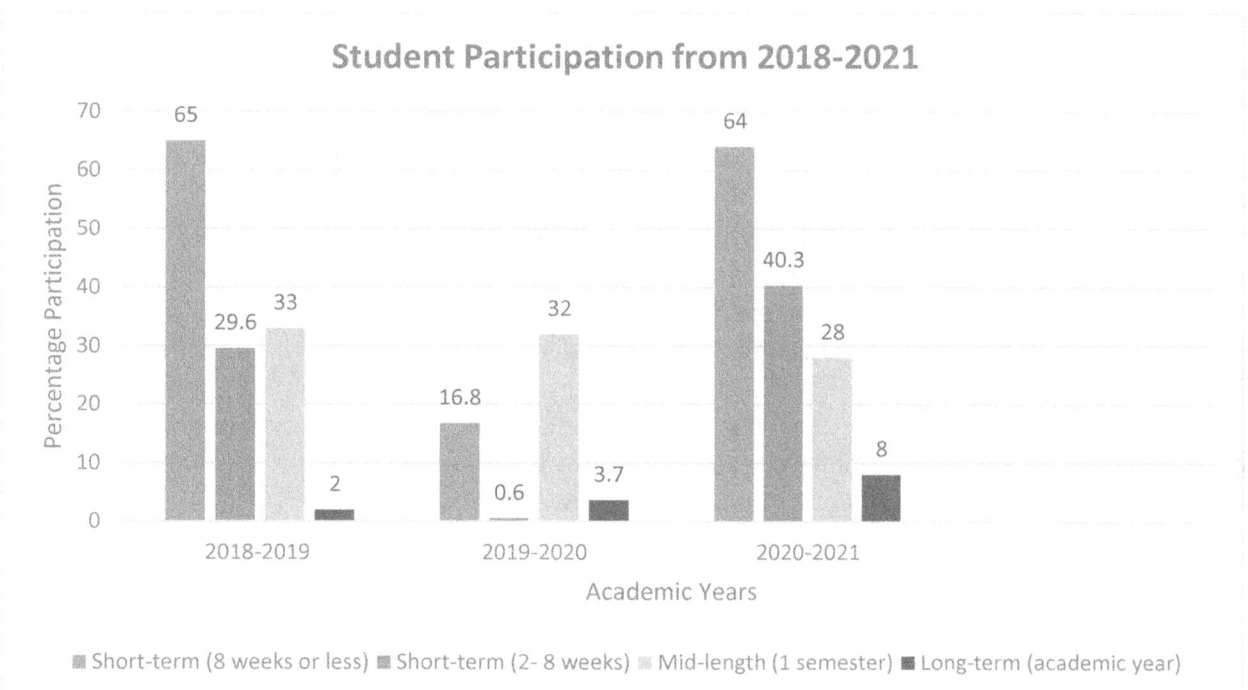

Figure 1.1: Percentage of Student Participation in U.S. Study Abroad 2018-2021

As is evident from the percentage participation in Figure 1.1, even though the total number of participants in study abroad programs in 2020-21 dropped by 91% over the previous year when COVID was at its peak, the percentage of participation, especially in the short-term programs, is comparable with pre-COVID lockdown data in 2018-19. Looking specifically at the percentages for the two-to-eight weeks summer short-term programs, which overlap with most of the faculty-led type of programs, the percentage of participation of 40.3% was higher in 2020-21 than even the pre-COVID lockdown year of 29.6%. These numbers suggest that despite the decline in study abroad participation during 2019-20, universities and colleges in the U.S. are working proactively toward a strong rebound for in-person study abroad programs. A positive momentum is particularly indicated in the two-to-eight weeks short-term summer programs category. According to the Spring 2022 Snapshot on International Education Exchange survey (Martel & Baer, 2022), approximately 90% of the surveyed institutions are offering faculty-led programs in 2022-23, 85% have options for study abroad through third-party providers, and 81% are providing direct exchange programs (Martel & Baer, 2022). Clearly, this is an exciting time for leading and administering short-term, faculty-led programs, making this volume a timely resource for all stakeholders involved with such programs.

With a focus on the design and implementation of short-term, faculty-led study abroad programs and with special emphasis on the integration of intercultural competencies (described later) into the course curricula, the chapter contributions in this book will be useful to both new and experienced study abroad program leaders and administrators to create new programs or reinvigorate existing programs with fresh ideas.

PURPOSE

The broad objective of this edited volume is to offer creative ways of integrating elements of intercultural competence into class activities, tasks, and assignments in short-term, faculty-led study abroad programs. Short-term study abroad programs cannot be mere substitutes for on-campus courses conducted overseas. Rather, through careful planning and delivery, short-term study abroad courses can effectively facilitate the development of students' intercultural competencies. The intercultural competencies, categorized in the areas of knowledge, skills, and attitudes, include characteristics and soft skills such as awareness of self and other cultures, creative thinking, problem-solving, empathy, tolerance towards ambiguity, and withholding judgment. By purposefully embedding these characteristics and soft skills in their course activities, faculty leaders can better assist their students in deepening intercultural and global competencies. These competencies can prepare the students for a changing global work environment and help them manage a more diverse workforce at home.

The purpose of this edited volume is three-fold. The first purpose is to present practice-based models of university courses from multiple disciplines and display a connection between course content and intercultural competencies in the specific context of short-term, faculty-led study abroad programs. The second purpose is to familiarize the readers with learning theories and conceptual models of intercultural competence that have guided the design and delivery of faculty-led study abroad programs in recent years. The final purpose is to spark new ideas and open pathways for future pedagogical innovations that enhance meaningful intercultural engagement in study abroad programs.

OVERVIEW OF THE BOOK

Panorama of Study Abroad Programs

Among the 15 faculty leaders who contributed to this volume, we have covered six of the eight academic colleges across our university, Middle Tennessee State University (MTSU). These six colleges include the College of Basic and Applied Sciences, College of Behavioral and Health

Sciences, College of Business, College of Education, College of Liberal Arts, and the College of Media and Entertainment (as seen in Figure 1.2). This volume serves as a collective resource for faculty across a range of disciplines. The College of Liberal Arts had the highest participation as compared with other colleges. To further internationalize the MTSU campus, these data indicate opportunities for other colleges to integrate study abroad within their existing program.

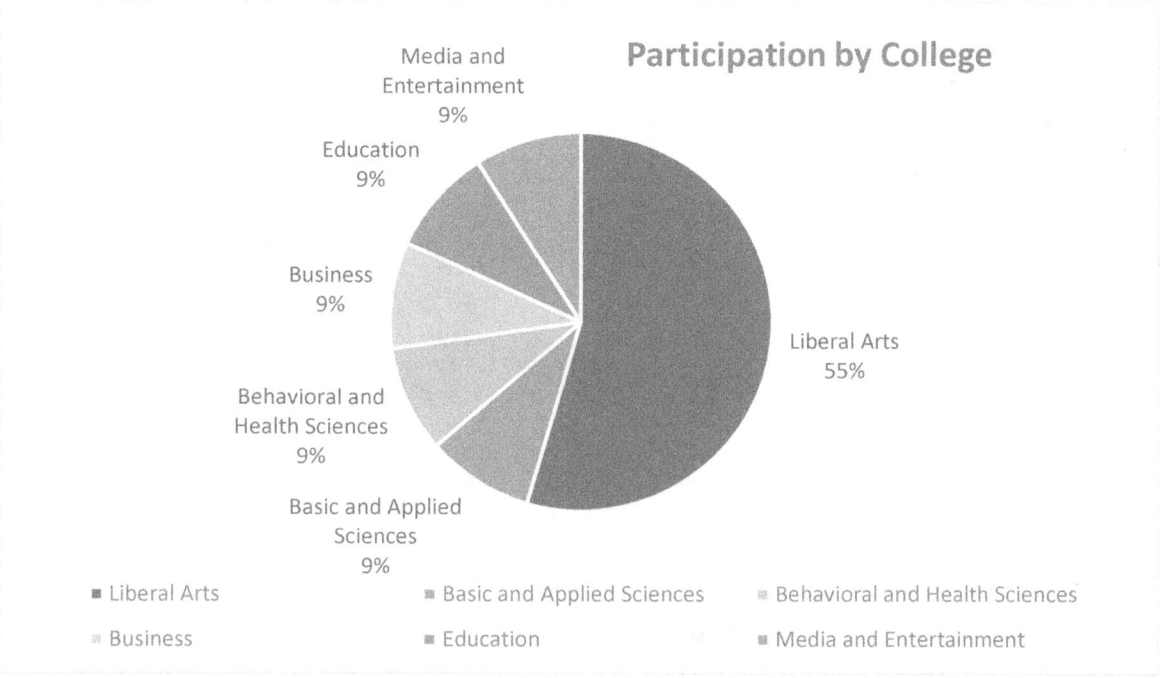

Figure 1.2: Participation by College: Percentage of the book's 11 study abroad case studies by academic college.

Faculty members who led the study abroad experiences described in this volume consist of veteran leaders with 20-plus years of experience as well as novice leaders. Program destinations include Asia (China, Japan, Singapore); Europe (Austria, France, United Kingdom, Scotland); Latin America (Cuba); and South America (Argentina). The participation rates by region represented in this book (see Figure 1.3) remain consistent with the 2020-21 NAFSA study abroad trends, where most study abroad occurs in Europe followed by Asia (NAFSA, n.d.)

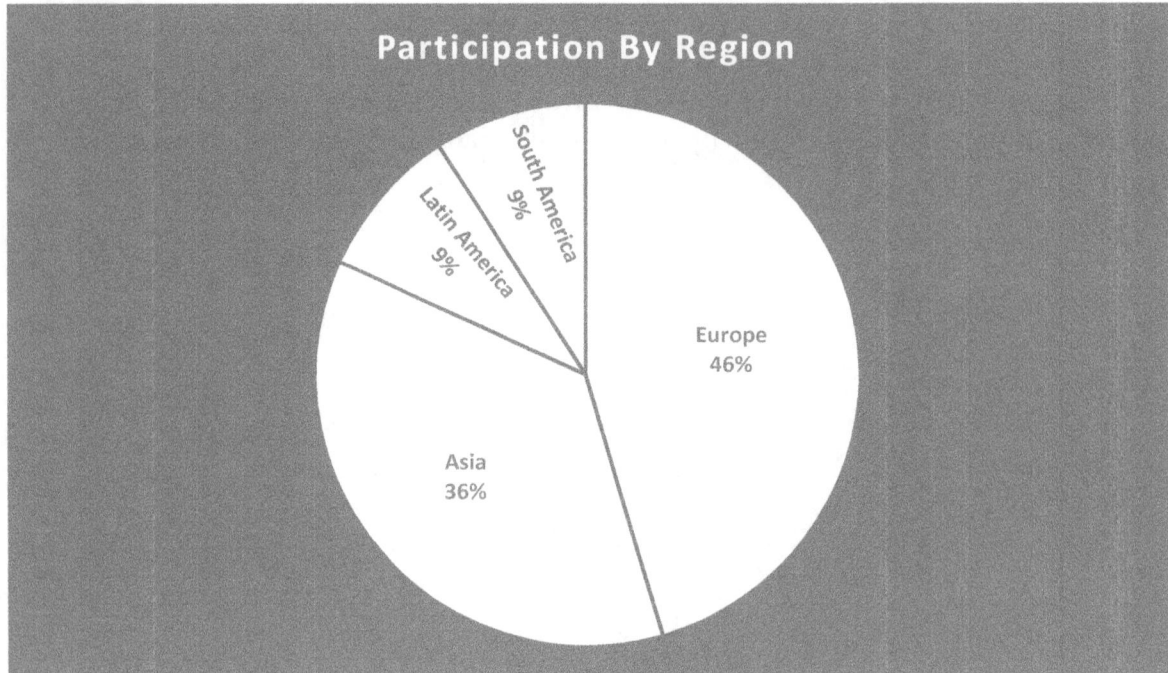

Figure 1.3: Participation by Region: Percentage of the book's 11 study abroad case studies by region of destination.

Delivery models include a mix of those teaching entirely in the country abroad (e.g., Chapter 5) and others with a blended model of in-country and overseas instruction (e.g., Chapter 12). Some of the programs are comprised of stand-alone courses within a single discipline (e.g., Chapter 4), while others identify as interdisciplinary with cross-listed courses (e.g., Chapter 7). Cross-listing a program to multiple disciplines increases the student participation rate and suggests a positive impact in terms of marketing the program.

The duration of travel for short-term, faculty-led programs usually ranges from one-week to a month. Summer is when most study abroad programs occur. Participation numbers for each program range from four to 18 students. The length of the study abroad program determines the costs. For this current discussion, most study abroad programs represented a three-week time frame. Figure 1.4 shows the duration of the study abroad programs that are included in this volume.

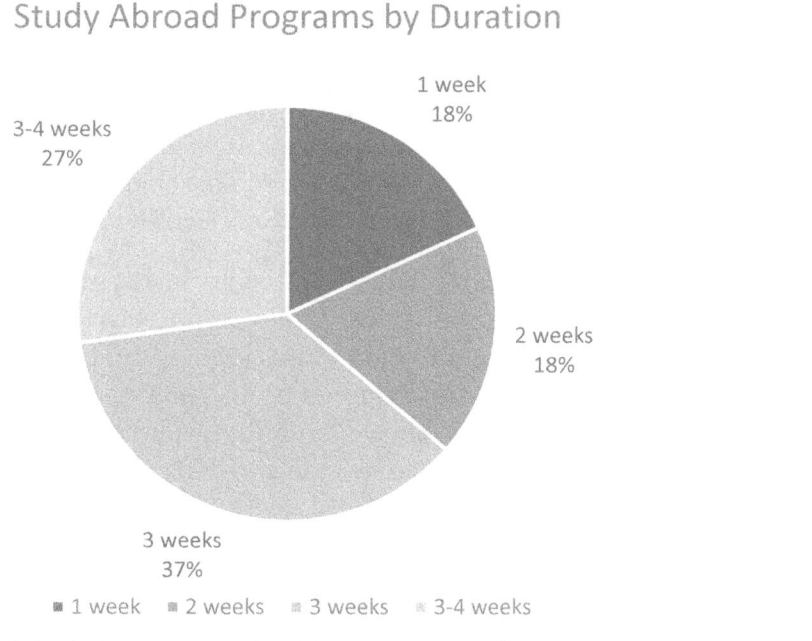

Figure 1.4: Duration of study abroad programs represented in this book.

Overview of Chapters

This book is arranged into three sections. Section I consists of three chapters including the introduction, administrative perspective, and theoretical framework for faculty-led study abroad programs. Chapter 1 (this chapter) by Priya Ananth and Seok Jeng Jane Lim provides an introduction and an overview of the book. Chapter 2 by Rehab (Rubie) Ghazal and Robert Summers offers an administrative perspective on the education abroad programs at Middle Tennessee State University with a focus on faculty support as well as on the importance of developing intercultural competence in students and faculty. In Chapter 3, Jason Lee Pettigrew and Priya Ananth lay out some of the influential conceptual models of intercultural competence as well as learning theories and pedagogical approaches that have guided study abroad facilitators in designing and implementing effective programs in recent years.

Section II showcases 11 contributions from 12 faculty leaders across six colleges (Chapters 4-14). Faculty leaders share details regarding their programs including course objectives, curriculum design, assessment procedures, and student feedback. Regardless of the academic discipline, each of the 11 chapters in this section demonstrates how intercultural competencies were strategically incorporated into the activities, tasks, and assignments of the study abroad curricula. Individual chapters adhere to a case study template detailing a unique aspect of the program, the course information, logistics, theoretical foundations, program itinerary, class activities, intercultural competencies, evaluations, and feedback and reflections from both students and faculty leaders.

In Chapter 4, Seok Jeng Jane Lim and Karen Nourse Reed, representing the College of Education, describe a two-week study abroad program in Lim's native country, Singapore. The curriculum focuses on administering Early Childhood Programs. The content examines early childhood settings and public preschool issues and provides an understanding of the state regulations, standards, and overall framework that impact early care and education in Singapore. A vital component of the program is the inclusion and assessment of intercultural and global competency skills at various points of the curriculum and the post-program data analysis of the competencies acquired by the students. This chapter also demonstrates collaboration between faculty members other than those leading a program.

Chapters 5-10 constitute contributions from faculty leaders in the College of Liberal Arts. In Chapter 5, Priya Ananth introduces ways to design a short-term, faculty-led study abroad program in Japan that purposefully integrates intercultural competencies in a course on traditional and modern Japanese culture. Sample activities, tasks, and assignments illustrate how intercultural competencies are flexibly woven into the curriculum. Student reflections describe gains in their intercultural competencies at the end of the program.

In Chapter 6, Mako Nozu from the University of South Florida shares her three-week summer program *USF Japan: Culture, History, and Society* offered by her home institution. Designed to facilitate successful knowledge of Japan, this course is open to anyone from any discipline and background. The purpose of the course is to nurture the participants' multicultural awareness by traveling across Japan and experiencing a variety of hands-on activities that adeptly incorporate intercultural competencies in knowledge, skills, and attitudes.

In Chapter 7, James Chaney describes his two-week study abroad program that explores contemporary Cuba and its geography. Using a thirteen-day study abroad program in Cuba as a case study, this chapter demonstrates how a short-term program designed around service learning, place-based education, and active learning activities can enhance the development of students' critical thinking, intercultural competence, and communication skill set. This course is cross listed with Global Studies and Political Science to encourage more recruitment and satisfy credit fulfillment.

In Chapter 8, Nancy Sloan Goldberg introduces her *MTSU Summer in Normandy* program. For 14 years, this program enabled more than 160 students studying French, both majors and non-majors, to expand their linguistic and cultural competencies through experiential learning. Education opportunities include classroom activities and visits to local cultural sites as well as a homestay with French families. The students used their enhanced linguistic and intercultural competency skills to construct deeper connections and understandings of the people they interacted with and the sites they visited, including service-learning experiences.

In Chapter 9, Stacey Graham describes *MTSU in Scotland*, a three-week study abroad program that provides an immersive experience building students' understanding of historic preservation while fostering intercultural competencies. Through hands-on preservation experiences, particularly through Edinburgh World Heritage and the City of Edinburgh Council, students attain both discipline-specific knowledge as well as intercultural competency skills. This discussion offers unique insights as it was conducted both before and after the COVID-19 pandemic lockdown.

In Chapter 10, Joseph E. Morgan describes his short-term study abroad program in music history conducted in Vienna, Austria. This educational experience describes an ideal synthesis of experiential, integrative, collaborative, and reflective approaches to education while aligning the course objectives with key intercultural competencies in order to grow students' understanding and development of new frames of reference.

In Chapter 11, Tony V. Johnston from the College of Basic and Applied Sciences introduces his program *International Agriculture* in Argentina. This chapter highlights the use of food as an opportunity for learning when teaching abroad and discusses ways in which food can be utilized as a powerful tool to develop intercultural competencies. The program has been replicated in different locations and countries.

In Chapter 12, Sesan Kim Sokoya from the College of Business presents his three-week study abroad program to China with content regarding international management and globalization. The model for the program is one week on campus followed by two weeks in China. The comparative management issues facing multinational corporations (MNCs) are included in this program, with special emphasis on the Chinese environment. The course and associated extra and co-curricular activities are designed to sensitize students to the differences in the environments in which MNCs operate as well as to enhance the intercultural competencies of the participating students.

In Chapter 13, Lee Miller Wade from the College of Behavioral and Health Sciences introduces the criminal justice system in London through a one-week study abroad program. This program provides three lectures on campus before departing for the intensive one-week program. The purpose of the London, England Criminal Justice Study Abroad program is to broaden students' understanding of the criminal justice system. This program integrates intercultural competency skills into the course activities and exposes students to the policing, courts, and corrections systems in Britain while providing comparisons with the U.S. system.

In Chapter 14, Christine C. Eschenfelder from the College of Media and Entertainment details a study abroad course describing the 75th Anniversary of D-Day in France from a journalist's perspective. Journalism students experienced newsgathering abroad and developed life skills in other countries. The chapter details a narrative with learning outcomes related to the intercultural competency goals of the course. This chapter also provides a weblink to original media content, a 20-minute documentary produced by the students called "Never Forgotten."

In Section III, Seok Jeng Jane Lim and Priya Ananth discuss the conclusions and provide closing thoughts on intercultural competencies across disciplines. They describe the nine categories of the most prevalent class activities, tasks, and assignments faculty leaders implemented to facilitate intercultural competencies in the preceding 11 chapters. Furthermore, these editors offer practical recommendations to encourage faculty leaders of short-term study abroad programs to promote enhanced intercultural engagement in their courses for the benefit of their students.

Note: A glossary of terms and definitions used in this book is provided in Appendix 1.1 at the end of this chapter.

REFERENCES

Ashwin, P., & McVitty, D. (2015). The meanings of student engagement: Implications for policies and practices. In A. Curaj, L. Matei, R. Pricopie, J. Salmi, & P. Scott (Eds.), *The European higher education area: Between critical reflections and future policies* (pp. 343-359). Springer. https://doi.org/10.1007/978-3-319-20877-0_23

Bennett, J. M. (2008). Transformative training: Designing programs for culture learning. In M. A. Moodian (Ed.), *Contemporary leadership and intercultural competence: Understanding and utilizing cultural diversity to build successful organizations* (pp. 95-110). Sage Publishing.

Deardorff, D. K. (2012). Framework: Intercultural competence model. In K. Berardo & D. K. Deardorff (Eds.), *Building cultural competence: Innovative activities and models* (pp. 45-52). Stylus Publishing.

Harvey, T. A. (2017). Design and pedagogy for transformative intercultural learning. In B. Kappler Mikk & I. E. Steglitz (Eds.), *Learning across cultures: Locally and globally* (pp. 109-138). NAFSA and Stylus Publishing.

Helms, R. M., Brajkovic, L., & Struthers, B. (2017). *Mapping internationalization on U.S. campuses: 2017 edition.* American Council on Education. https://www.acenet.edu/Documents/Mappaing-Internationalization-2017.pdf

Laux, B. (2019). *Intercultural learning in education abroad: Current research trends.* College of Professional Studies. Northeastern University.

Martel, M., & Baer, J. (2022). *Spring 2022 snapshot on international educational exchange.* Institute of International Education. https://www.iie.org/wp-content/uploads/2022/12/SpringSnapshot_Final.pdf

NAFSA. (n.d.). *Trends in U.S. study abroad.* https://www.nafsa.org/policy-and-advocacy/policy-resources/trends-us-study-abroad

Open Doors. (2022a). *U.S. study abroad for academic credit trends.* https://opendoorsdata.org/data/us-study-abroad/u-s-study-abroad-for-academic-credit-trends/

Open Doors. (2022b). *Duration of study abroad.* https://opendoorsdata.org/data/us-study-abroad/duration-of-study-abroad/

Quote #571 (n.d.). Quotery. Retrieved from https://www.quotery.com/quotes/twenty-years-now-will-disappointed

Soler, M. C., Kim, J. H., & Cecil, B. G. (2022). *Mapping internationalization on U.S. campuses: 2022 edition.* American Council on Education. https://www.acenet.edu/Documents/Mapping-Internationalization-2022.pdf

Weimer, M. (2013). *Learner-centered teaching: Five key changes to practice.* John Wiley & Sons.

APPENDIX 1.1

Glossary of Terms and Definitions

Activities refer to the in-class or out-of-class engagements that students are expected to complete individually or as a group. These engagements are directly tied to the academic course content—for example, in-class discussions, teaching a mini-lesson, and site visits.

Assignment refers to assigned work either at home or in-class for testing and evaluation—for example, group research projects, class presentations, and video projects.

Attitudes include empathy, curiosity, discovery, risk-taking, withholding judgment, open-mindedness, tolerance for ambiguity, stepping outside the comfort zone, resilience, patience, respect, flexibility, and adaptability.

Education abroad accounts for service learning, internships, research experiences, and other non-classroom-based activities that take students to other countries and contribute to their learning and development (Helms et al., 2017, p. 3).

Faculty-led study abroad programs are typically short-term programs that are led by one or more faculty leaders from the home institutions.

Formative assessment is the process of providing feedback to students during the learning process. These are often low-stakes activities that allow the instructor to check student work and provide feedback. An instructor writing comments and suggestions on a draft version of a paper is an example of formative assessment (Weimer, 2013).

Intercultural competence refers to a set of cognitive, affective, and behavioral skills and characteristics that support effective and appropriate interaction in a variety of cultural contexts (Bennett, 2008). The following intercultural competency characteristics in knowledge, skills, and attitudes will be used in each chapter. These items have been adapted from Deardorff (2012).

Intercultural curriculum is broadly defined as a structure or framework through which educators intentionally facilitate intercultural learning (Harvey, 2017).

Intercultural learning refers to the teaching and learning methods, activities, and processes that facilitate the development of intercultural competence in a study abroad context (Laux, 2019).

Knowledge refers to cultural self-awareness/understanding, understanding others' worldviews, culture-specific knowledge, and academic content knowledge.

Short-term study abroad refers to study abroad programs, eight-weeks or less, occurring during the academic year as well as all types of summer programs (fewer than two-weeks, two-to-eight weeks, more than eight-weeks) (Open Doors, 2022b).

Skills include creative thinking, problem-solving, leadership, articulation, teamwork, technology skills, listening, observation, interpretation, analysis, evaluation, relation, and communication skills.

Student engagement describes the ways in which students take part in the learning process and the development of their own knowledge. An increase in student engagement is thought to be linked to an increase in student learning. Student engagement is often tied to active learning techniques and student motivation (Ashwin & McVitty, 2015).

Summative assessment is the process of measuring a student's learning at the conclusion of a course (or a portion of the course). Summative assessments are typically associated with grades and can take the form of quizzes, exams, or papers.

Tasks refer to engagements that are not directly tied to the academic course content but need to be completed to accomplish the program's overall goals. For example, using public transportation, going to the grocery store, and using the ATM machine.

Chapter 2

Supporting Intercultural Competence Through Education Abroad at a Public University: Thoughts from Two Administrators

Rehab (Rubie) Ghazal and Robert Summers

With the turn of the century, we have witnessed many changes in the corporate and educational markets. Even before the world was hit by a pandemic that left us all grappling with a virtual work environment in 2019, many industries had virtual teams in place working with members from two or more cultures (Anthony, 2022; RW3 Culture Wizard, 2018). The corporate world, in our opinion, is just catching up with what academia discovered decades ago—the importance of understanding different cultures. Surveying corporate employees in 2016 and later in 2018, RW3 Culture Wizard (2018) found that 89% of the virtual teams in the world included more than two cultures. This has brought to the surface more questions concerning cultural diversity and intercultural communications. Although 76% of the survey participants valued cultural diversity and indicated that it ultimately improved their overall output, around one-fifth believe that at one point, a misunderstanding resulting from cultural differences has cost their companies an opportunity. The corporate world now realizes that the need to build cultural bridges and establish communication is key in understanding today's global economy. Universities, on the other hand, were pioneers in recognizing the importance of international consciousness and established education abroad programs that help to better understand the differences and to build stronger cultural awareness. This chapter will start with a brief overview of the history of education abroad in the United States followed by a section on education abroad at Middle Tennessee State University (MTSU) and how the Office of International Affairs (OIA) has engaged in developing intercultural competencies campus-wide, added faculty incentives, and conducted assessment of the different programs. Finally, we highlight our points of pride and the challenges that we witness with faculty experience.

EDUCATION ABROAD IN THE U.S.: A BRIEF OVERVIEW

One might think that the focus on multiculturalism and internationalization are recent endeavors; however, the interest was sparked in the mid-20th century as a post-world war effort to promote peace and mutual understanding. The League of Nations (later the United Nations) as well as independent nonprofit, nongovernmental national organizations, such as the Institute of International Education (IIE), America Mideast for Educational and Training Services (AMIDEAST), and the Association of International Educators (NAFSA), were influential in the initial efforts. The IIE founders, for example, "believed that we [the U.S.] could not achieve lasting peace without greater understanding between nations—and that international educational exchange formed the strongest basis for fostering such understanding" (IIE, 2022). Other institutions, such as the Council on International Education Exchange (CIEE), the America Council on Education (ACE), the American Association of Colleges and Universities (AAC &U), and the Forum on Education Abroad have supported universities in their efforts to internationalize their campuses through programs, advocacy, and curriculum. Their programs include annual meetings, conferences, forums, and training opportunities for faculty and administrators. Some sessions focus on different elements of designing a study abroad course as well as practical tips on curriculum development and course assignments, while more extensive programs like the ACE Internationalization Lab create a learning environment and guided assessment for institutions to evaluate their efforts over the span of a two-year, cohort-based model. Table 2.1 lists a sample of annual conferences and events with a focus on international education and study abroad.

Table 2.1. Conferences and Events with Focus on International Education / Study Abroad

Organization - Conference	Website*
Association of International Education Administrators - AIEA Annual Conference	https://www.aieaworld.org/
The Forum on Education Abroad - Annual Conference (virtual and in-person)	https://forumea.org/
American Council on Education - ACE Annual Meeting	https://www.acenet.edu
NAFSA: Association of International Educators - NAFSA Annual Conference & Expo!	https://www.nafsa.org/
Diversity Abroad - Annual Global Inclusion Conference	https://conference.diversitynetwork.org/

*These website links were active at the time of publication.

Historically speaking, one key advocacy win for international education was the Higher Education Assistance Act of 1965 which gave institutions the ability to allow students to use financial aid to study abroad (Hoffa, 2007). With financial challenges addressed, different forms of education abroad have emerged and continue to grow, shaping the student learning experience not only at the undergraduate level but also at the graduate level. More federal legislation made federal financial aid explicitly available for study and experience abroad (History and Purposes of Study Abroad, 2012) with the help of selective scholarships such as the Benjamin Gilman International Scholarship, the Fulbright Scholarship, and others.

Education abroad experiences have ranged from short-term, spring co-curricular activities of one-to-two weeks to full course credits over the span of three-to-five weeks, to a full semester or year abroad at a partner institution. In addition, efforts have been made over the years to accommodate majors previously not present in the education abroad programs (De Winter & Rumbley, 2010). These efforts are intended to help diversify the student population (Stallman et al., 2010) and to expand the geographic locations to include developing countries and not just European ones (Ogden et al., 2010) while keenly focusing on knowledge building, course-related activities, and experiential learning.

With regards to the types of education abroad programs based on the length of stay, each serves distinct and important functions. For example, longer education abroad experiences like the ones available through exchange agreements seem to have a stronger impact on the participants' development as globally informed students (Schenker, 2019). Students who studied abroad for a semester reported better outcomes in numerous categories: contributing to class discussion; including diverse perspectives in discussions and assignments; synthesis of ideas; less rote memorization of course material; empathy; acquiring a broad general education; critical thinking; and working effectively with others (Coker et al., 2018).

Like long-term programs, short-term study abroad experiences also allow participants to gain firsthand experience with other cultures and increase their fluency in another language they are learning. This usually leads to higher levels of cultural understanding and raises the participants' global perspective. Both are critical when working with multicultural teams, which many employers look for in potential employees (Gaia, 2015). Short-term programs may also serve as an introduction to those looking to engage in a longer experience, providing students with the societal knowledge and confidence to join another university for a semester abroad (Gaia, 2015). Finally, traveling with a trusted faculty member can be a good first step for students who have never traveled abroad. As they take part in this guided experience, they can build confidence to explore the world beyond the campus (Gaia, 2015). Interest in short-term programs has consistently increased over the past two decades; in the academic year 2004-2005, short-term programs accounted for 51.4% of all education abroad programs, and ten years later in 2014, the percentage increased to 60% (Hulstrand, 2015). Most recently, the Open Doors report for the academic year 2020-2021 released by the Institute of International Education (IIE) stated that despite the general decline in the number of students traveling abroad, short-term programs still accounted for almost 65% of all education abroad programs (IIE, 2022).

EDUCATION ABROAD AT MTSU

For the past decade, MTSU has encouraged students to engage with the world beyond campus. Our mission at the Office of International Affairs (OIA) is to "provide leadership for the comprehensive internationalization of [the university] by fostering growth and development of our international programs and services" (MTSU OIA, 2022a). In our Impact Report, we highlight four strategic goals: to equip our students to be successful on an international level; to be a community leader in internationalization; to provide excellent service to all stakeholders; and to be innovative and nimble in our internationalization efforts (MTSU OIA, 2022a). Since 2016, we have had roughly 1,300 students participate in Faculty-led Signature Programs and 220 in long-term exchange programs, providing over a million dollars in scholarships (MTSU OIA, 2022a). In the past five years, more MTSU students have opted for short-term signature programs as compared to longer-term programs. In 2021-2022, 221 out of 265 students went on MTSU faculty-led programs, constituting 84% and the remaining 16% opted for long-term programs.

This ratio is also representative of the distribution of students who decide on a provider program. Figure 2.1 shows the number of students who went on an MTSU Signature Faculty-led Program from 2015 to 2022. MTSU Signature Faculty-led Programs are short-term programs led by MTSU faculty who teach courses specifically designed with an international experience. During the years 2019-2021, programs went from having 19 to zero yearly participants due to the COVID-19 pandemic when traveling was restricted. Out of the 24 countries, the top five destinations at MTSU were: Italy (21%), France (10%), Spain (9%), the United Kingdom (8%), and Austria (6%). Anecdotally, faculty mostly at the associate or full professor level typically lead the programs abroad.

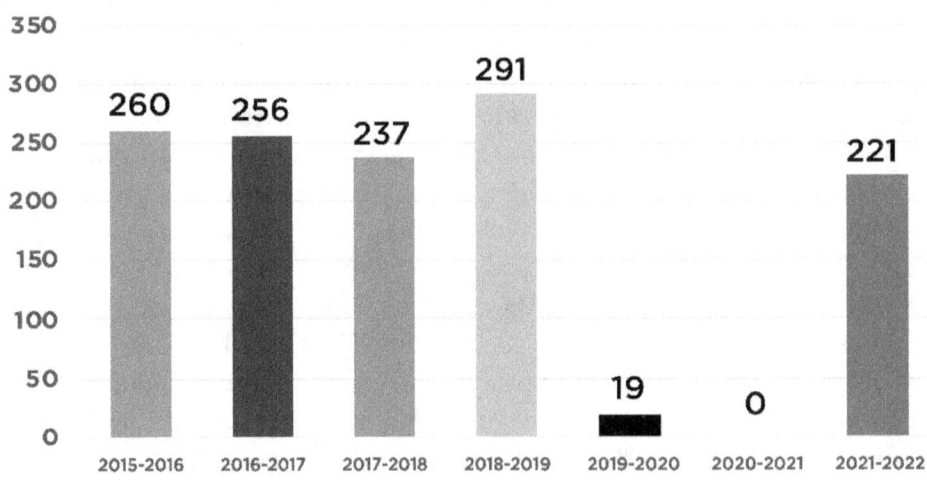

Figure 2.1: Number of Students who Participated in Faculty-Led Programs at MTSU during the Academic Years 2015-2022

Most students participate in study abroad during their sophomore or junior years, regardless of program. It is an MTSU policy not to allow freshmen to participate during their first two semesters; however, they can do a Signature Program during the following summer. Even though most majors do not require an education abroad experience, programs under the Liberal Arts seem to offer flexibility in what students can study overseas. Figure 2.2 shows the number of participants by college from 2015 to 2022.

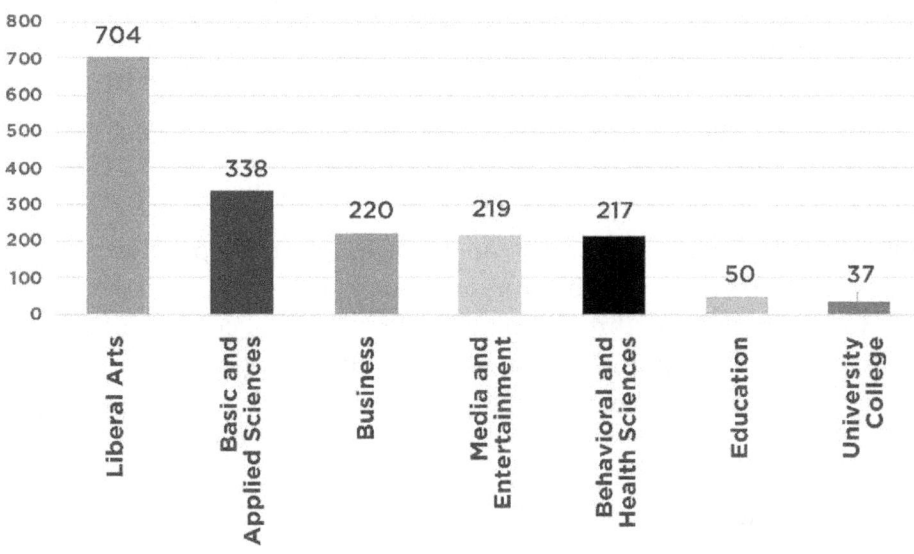

Figure 2.2: Number of MTSU Study Abroad Participants by College during the Academic Years 2015-2022, excluding 2020 and 2021.

An example of flexibility can be seen with the Global Studies Concentration of Global Studies and Human Geography which requires an education abroad experience, and that program accepts nearly everything taken abroad. Other flexible majors include History, Anthropology, Communications, and Sociology. Additionally, area studies degrees, such as Latin American Studies and Africana Studies, are also flexible if the student is studying within their areas. If a student elects to study a language abroad, that is also a straightforward process in figuring out how the credits will fit into a student's degree plan.

PREPARING FACULTY LEADERS FOR SHORT-TERM PROGRAMS

Much of the study abroad research has focused on the students' experiences, preparedness, and development but not as much on the faculty (Matthew & Lawley, 2011). Research on faculty suggested formal professional development and cultural training for those aspiring to lead study abroad programs (Dunn & Wallace, 2004), while others suggested informal training and opportunities for mentorship (Gribble & Ziguras, 2003). Faculty generally agreed that a pre-departure introduction to their students and host culture would be beneficial (Smith, 2012).

At MTSU, interested faculty can attend formal workshops through the Learning Teaching and Innovative Technologies Center (LT&ITC) and the Office of International Affairs (OIA). For example, a workshop titled "Internationalizing Our Campus: It is Closer than

You Think" recently led by one of the co-authors in this volume, Dr. Tony Johnston, along with four MTSU faculty, gave an overview of some of the current partnerships that they established in South America and how to integrate internationalization into the curriculum (Johnston et al., 2022). At another workshop titled "Explore Education Abroad with MT Engage," three MT Engage faculty shared signature assignments and takeaways from their experiences of teaching Education Abroad MT Engage courses in summer 2022 (Houghton et al., 2022). MT Engage is part of MTSU's Quality Enhancement Plan 2016-2021 and seeks to create a culture in which students become actively engaged in their learning (MTSU, 2022).

In addition to the faculty workshops, mentorship programs provide valuable input to faculty who are new to teaching with the world as their classroom. Seasoned faculty can help in the early conceptualization phase, through planning for the trip, communicating with students, parents, host agencies, and campus administrators, and finally program implementation and evaluation. Expert colleagues can help new faculty to decide on the appropriate program length, understand the time commitment, and plan day-to-day activities. Pasquarelli (2017) suggests that faculty must consider the specific knowledge that the students need to understand the context abroad and the process of how learning takes place abroad. In the past, MTSU study abroad leaders have collaborated to identify students' needs and design course structure during the faculty workshops and informal mentoring sessions to create the most rewarding experience.

Faculty Support (Pre-, During, Post-Program)

Preparation for faculty-led study abroad programs begin somewhere between 12 and 18 months before departure and includes coordination with MTSU's Office of Education Abroad (OEA). Table 2.2 shows an example of the timeline for running a summer faculty-led program at MTSU. The information has been adapted from the Education Abroad Handbook (MTSU OIA, 2022b).

Often, developing an education abroad program begins as a discussion among colleagues in the academic departments. Veteran education abroad faculty act as study abroad evangelists, recruiting coworkers. Faculty members also approach the International Affairs team with proposed ideas about leading a class abroad. These conversations lead to faculty members receiving a copy of our study abroad proposal and an invitation to attend one of our interest workshops. These workshops for faculty begin early in the spring semester and prepare faculty for proposal submission. Faculty usually spend the summer semester working on the curriculum and travel activities to include in the proposal.

Table 2.2. Timeline for Summer 2022 MTSU Signature Study Abroad Programs

Timeframe	Action
Summer 2020 to Spring 2021	Faculty meets with VPIA and Director of Education Abroad to discuss possibilities
Summer 2020 to Late Summer 2021	Faculty develops the program
September 1, 2021	Summer program proposal deadline
October 2021	Faculty Financial Meeting to discuss study abroad budget and finance questions – optional
October 2021	New faculty leader program briefing with the VPIA and OEA to discuss the program process
Program approved date to Fall 2021	Faculty works with OEA for program marketing
Program approval date to Fall 2021	Faculty submits Travel Authorization (TA); opens EAR fund
Program approval to February 2021	Faculty recruits, accepts participants, collects deposits
October 2021	Faculty Financial Meeting to discuss budget and finance
October 2021	New faculty leader program briefing with the VPIA and OEA to discuss the program process (if not already attended)
November 2021	Study Abroad Fair
December 2021	OEA Commitment Scholarship Deadline
February 2022	Office of Education Abroad Scholarship deadline
February 2022	Faculty Financial Meeting to discuss program budget and finance questions (optional)
Mid-February to early March 2022	Faculty decides if program will run based on committed participants (deposits & payments)
Late February to early March 2022	Vendor payments begin
March or April 2022	Mandatory MTSU pre-departure orientation
April 2022	Emergency guidelines and procedures meeting with VPIA;
May to August 2022	Faculty leads MTSU Signature Program

The proposal (MTSU OIA, 2022c) contains sections where faculty leaders provide a background and rationale for the program, a detailed day-by-day itinerary, a risk mitigation plan, a comprehensive budget, a complete academic syllabus, and a faculty vita. A completed proposal is reviewed by the departmental chairperson, the director of education abroad, the college dean, and the vice provost for International Affairs. The chairperson and deans focus on issues of academic integrity while the director of Education Abroad and the vice provost of International Affairs focus on budgeting, logistics, and risk mitigation. Program approvals for summer programs occur in mid-fall. Appendix 2.1 shows a flow chart of the suggested process for proposal submission and pre-departure key events.

The content of education abroad workshops for faculty focuses mainly on marketing, finances, and risk mitigation. Staff in the Office of Education Abroad help faculty to understand how to effectively market their programs. Notably, all program leaders are given a budget of $300 to support their marketing efforts. Representatives from the university's business office attend and present on financial policy, travel authorization forms, and issues of payment and reimbursement. The director of education abroad speaks to issues of health, safety, and risk management. We pay special attention to student health insurance, the overseas network of providers, and how one accesses health services.

Before departure, both faculty and students attend a pre-departure orientation. The faculty orientation mostly focuses on health and safety measures and the process of handling and reporting emergency cases. During the student orientation, the staff gives an overview of what to expect at the airport when leaving and upon arrival, how to handle transportation and money exchange, and where to go in case of emergency. We also put the students into groups by program and discuss cultural norms and customs to lessen the potential culture shock and help students avoid embarrassment. The idea highlighted is that intercultural learning is an experience that starts before the program begins and continues beyond the end of the program.

During the program, the support that the Office of International Affairs offers is limited to cases of emergency, such as natural disasters, civil unrest, and, as we all witnessed, a global pandemic. In other rare cases, a senior administrator might need to travel to help with an emergency case where a student or faculty member got sick or was hospitalized. After the program concludes, the office usually sends an end-of-program evaluation form and summarizes the findings to share with the program leaders, the department chairs, and college deans. They also schedule optional meetings with faculty to go over lessons learned.

Faculty Incentives

Preparing for and running a study abroad program can be a daunting task; however, it is also rewarding. Most faculty take the opportunity to energize their curriculum and give their students a hands-on experience with the content they deliver. Everyone usually comes back more refreshed and motivated with new ideas and insights. To encourage faculty at MTSU, the provost offers the Faculty Professional Development Travel Grant, and the International Affairs Office offers travel funds for reconnaissance trips. Additional grant opportunities for curriculum development and course design can usually be obtained through the teaching and learning centers and the department chair and college deans' funds. Anyone reading this chapter would expect faculty recognition to be a straightforward matter. Unfortunately, it is not. Most universities and colleges do not have a formal policy to acknowledge study abroad in the tenure and promotion process. Faculty sometimes get creative by including the extensive work of preparing and leading a study abroad program in the service section of the tenure and promotion portfolio.

BUILD INTERCULTURAL COMPETENCIES CAMPUS-WIDE

OIA leadership has a strong commitment to having our students develop intercultural competence. We firmly believe that one of the best ways for this to occur is for all our students to have an international experience. By doing this, the university equips our students to be successful on an international level. After they come back, we also encourage them to join one of the on-campus communities that International Affairs supports: the International Buddy Program, the Global Ambassador Program, or the Student Society for International Education.

While one of the most poignant ways for students to have an international experience is through study abroad, there are also other, more accessible ways for students to have international experiences and develop intercultural competence. For instance, there are several MTSU centers that play a key role in advancing the internationalization agenda, including the Center for Chinese Music and Culture, the Middle East Center, and the Center for Asian Studies. International Affairs, in collaboration with community organizations and MTSU centers, hosts a region-wide international festival every year. This takes place on campus and students are given free admission. Also, we host a variety of events where we celebrate multicultural holidays. In the spring we host *Holi* and provide our students an opportunity to celebrate with their Hindu peers. During Ramadan, we host a campus wide *Iftar*. Attendance at these, and other similar events, has surpassed our expectations, and they are a start toward global learning without traveling abroad or leaving campus.

Olson et al. (2006) define global learning as the "knowledge, skills, and attitudes that enable students to understand world cultures and events; analyze global systems; appreciate cultural differences; and apply this knowledge and appreciation to their lives as citizens and workers" (p. v). We understand that to have a successful experience, it is important to recognize and build intercultural competencies not only for our students but also for our faculty leaders. Hoekje and Stevens (2017) compare the campus community to an ecosystem of interrelated components and state that the faculty are an integral part of this complex social organization. The faculty are the first lens through which students view the outside world. Students consider them role models who display desirable and undesirable intercultural competencies. For example, some of the desired competencies that are valuable when leading a study abroad program are the faculty's appreciation of diversity and their ability to manage the dynamics of difference. This usually requires cognitive flexibility, quick decision-making, and clear communication skills. On the other hand, being stubborn and unwilling to consider alternative ideas and perspectives would defy the purpose of the program and cause it to fail. Since trying to build such competencies can be tricky when working with faculty, we lean on partnering with the LT&ITC and informal peer mentorship to support faculty who need capacity building. Additional programs, such as a community book club, featuring keynote speaker lectures, celebratory events, and specialized workshops, are also being considered for the future.

REFLECTIONS AND CAVEATS

Even with the importance that the university places on education abroad, there remain some challenges to overcome. Given the federal and state guidelines that require grants, scholarships, and loans to be used toward coursework that leads to degree completion, students, faculty, and advisors are particularly concerned with education abroad following a graduation roadmap. This has led to a robust system of checks and balances to ensure that the classes that students take while they are abroad meet federal and state guidelines for aid and degree completion. Moreover, the Office of International Affairs conducts a series of workshops targeted at advisors that help them navigate these compliance issues and therefore protect students' financial aid for study abroad.

As the university has experienced an increase in both incoming and outgoing mobility, we have also experienced an increase in student health issues. Certainly, given the COVID-19 pandemic, physical student health and virus transmission and prevention have been important. At the same time, issues of student mental health have been of concern. Luckily, we have a robust risk mitigation plan that includes accommodations for student mental health. We work with student health services to vaccinate all students who want to be vaccinated, and we can provide vaccinations to exchange students who are not able to secure them in their home countries. We work with the counseling center to offer remote support to students who are quarantined or who are not comfortable with seeking counseling in a public setting. These efforts have proved to be successful and have continued after face-to-face classes and activities have resumed.

LOOKING AHEAD

As we reflect on the opportunities and challenges facing education abroad at MTSU, we find ourselves considering the following important elements:

Communication

Communication is key at all stages of the education abroad experience. This includes communicating with faculty who are interested in establishing an education abroad program. The communication of policies and procedures is vital in ensuring a smooth experience. This takes place over time through different channels, emails, guidebooks, mandatory faculty orientation, and mandatory student orientation and workshops. Communication also includes promotional events and activities, such as the International Education Week celebration with at least one day dedicated to education abroad programs. Other events that draw and indirectly expose the campus community to different cultures and communicate a commitment to cultural understanding include mini talent shows, international scavenger hunts, calligraphy, international movie night, or an African drumming workshop.

Constant Assessment, Monitoring, and Evaluation

Tyson (2017), in discussing the marketing of short-term programs, states what we all know as obvious: if there are no students, we have no program. In assessing the potential success of any program, he recommends using a business model of analysis, the 4 Ps (product, place, promotion, price). Assessing the education abroad program as a *product*, where the program is going as the *place*, the campaign *promoting* the program, and the *price* of the program would give a quick assessment of the value proposition offered to the students, the faculty, and the campus.

As we plan the program, assessing the different program elements before, during, and after the program helps us better understand the benefits, challenges, and lessons learned for future programs. For example, every year, the office reviews the faculty handbook, assessing if there really is a magic number of participants that would provide a robust academic experience while making the program succeed financially. The curriculum committees, chairs, and deans are heavily involved in assessing the academic components, reconciling hours spent face-to-face versus the hours needed as per accreditation requirements.

Most of the time, we use post-program student and faculty reflections and suggestions compiled from student videos, student feedback, student evaluation, and student grade equivalency in our preparation for the next cycle. Different layers of evaluation are also monitored for feedback: course evaluation, faculty evaluation, and study abroad office advising session notes (see Appendix 2.2 for a sample faculty post-program survey). One aspect that we have not thought about in the past that we plan to consider in the future is examining the reasons behind choosing one program type over the other that could be included in future student surveys. The response might help to shed light on the participation of specific short-term programs and in future marketing of the program.

SUGGESTIONS FOR FACULTY AND ADMINISTRATORS

For many who have not led a program abroad or taught a course with an international focus, the time and effort that goes into building a study abroad may be lost. We have all heard others on campus referring to study abroad courses as trips abroad or excursions, but the reality is far from this simple notion. As we conclude this chapter, we want to acknowledge the faculty who have contributed to our robust Signature Programs overseas and thank them for pushing through over the years. We want to remind them and any other faculty who are hoping to run a program in the future that it takes a village and that our office and offices like ours in different universities are there to help. The faculty should not attempt to start this journey or continue this road alone.

In our over 25 years of serving in administrative roles overseeing study abroad, we have seen both effective and ineffective programs. As we think through the effective programs, two things come to mind. Faculty leaders who run effective programs are nimble. They do not become overly concerned when a flight is canceled. They understand that other flights are available. They do not become unruly when the water in their foreign dorm room is not as warm as the shower of their home. They understand that things are different in a foreign country, and they help their students to understand the same. Faculty leaders who run effective programs are also academically centered. They understand that the academic component of studying abroad is the most important part. They work hard to be sure that the context of their trip ameliorates the academics of their class. While the touristic adventure of the travel is important, it is secondary to curricula.

The contrary can be said of ineffective programs. They are sometimes led by faculty leaders who have a difficult time tolerating ambiguity. This leads to problems dealing with the cultural dissonance surrounding international travel. They become irritated when something unexpected happens. Sometimes this occurs before, during, or after travel, and this perspective influences their students. Ineffective programs often focus more on the travel aspect of studying abroad. Ineffective program leaders set up tours that only peripherally address academics. While students may initially be excited by the prospects of a trip abroad, they quickly understand that the purpose of the trip is not necessarily academic.

CLOSING THOUGHTS

As we continue to deliver on our mission to promote comprehensive internationalization at MTSU, we believe that two key strategic goals are particularly relevant to education abroad:

firstly, an intentional effort to support and expand a wide variety of programs such as services to support international internships, noncredit international services, and service learning abroad; and secondly, a campus-wide commitment to provide and facilitate programming that supports intercultural competence, inclusion, acceptance, tolerance, and empathy. Working closely with the faculty, the administrators, and key stakeholders would ensure the attainment of these two strategic goals.

REFERENCES

Anthony, J. (2022). *70 virtual team statistics you can't ignore: 2021/2022 data analysis, benefits & challenges*. Finances Online. Retrieved October 5, 2022, from https://financesonline.com/virtual-team-statistics.

Coker, J. S., Heiser, E., & Taylor, L. (2018). Student outcomes associated with short-term and semester study abroad programs. *Frontiers: The Interdisciplinary Journal of Study Abroad*, *30*(2), 92–105. https://doi.org/10.36366/frontiers.v30i2.414

DeWinter, U. J., & Rumbley, L. E. (2010). The diversification of education abroad across the curriculum. In W. W. Hoffa & S. C. DePaul (Eds.), *A history of U.S. study abroad: 1965 – present* (pp. 55–114). Carlisle: A special publication of Frontiers: The Interdisciplinary Journal of Study Abroad.

Dunn, L., & Wallace, M. (2004). Australian academics teaching in Singapore: Striving for cultural empathy. *Innovations in Education and Teaching International*, *41*(3), 291-304. https://doi.org/10.1080/1470329041001733285

Gaia, A.C. (2015). Short-term faculty-led study abroad programs enhance cultural exchange and self-awareness. *The International Education Journal: Comparative Perspectives*, *14*(1), 21–31.

Gribble, K. & Ziguras, C. (2003). Learning to teach offshore: Pre-departure training for lecturers in transnational programs. *Higher Education Research & Development*, *22*(2), 205–216. https://doi.org/10.1080/07294360304115

Hoekje, B. J., & Stevens, S. G. (2017). *Creating a culturally inclusive campus: A guide to supporting international students*. Routledge. https://doi.org/10.4324/9781315226729

History and Purposes of Study Abroad. (2012). *ASHE Higher Education Report*, *38*(4), 13–26. https://doi.org/10.1002/aehe.20004

Hoffa, W.W. (2007). *A history of US study abroad: Beginnings to 1965*. Forum on Education Abroad.

Hoffa, W.W., & DePaul, S. C. (2010). *A history of U.S. study abroad: 1965-present*. Forum on Education Abroad.

Houghton, S., Saul, T., O'Neill, T., & Myatt, J. (2022, October 19). *Explore education abroad with MT Engage*. Workshop at Middle Tennessee State University, Murfreesboro, TN, United States.

Hulstrand, J. (2015). Best practices for short-term, faculty-led programs abroad. *International Educator*, *24*(3), 58–64. Retrieved from https://www.nafsa.org/professional-resources/publications/international-educator-may-june-2015.

Institute of International Education. (2022). *Open Doors report on international educational exchange*. Retrieved from http://www.opendoorsdata.org.

Johnston, T., Eschenfelder, C., Harden, V., Julian, K., & Zaza, S. (2022, April 19). *Internationalizing our campus: It is closer than you think*. Workshop at Middle Tennessee State University, Murfreesboro, TN, United States.

Matthews, J., & Lawley, M. (2011). Student satisfaction, teacher internships, and the case for a critical approach to international education. *Discourse: Studies in the Cultural Politics of Education, 32*(5), 687–698. https://doi.org/10.1080/01596306.2011.620752

Middle Tennessee State University. (2022, April 5). *About us*. MT Engage. https://www.mtsu.edu/mtengage/about_us.php

Middle Tennessee State University Office of International Affairs (OIA) (2022a). *Annual impact report 2021-2022*. Retrieved from https://issuu.com/mtsumag/docs/mtsu_ia_annual_report_2021-22.

Middle Tennessee State University Office of International Affairs (OIA) (2022b). *Education abroad handbook: MTSU signature faculty-led programs*. Retrieved from https://mtsu.studioabroad.com/_customtags/ct_FileRetrieve.cfm?File_ID=898427.

Middle Tennessee State University Office of International Affairs (OIA) (2022c). *MTSU signature faculty-led education abroad program proposal new and recurring programs*. Retrieved from https://mtsu.studioabroad.com/_customtags/ct_FileRetrieve.cfm?File_ID=611984.

Ogden, A. C. (2010). Education abroad and the making of global citizens: Assessing learning outcomes of course-embedded, faculty-led international programming (Publication No. 3420254). [Doctoral dissertation, The Pennsylvania State University]. ProQuest Dissertations and Theses Global.

Olson, C. L., Green, M. F., & Hill, B. A. (2006). *A handbook for advancing comprehensive internationalization: What institutions can do and what students should learn*. American Council on Education. https://goglobal.fiu.edu/_assets/docs/handbook_advancing-comprehensive-internationalization.pdf

Pasquarelli, S. L. (2018). Laying the groundwork: Faculty preparation for teaching abroad. In Pasquarelli, S. L., Cole, R. A., & Tyson, M. J. (Eds.), *Passport to change: Designing academically sound, culturally relevant, short-term, faculty-led study abroad programs* (pp. 201-221). Stylus Publishing.

RW3 Cultural Wizard: Become One. (2018). *Virtual teams survey: 2018 executive brief*. CultureWizard. Retrieved October 5, 2022, from https://cdn2.hubspot.net/hubfs/466336/Virtual%20Teams%20Survey-Executive%20Summary--Final%20(2018).pdf.

Schenker, T. (2019). Fostering global competence through short-term study abroad. *Frontiers: The Interdisciplinary Journal of Study Abroad, 31*(2), 139–157. https://doi.org/10.36366/frontiers.v31i2.459

Smith, K. (2012). Exploring flying faculty teaching experiences: Motivations, challenges, and opportunities. *Studies in Higher Education, 39*(1), 117–134. https://doi.org/10.1080/03075079.2011.646259

Stallman, E., Woodruff, G. A., Kasravi, J., & Comp, D. (2010). The diversification of the student profile. In W. W. Hoffa & S. C. DePaul (Eds.), *A history of US study abroad: 1965-present*. Forum on Education Abroad.

Tyson, M. (2017). Marketing short-term programs: No students, no program. In Pasquarelli, S. L., Cole, R. A., & Tyson, M. J. (Eds.), *Passport to change: Designing academically sound, culturally relevant, short-term, faculty-led study abroad programs* (pp. 183-200). Stylus Publishing.

APPENDICES

Appendix 2.1 Proposal Submission and Pre-departure Preparation

This is a suggested, sequential workflow for the study abroad program proposal and departure preparation requirements.

1. Read through the Signature Faculty-led Program Handbook.
2. Review the existing study abroad programs to ensure a program will not be duplicated (see the Office of Education website at https://mtsu.studioabroad.com/. From there, select Program Search or contact the OEA since some programs may not be listed at the time of search).
3. Meet with the Director of Education Abroad.
4. Attend planning workshops, review the website, and find the documents which need to be submitted for an MTSU signature Study Abroad Program.
5. Submit the proposal.
6. Market the program during Study Abroad Fair and through marketing materials.
7. Follow up with students: course registration, scholarship application, financial aid, etc.
8. Pre-departure orientation for faculty and students.
9. Finalize last-minute details with the Office of Education Abroad/provider.
10. Run program-safe travels.

Appendix 2.2: Sample Faculty Post-Program Survey

Faculty Leader – Education Abroad Post-Program Survey

Thank you for taking the time to complete this short survey regarding your MTSU Signature Program experience. Your answers will remain anonymous. The data collected here will be used by Education Abroad to improve future programs for your students and Faculty Leader colleagues.

1. The support I received from the Education Abroad Office concerning travel arrangements was adequate.
    - Strongly agree
    - Agree
    - Neither agree nor disagree
    - Disagree
    - Strongly disagree
2. The support I received from the Education Abroad Office concerning finances and contracts was adequate.
    - Strongly agree
    - Agree
    - Neither agree nor disagree
    - Disagree
    - Strongly disagree

3. The support I received from the Education Abroad Office concerning safety and risk management was adequate.
    - Strongly agree
    - Agree
    - Neither agree nor disagree
    - Disagree
    - Strongly disagree
4. What was the best part of the support you received from the Education Abroad Office?
5. How might the support you received from the Education Abroad Office be improved?
6. Is there anything else you would like to add?

We thank you for your time spent taking this survey. Your response has been recorded.

Chapter 3

Intercultural Competence & Theoretical Framework

Jason Lee Pettigrew and Priya Ananth

The purpose of this book is to present practice-based models of courses from multiple disciplines with a focus on the design and implementation of short-term, faculty-led study abroad programs. These programs interweave course content and intercultural competencies. In this chapter, we will examine the research literature on the facilitation and development of intercultural competencies in study abroad programs. Additionally, we will review the foundations of intercultural competence learning theories, conceptual models, and pedagogical approaches that are at the core of many discussions involving study abroad programs.

We will begin this chapter by first presenting a few representative definitions of the term "intercultural competence." Bennett (2008) defines intercultural knowledge and competence as "a set of cognitive, affective, and behavioral skills and characteristics that support effective and appropriate interaction in a variety of cultural contexts" (p. 97). Deardorff and Arasaratnam-Smith (2017) define the terms effectiveness and appropriateness as "the ability to achieve one's goals in a particular exchange" and "the ability to do so in a manner that is acceptable to the other person" (p. 9). Bennett's definition is corroborated by Hammer (2009) as follows:

> Building intercultural competence involves increasing cultural self-awareness; deepening understanding of the experiences, values, perceptions, and behaviors of people from diverse cultural communities; and expanding the capability to shift cultural perspective and adapt behavior to bridge across cultural differences. (p. 116)

Scholars generally agree that intercultural competences have cognitive, affective, and behavioral dimensions. Spitzberg and Changnon (2009) offer the following definition: "Intercultural competence is the appropriate and effective management of interaction between people who ... represent different or divergent affective, cognitive, and behavioral orientations to the world" (p. 7). Deardorff and Arasaratnam-Smith (2017) summarize all the above points in their definition of intercultural competence as "the process of developing targeted knowledge, skills, and attitudes that lead to visible behavior and communication that are both effective and appropriate in intercultural interactions" (pp. 114-115). For the purposes of this book, we will employ Bennett's (2008) definition of intercultural competence which captures the essence of the term well: *Intercultural competence* is "a set of cognitive, affective, and behavioral skills and characteristics that support effective and appropriate interaction in a variety of cultural contexts" (p. 97).

We will consider this definition throughout the rest of this chapter, which is divided into the following parts: foundational learning theories; conceptual models of intercultural competence; facilitation of intercultural competence during study abroad; intercultural competence development within the larger scope of campus internationalization; and pedagogical approaches and best practices relevant in the context of study abroad.

INTERCULTURAL COMPETENCE LEARNING THEORIES

Three learning theories have influenced the design and delivery of intercultural interventions in study abroad contexts in the past few decades. The three learning theories, namely constructivist, experiential, and transformational learning theories, all emanate from a learner-centered approach and maintain that effective learning occurs only when learners intentionally construct knowledge prompted by the transformation of their own unique experiences. These learning theories are at the core of curriculum design and implementation in many study abroad programs in recent years.

Constructivist Pedagogies

The constructivist pedagogies maintain that reality is socially constructed and how we make meaning of the world is highly culturally influenced (Berger & Luckmann, 1966). How individuals will make meaning of these events will differ depending on the cultural groups that have influenced their lives. Intercultural curricula that are constructivist in nature encourage learners to come into awareness of their own processes of making meaning and help them recognize and appreciate how others may make meaning differently (Harvey, 2017, p. 111). In other words, constructivism is based on the assumption that a learner processes new information based on what is previously known (Pasquarelli, 2018, p. 42). Constructivism takes the theoretical position that the world we know is constructed in our mind through our ongoing perception of and interaction with external reality. As our interactions with that reality become more complex, we are gradually pressed to construct more comprehensive worldviews (Stuart, 2012, p. 64).

Vygotsky's (1978) work in the area of mediated social experience alludes to the constructivist view of learning where the role of social reconstruction of knowledge is highlighted in human learning. According to Pasquarelli (2018), the constructivist approach suggests that learning occurs through interpersonal interactions (Vygotsky's mediated social activity) and intrapersonal examination (metacognition and self-regulation) of behavior and knowledge during a learning event. Study abroad programs provide an ideal context for learning derived from mediated social activity, such as community discussions, small- and whole-group dialogues, debates, and community forums to drive us to deeper meanings of what we see, encounter, and experience on a daily basis (Pasquarelli, 2018, p. 47).

Bennett (2012) refers to Thomas Kuhn's (1967) interpretation of constructivism and perspectives in that our "perspective *constructs* the reality that we describe" (p. 99). He goes on to explain that:

> In a constructivist paradigm, the observer interacts with the reality via his or her perspective in such a way that reality is organized according to their perspective. Kelly (1963) suggests that experiences by themselves do not carry much meaning unless people "make something out of them." (p. 99)

In other words, unless one engages with the experience to construct meaningful perspectives, one does not gain much from that experience.

Experiential Learning Theory

Kolb defines experiential learning as "the process whereby knowledge is created through the transformation of experience. Knowledge results from the combination of grasping and transforming experience" (Kolb, 1984, p. 41). Kolb's recursive learning cycle includes the following: undergoing concrete experiences, observing and reflecting on the experiences, forming abstract concepts or generalizations about those experiences, and trying out those generalizations in new contexts.

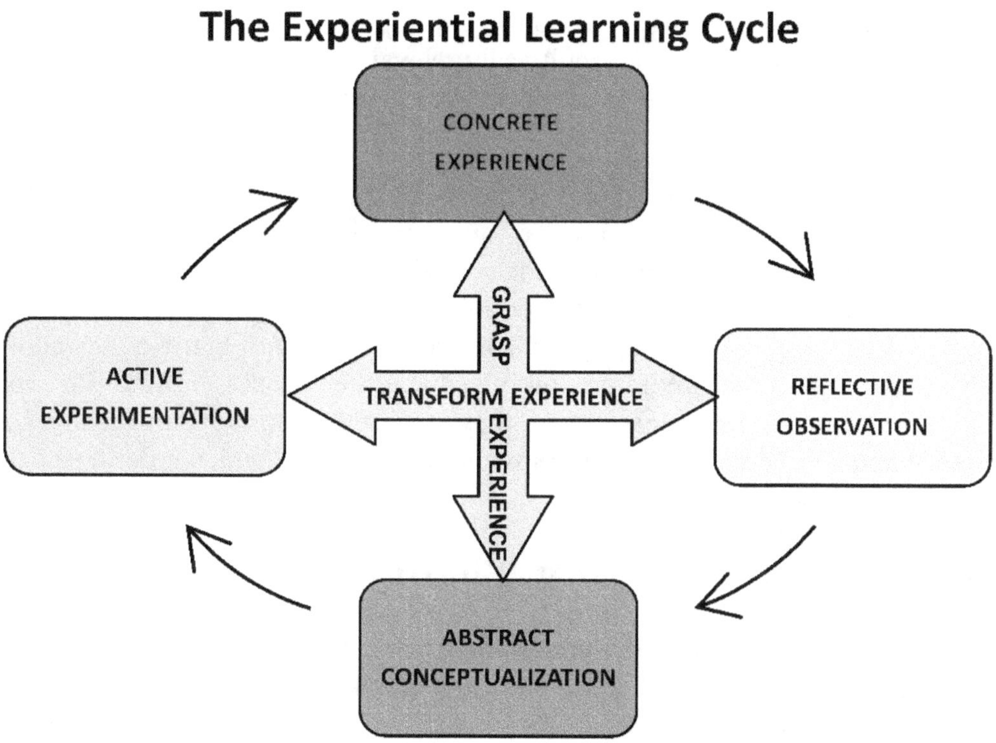

The Experiential Learning Cycle

Figure 3.1: The Experiential Learning Cycle. Reprinted from Student Learning Abroad: What Our Students Are Learning, What They're Not, and What We Can Do About It, edited by Michael Vande Berg, R. Michael Paige, and Kris Hemming Lou. Sterling, VA: Stylus. Reprinted with permission.

According to Passarelli and Kolb, a learner in this learning cycle touches all the bases, experiencing, reflecting, thinking, and acting, in a recursive process that is sensitive to the learning situation and to what is being learned (Passarelli & Kolb, 2012). This postulate is based on the idea that the experiential learning cycle is in fact a learning spiral. When a concrete experience is enriched by reflection, given meaning by thinking, and transformed by action, it becomes richer, broader, and deeper (Passarelli & Kolb, 2012). Continuous recurrences of the spiral learning process lead to more explorations and transfer of experiences to other contexts, thus enabling higher levels of learner development in the form of affective, perceptual, symbolic, and behavioral complexities.

Passarelli and Kolb (2012) explain each of these complexities in the context of study abroad as follows. Affective complexity arises from increasingly meaningful interactions with diverse people, especially when students are attuned to how they feel in the context of their relationships. Increases in openness to experience, sensitivity to beauty and aesthetics, bodily awareness, and the ability to be fully present in the moment contribute to the development of affective complexity. Students develop perceptual complexity as they learn to notice detail, attend to multiple stimuli, and embrace a multiplicity of viewpoints. The ability to locate oneself among an array of external data also contributes to perceptual complexity. Symbolic complexity can be marked by the mastery of a new language. Additionally, symbolic complexity can also be developed as students organize their experience into preexisting knowledge structures and begin to engage in systems of thinking, understanding interconnections among stimuli, analysis, and model building. Finally, the development of behavioral complexity occurs as students experiment with new, culturally relevant practices. Greater behavioral complexity is associated with increased flexibility in executing actions that match the demands of the environment.

The role of the teacher in the experiential learning spiral is that of a facilitator, that is someone who helps the students to become "autonomous, self-directed, and self-regulating learners" (Harvey, 2017, p. 113) and not someone who simply transfers their knowledge to the students. The scholars who support Kolb's experiential learning theory, notably John Dewey, Jean Piaget, Lev Vygotsky, and others, offer a constructivist view of knowledge and learning that emphasizes the importance of organizing the educational process around the experience of learners. This entails meeting students "where they are" in their understanding and building their confidence and competence to the point where they become independent, self-directed learners (Passarelli & Kolb, 2012, p. 150).

Transformational Learning Theory

Mezirow (1991) posits that immersion in uncomfortable or disruptive situations, in tandem with deep reflection, critical thinking, and active learning, enables students to reassess their assumptions about the world and arrive at transformative perspectives with increasingly robust frames of reference (Strange & Gibson, 2017). In other words, in transformational learning theory, a specific disorienting dilemma sparks the need to understand an experience that is different and unexpected (Savicki & Price, 2018). Reflection can be employed to think about an event in an unconventional manner, thus paving the way for the students' meaning frame to expand, which is the definition of transformation (Hunter, 2008).

Regarding transforming perspectives during the learning process, Mezirow (2000) offers useful insights into the ways that emotional responses to crises can serve as catalysts that lead to "frame shifts," a key component at the core of intercultural competence. For Bennett (2012) "the crux of communication … [is] the ability to transcend our own limited experience and embody the world as another is experiencing it" (p. 102). For Hammer (2009), cultural adaptation is the capability of shifting perspectives to another culture and adapting behavior according to cultural context. This type of change in perspective and behavior requires self-reflection on the student's premises, presuppositions, and assumptions regarding the event (and host culture).

Hawks (2021) summarizes the basic constructs of the transformational learning theory by stating that this theory is valuable to: a) cultivate experiential intelligence, holistic learning, and transformative perspectives; b) question and rethink assumptions about one's own worldview; c) be immersed in disruptive experiences and active learning; d) use critical thinking and reflection to foster understanding; and e) transform global perspectives and develop new frames of reference (as shown in Table 2 in Hawks, 2021). In other words, transformative learning theory can be considered beneficial for reframing higher-education pedagogy in times of systemic global dysfunction, such as the COVID-19 pandemic and ensuing study abroad dilemmas.

It may be useful to distinguish between a learning theory and a conceptual model. Often, the terms theory and model are used interchangeably, but we will make a distinction here. A theory is a set of ideas or concepts that "usually describes, explains and/or predicts phenomena" (Picciano, 2017, p. 166). A model, on the other hand, is a "visual representation of reality or a concept" (Picciano, 2017, p. 166). For our purposes, the three learning theories delineated in this section provide theoretical explanations of how intercultural learning occurs in study abroad contexts. The conceptual models in the following section will offer a visual picture of how these theories are put into practice. The learning theories and conceptual models together form the foundational framework within which an academic curriculum is designed and implemented.

CONCEPTUAL MODELS OF INTERCULTURAL COMPETENCE

Terms such as *intercultural competence* trace back to the 1970s, and a wide variety of conceptual models have been developed since the 1990s. These models describe the different elements that contribute to intercultural growth and transformation and can be categorized as compositional models, co-orientational models, developmental models, adaptational models, and causal process models (Spitzberg & Changnon, 2009). In this section, we will touch on a few influential models that are useful for reflecting on intercultural competence development with an eye toward education abroad. For an extensive overview of models, see Spitzberg and Changnon (2009). As Deardorff has observed, "three common themes can be found in most Western models of intercultural competence—empathy, perspective taking, and adaptability" (2009, p. 265).

Byram's Intercultural Communicative Competence Model

An early, influential framework of intercultural competence is Byram's (1997, revisited in 2009) co-orientational Intercultural Communicative Competence Model. This model posits that intercultural competence involves five factors (or *savoirs*): knowledge of self, others, and the processes of interaction (*savoirs*); attitudes that relativize the self and value others (*savoir être*); skills of interpreting and relating (*savoir comprendre*); skills of discovery and interaction (*savoir apprendre/faire*); and critical cultural awareness (*savoir s'engager*) (Byram, 1997, pp. 33-34). In the study abroad context, when we interact with an individual from another culture, we bring with us knowledge about our own and other cultures, about the process of interaction, and our cultural norms of behavior in specific situations. Byram's (1997) model underscores that learners must also be able to employ skills of interpreting and relating in order to navigate intercultural encounters and relate comparable concepts between cultures. Skills of discovery and interaction involve building up new cultural knowledge that is encountered in texts or real-time social interactions. This model also emphasizes the cultivation of productive attitudes such as curiosity, openness, and the readiness to suspend judgment, which will lead to more successful intercultural interactions. Finally, critical cultural awareness involves the ability to critically evaluate and relativize cultural products, practices, and perspectives in one's own and other cultures. Byram (1997) describes "intercultural competence" as the ability to apply these skills and knowledge to communicate in one's *own* language with people from another culture, while "intercultural *communicative* competence" involves doing so in another language (pp. 70-71). For a pictorial representation of Byram's conceptual model of intercultural communicative competence, refer to the original figure 18.1 (Byram, 2009, p. 323).

Deardorff's Process Model of Intercultural Competence

While Byram's (1997) model continues to be an influential touchstone, Deardorff (2006) conducted the first study to document some consensus about how to define and measure intercultural competence as a student learning outcome of universities' internationalization efforts. Deardorff carried out a Delphi study in order to seek consensus among the opinions of 23 intercultural scholars as well as university administrators. The participants identified their top-rated definition of intercultural competence: "the ability to communicate effectively and appropriately in intercultural situations based on one's intercultural knowledge, skills, and attitudes" (pp. 247-248). Based on the elements of intercultural competence that 80% or more of the participants agreed on, Deardorff (2006) generated a compositional model, the Pyramid Model of Intercultural Competence, and a causal process model, the Process Model of Intercultural Competence (Figure 3.2).

Applied to a study abroad context, Deardorff's Process Model emphasizes prerequisite attitudes that are the starting point for intercultural competence development: respect for cultural diversity, openness, curiosity, an interest in discovering new cultures, and the willingness to withhold judgment and accept ambiguity. Students who go abroad without having cultivated these attitudes are less likely to make significant progress. Study abroad professionals also need to provide opportunities for students to acquire new cultural knowledge and develop cultural self-awareness and sociolinguistic awareness.

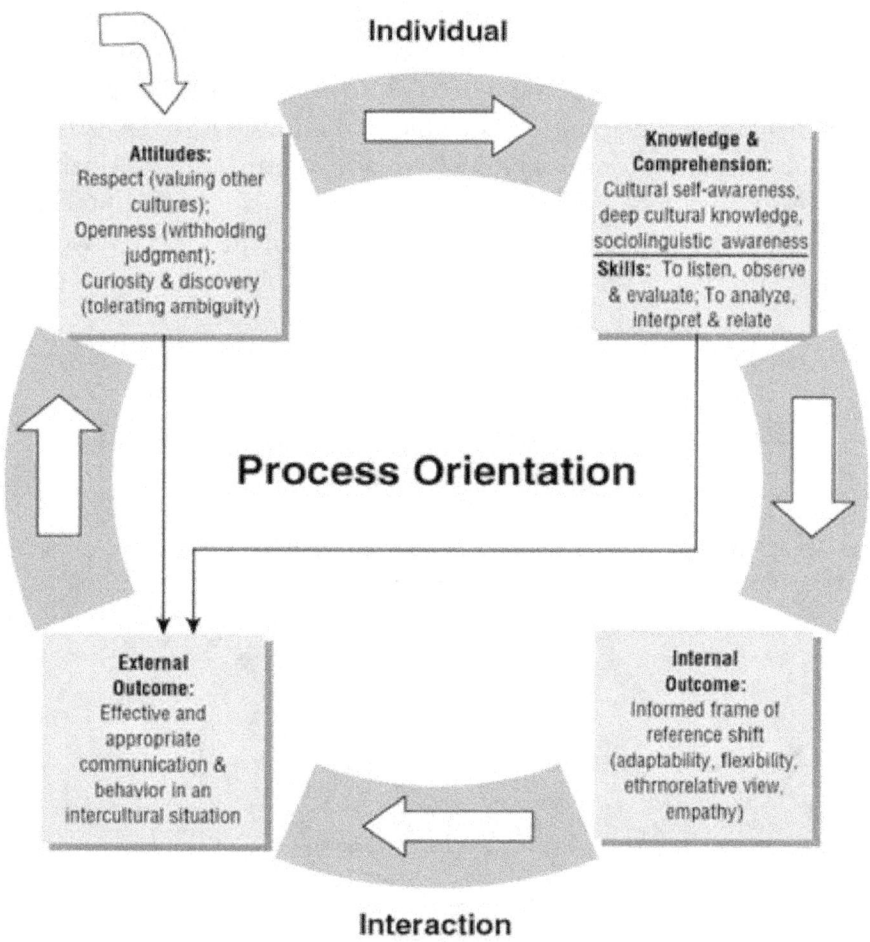

Figure 3.2: Process Model of Intercultural Competence. From "Identification and assessment of intercultural competence as a student outcome of internationalization," by D.K. Deardorff, 2006, Journal of Studies in International Education, 10(3), 241-266. Copyright 2006 by Sage Publications. Reprinted with permission.

Beyond attitudes and knowledge, students must also continually work to develop and apply specific skills as they interact across cultures in new situations: listening, observing, interpreting, analyzing, evaluating, and relating. This ongoing interplay between personal attitudes, knowledge, and skills will allow students to continually improve on both internal and external outcomes. The internal outcome eventually leads to an informed frame of reference shift that involves empathy, adaptability, flexibility, and an ethnorelative worldview (Deardorff, 2006, p. 256). The external outcome of intercultural competence involves the ability to communicate effectively and to behave in culturally appropriate ways in intercultural situations (p. 255). This model emphasizes the ongoing process of developing intercultural competence, as improvements to each individual component will continually impact the outcomes (Deardorff, 2006).

Another influential framework is M. J. Bennett's (1993) Developmental Model of Intercultural Sensitivity (DMIS) (Figure 3.3), which was also adapted for Hammer's (2012) Intercultural Development Continuum. M. J. Bennett's (1993) model emphasizes stages of personal growth and proposes "a continuum of increasing sophistication in dealing with cultural difference," ranging from ethnocentric stages, in which one's own culture and worldview are viewed as universal and uniquely valid, to ethnorelative stages, in which other cultures' beliefs and behaviors are accepted as viable in their own right (p. 22). The DMIS establishes six perceptual orientations, including two ethnocentric stages (Denial and Defense), a transitional stage (Minimization), and three ethnorelative stages (Acceptance, Adaptation, and Integration) (Bennett, 1993, p. 29). Individuals must reconcile different aspects of their perception of cultural differences in order to advance along the continuum.

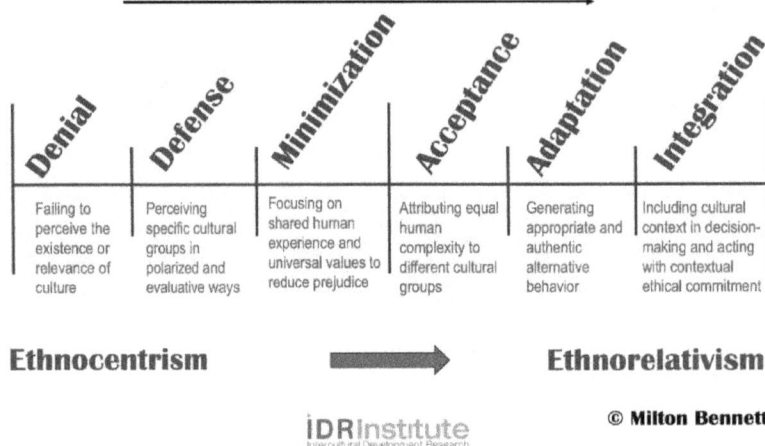

Figure 3.3: The Developmental Model of Intercultural Sensitivity. From Basic concept of intercultural communication: Paradigms, principles, & practices by M. Bennett (2013), Boston: Intercultural Press; www.idrinstitute.org; used with permission of the publisher.

Hammer's Intercultural Development Continuum

Hammer's (2012) Intercultural Development Continuum adapts the DMIS, also emphasizing the stages of Denial, Polarization, Minimization, Acceptance, and Adaptation as individuals move from a monocultural mindset towards an intercultural mindset. In its application to education abroad, this model advocates for intercultural competence development as a primary mission and stresses the use of specific pedagogical strategies to help students navigate each stage of growth.

Individuals with a Denial mindset have a lack of awareness and/or understanding of culture and its relevance, as well as a diminished ability to notice, understand, and respond appropriately when they encounter different cultural values and behaviors. They generally view their own culture as the only viable one, and they often apply stereotypes or broad generalizations about other groups, avoid interactions with people from other cultures, and can quickly become overburdened with feelings of misunderstanding, confusion, and frustration in a new cultural environment. To help study abroad students overcome a Denial mindset, Hammer (2012) suggests facilitating increased interaction with diverse peoples and providing opportunities for reflection on cultural similarities and observable differences (pp. 120-121).

During the Polarization stage, individuals have a judgmental *us versus them* mindset which "can take the form of Defense ('My cultural practices are superior to other cultural practices') or Reversal ('Other cultures are better than mine')" (Hammer, 2012, p. 121). During the Polarization stage, study abroad facilitators can help students identify commonalities and recognize when they adopt a polarizing attitude toward cultural differences without fully understanding them. Individuals with the transitional Minimization mindset often have limited cultural self-awareness, tend to believe in the basic similarity of all peoples, and concentrate on "cultural commonality and universal values and principles that can mask a deeper understanding and consideration of cultural differences" (Hammer, 2012, p. 122). The development strategy at this stage is to help students increase their cultural self-awareness, engage in a deeper analysis of cultural differences, and reflect on issues related to power and privilege (Hammer, 2012).

Both the Acceptance and Adaptation stages represent an ethnorelative worldview. Individuals with an Acceptance orientation understand their own culture as just one of many equally valid cultures and that values and behaviors exist in a cultural context. They can appreciate and value cultural differences and commonalities, but they may be unsure about how to adapt appropriately and have difficulty reconciling behaviors that may be viewed as unethical in their own culture. The pedagogical strategy at this stage is to help students develop strategies for making ethical judgments and to increase their engagement in intercultural interactions so that they can gain more knowledge and adaptation skills (Hammer, 2012, pp. 123-124). An Adaptation orientation involves the ability to shift one's cultural frame of reference, change behavior appropriately to accommodate others' expectations, and engage in meaningful interactions with conscious consideration of adaptation strategies (Hammer, 2012, p. 124). Bennett's model also includes the Integration stage, which involves internalizing aspects of other cultural worldviews and developing the ability to move between cultures and act as a cultural intermediary.

Regarding this model's implications for study abroad facilitators, research using Hammer and Bennett's Intercultural Development Inventory assessment tool has found that mere immersion in another culture only results in marginal gains in intercultural competence development when students are left to their own devices (Hammer, 2012, p. 126). Research has shown that to produce larger gains, programs should encourage active involvement in the host community and include thoughtful pedagogical interventions before, during, and after the trip abroad, such as cultural mentoring and guided reflection on cultural comparisons and critical intercultural experiences (Hammer, 2012, p. 133).

FACILITATING INTERCULTURAL DEVELOPMENT DURING STUDY ABROAD

Stage-Appropriate Interventions and Self-Reflection

Much like Hammer's suggested pedagogical interventions for different stages of development, Bennett (2008) underscores the importance of exploring stage-appropriate topics based on the Developmental Model of Intercultural Sensitivity (DMIS) and Sanford's (1966) model of challenge and support. Sanford's (1966) model underscores "the essential balance required between the challenges any individual faces in a new situation and the level of support required for that person to adjust effectively" (Bennett, 2009, p. 131). This approach considers the risk of challenging study abroad participants who are in the ethnocentric stages of development with lessons that may make them feel threatened or alienated. They may put up resistance or simply disconnect from learning if they perceive the intervention to be a strong challenge to their worldview and mindset. Similarly, a student in the ethnorelative stages of development may become bored and disconnect from a basic exercise about the importance of noticing and valuing cultural differences. Bennett's summary of the principal intercultural competencies that one must develop is also useful to consider when planning targeted pedagogical interventions:

- The cognitive dimension, or *mindset*, includes knowledge of culture-general maps or frameworks, of specific cultures, of identity development patterns, of cultural adaptation processes, and of cultural self-awareness.
- The behavioral dimension, or *skillset*, includes the ability to empathize, gather appropriate information, listen, perceive accurately, adapt, build relationships, resolve problems, and manage social interactions and anxiety.
- The affective dimension, or *heartset*, of attitudes and motivation includes first and foremost, curiosity, as well as initiative, non-judgmentalness, risk taking, cognitive flexibility, open-mindedness, tolerance of ambiguity, flexibility, and resourcefulness (Bennett, 2008, p. 97).

The vast majority of students who are embarking on their first trip abroad, especially those who have had limited experience with other cultures, will be in the ethnocentric stages of development, so careful planning of supportive, low-risk interventions is advisable at the outset. For learners at the Denial stage, this might entail introducing them to the concept of culture, instructing them on how to recognize cultural differences, and acquainting them with how intercultural competence is relevant to their future careers (Bennett, 2008, p. 101). At the Defense stage, the primary goal is to promote recognition of cultural similarities, help learners manage anxiety, and develop patience and tolerance in intercultural encounters (Bennett, 2008, p. 102). Learners at the transitional Minimization stage tend to overemphasize universal similarities among cultures, so the goal is to help them develop cultural self-awareness, open-mindedness, listening skills, and deeper cross-cultural knowledge and understanding through exercises like "Description, Interpretation, and Evaluation" or DIE (Bennett, 2008, pp. 102-103). These exercises ask people to observe a photograph, object, or other stimulus that has cultural significance, but not for the participants. People are asked to "first 'describe' what they see, then 'interpret' possible meanings, and finally to 'evaluate' by giving their value judgments" (Nam & Condon, 2010, p. 81). The exercise fosters cultural self-awareness, promotes frame-shifting when encountering the unfamiliar, and helps individuals recognize the difference between objective descriptions, subjective judgments, and emotionally laden reactions based on one's own cultural worldview (Nam & Condon, 2010). While most first-time study abroad participants are not likely to fall into the ethnorelative stages of development, the process and cultural content of interventions at those levels can present a deeper challenge to their cultural norms and worldviews without running the risk of causing students to disengage from learning.

Unquestionably, one of the most important early pedagogical interventions is to help learners understand the components of intercultural competence, build self-awareness of their current strengths and weaknesses, and reflect on how they can cultivate the necessary attitudes, knowledge, and skills. Deardorff (2012a) provides advice on how to introduce these concepts using the Process Model of Intercultural Competence, emphasizing that development is a lifelong process and that each area of competence must be intentionally cultivated. Critical reflection is an essential tool, and Deardorff provides a sample self-reflection questionnaire that can be used as a starting point with new learners (Appendix 3.1), as well as a questionnaire that encourages educators to reflect on interculturally competent teaching (pp. 50-52). This type of self-reflection questionnaire not only raises learners' self-awareness but can also help study abroad facilitators tailor their interventions to their students and determine what components of intercultural competence to focus on. Once learners understand the basics of intercultural competence, facilitators can design interventions that focus on improving the individual components.

Deardorff (2012b) suggests helping learners question their own assumptions about intercultural situations with techniques like the OSEE (Observe, State, Explore, Evaluate) exercise (p. 58). The OSEE technique helps students to develop the essential skills to move beyond their assumptions, respond more objectively in intercultural situations, and understand the perspective and rationale underlying others' behaviors. The process involves 1) **O**bserving (and listening to) what is happening in a particular situation, 2) **S**tating objectively what is happening, 3) **E**xploring different explanations for what is happening, and 4) **E**valuating which explanation is the most likely (Deardorff, 2012b, pp. 58-59). The evaluation step can also encourage learners to build up culture-specific knowledge through follow-up research or conversations with people across cultures. This OSEE technique can be used in a variety of ways, such as to explore photos, film clips, critical incidents, or to reflect on behaviors that may differ from the learner's cultural conventions.

Cultural Mentoring

Hammer's (2012) research has called into question the so-called immersion assumption, which presupposes that merely being immersed in another culture is sufficient for intercultural learning. However, to experience meaningful growth, study abroad participants ideally need some form of cultural mentoring, which can be defined as "an intercultural pedagogy in which the mentor provides ongoing support for and facilitation of intercultural learning and development" (Paige, 2013, p. 6). Paige and Goode (2009) make several recommendations for study abroad facilitators to provide effective cultural mentoring. First, it is important to note that faculty often come to the table with an uneven understanding of intercultural concepts and theories. Faculty need to be provided with training so that they can better facilitate intercultural competence development among their students (Paige & Goode, 2009). In fact, students often participate in study abroad programs that do not include any formal preparation for second language learning or intercultural competence development, which will produce lackluster results. Paige and Goode (2009) recommend that facilitators be familiar with Deardorff's (2006) process model of intercultural competence (see Figure 2.2), Bennett's developmental model of intercultural sensitivity (see Figure 3.3), and Paige's model of intensity factors in intercultural experiences. Paige (1993) presents ten variables that have the potential to cause significant stress for students while abroad:

1. the degree of cultural differences between the two cultures;
2. an ethnocentric mindset;
3. "culture fatigue" during longer-term cultural immersion;
4. a sense of cultural isolation;
5. a lack of essential linguistic competence;
6. a lack of prior intercultural experience;
7. unrealistic expectations about the host culture and themselves;
8. feelings of being more or less visible in another culture;
9. status dislocations;
10. issues of power and control

In essence, study abroad faculty need to account for and address these common stress factors of intercultural experiences and engage students in ongoing cultural mentoring that is rooted in intercultural models and theories. This calls for an intentional approach to intercultural learning and development, including orientation sessions before departure, cultural mentoring, and opportunities for reflection while abroad, as well as follow-up sessions after returning home.

Since face-to-face mentoring is not always possible, online cultural mentoring can provide another avenue for enhancing students' intercultural learning while abroad. Giovanangeli et al. (2018) call attention to the positive impact that cultural mentoring can have on intercultural competence development, describing the process for online mentoring during the "In-Country Studies" (ICS) program developed at an Australian university. They recommend a style of "formation mentoring" that goes beyond giving students useful information and advice about living in the host country, focusing instead on creating an online space for discussion and storytelling in which students engage in reflection and critical questioning to work through any issues and "threshold experiences" that they may encounter, which leads to greater consciousness and intercultural awareness (Giovanangeli et. al, 2018).

This program incorporates mentoring via an online course that students take while they are abroad. The course requires students to reflect on their intercultural awareness and engagement and develop a research project that involves fieldwork and data collection in the host country (p. 90). Faculty members work with students asynchronously using group and private emails, via synchronous communication technologies such as Zoom or Skype, and in one face-to-face meeting in the host country. This predominantly online cultural mentoring program encourages students to engage with the host society, reflect on intercultural encounters, and "refine and challenge their ideas as they carry out the reflective and research-based assessment tasks" (Giovanangeli et al., 2018, p. 91). Whether cultural mentoring takes place in person or online, research has made clear that its positive impact should not be overlooked.

Interventions in Pre, Mid-, and Post-Sojourn Phases

In principle, support for intercultural learning should not be limited to the time students spend immersed in the host culture. For instance, Hepple (2018) explores the benefits of pre-departure intercultural workshops, highlighting the approach that was implemented as part of the Global Networking Intercultural Capabilities (GNIC) program at the Queensland University of Technology in Brisbane, Australia. One point of concern related to the immersion assumption is that "study abroad researchers have found that mere *exposure* to other cultures, without adequate intercultural preparation beforehand, often leads to the deepening of existing prejudices rather than a more open mindset" (p. 19). The GNIC program addressed this potential problem by creating a series of three two-hour, pre-departure workshops that explore culture-general issues, adapting resources that were developed by the Intercultural Education Resources for Erasmus Students and Their Teachers (IEREST) project (http://www.ierest-project.eu).

The GNIC workshops incorporated three activities from the IEREST resources, one related to going abroad and connecting with a new community, one about encountering different values and navigating prejudices, and a final activity related to developing intercultural communication skills. These workshops emphasized peer learning by bringing local students and international students together and sought to enable the participants to "explore the ways in which individuals construct and negotiate their own and others' identities; recognize and analyze misunderstandings and misrepresentations caused by essentializing and stereotyping; set realistic personal goals for their study abroad; identify and develop more effective and appropriate intercultural communication skills" (Hepple, 2018, p. 21). An analysis of the perceptions of workshop facilitators and students revealed the value of peer learning for local and international students, the benefits of guided reflection, and the advantages of helping students set their personal goals for their study abroad period.

Beyond the pre-departure phase, support for intercultural competence development can be implemented while students are abroad and even after they return home. For example, Weber Bosley (2017) describes the development, implementation, and assessment of a three-stage study abroad intervention called FRILA (Framework for Reflective Intervention in Learning Abroad) that she developed at Bellarmine University in Kentucky. Drawing on personality theory, social constructivism, Bennett's (1993) Developmental Model of Intercultural Sensitivity (DMIS), and Kolb's (1984) experiential learning theory, FRILA involves interventions at the pre-sojourn, sojourn, and post-sojourn stages. Before going abroad, all students take part in a workshop to learn about intercultural concepts, examine their own core values, and participate in group activities that lay the groundwork for fieldwork exercises to be completed abroad. Students also complete a pre-sojourn Intercultural Development Inventory (IDI) assessment, which allows the instructor to tailor instruction to each student's developmental stage (Weber Bosley, 2017, p. 162). During the intercultural experience, students take an online course that is also offered to international exchange students on the Bellarmine campus. Students are grouped with peers who are within a similar developmental range on the DMIS and complete weekly experiential and reflective assignments that are "designed to simulate engagement with the host culture" and compel them to engage in activities that move them out of their comfort zone (Weber Bosley, 2017, p. 163).

After returning home, the final phase involves workshops that build an understanding of the transferability of intercultural skills and encourage continuous development via interactions with diverse groups within their home country. Weber Bosley tracked the impact of FRILA on intercultural learning over a four-year period, analyzing qualitative data from student assignments and reflections and comparing pre-sojourn and post-sojourn IDI scores for students who completed a study abroad program with the scores of students who did not. The IDI was given to 1,802 random students from freshman to senior year to track their intercultural competence development. The average freshman score was 81.89 (in the Polarization stage) while the average senior score was 87.19 (at the low end of the Minimization stage), a gain of 5.29 points (p. 164). However, the average score for seniors who participated in study abroad and completed the three-stage FRILA intervention was 100.37 (at the mid-point of the Minimization stage), a gain of 18.48 points over the average freshman year score (p. 164). By comparison, the comprehensive Georgetown Consortium Study (2003-2005) of IDI results before and after study abroad without any pedagogical intervention showed an average gain of only 1.27 points (Weber Bosley, 2017, p. 165). These quantitative data, which can be supported by qualitative data from student reflections and assignments that highlight their progress, reveal the importance of implementing well-designed pedagogical interventions to enhance intercultural learning for students, ideally at all stages of study abroad.

Intercultural learning also need not end when students return home, since advances in computer-mediated communication provide numerous ways to maintain contact with individuals from the host culture. For example, Lee (2018) highlights the use of asynchronous and synchronous telecommunication tools such as Wikispaces, blogs, VoiceThread, and Zoom to promote cross-cultural dialogue and continue to improve students' intercultural competence and target language skills in the post-sojourn phase, weighing the benefits and challenges of this approach. Lee (2018) partnered with a university in Spain to connect study abroad returnees in an advanced Spanish class with native-speaker peers who were enrolled in an advanced English class. Throughout the semester following the U.S. students' study abroad experience in Spain, the groups used various computer-mediated communication tools to complete four task-based activities to get to know each other, share opinions about language learning, explore and discuss typical stereotypes about their home countries, and explore major cultural themes in movies, providing each other with ongoing peer feedback (Lee, 2018, p. 141). At the end of the semester, the participants reflected on the impact of telecollaborative exchange on their intercultural learning, and the researchers analyzed blog posts and oral recordings to identify recurring themes. Eighty percent of the students indicated that they benefited from the project and improved their cross-cultural awareness. Students also commented that they gained the confidence to communicate with people from other cultural backgrounds, learned about cultural differences and similarities, and some developed intercultural friendships beyond the assignments (Lee, 2018, pp. 144-145). While these types of post-sojourn exchanges may be challenging to organize, they can provide a way to capitalize on the heightened enthusiasm for the host culture that students naturally experience after a trip abroad.

Student Learning Outcomes (SLOs) for Intercultural Competence Development

In addition to designing and implementing sound pedagogical interventions, it is also vital to develop specific and measurable student learning outcomes for study abroad programs that address intercultural competence development. To find out how and to what extent faculty address intercultural learning, Niehaus et al. (2019) conducted a review of 663 student learning outcomes (SLOs) across a sample of 84 syllabi for faculty-led, short-term study abroad (FLSTSA) courses from around the United States. Short-term study abroad programs (those lasting eight weeks or less) are becoming more and more prominent in institutions' internationalization efforts to develop globally competent students, but research findings on their efficacy in enhancing intercultural competence have been mixed (Niehaus et al., 2019, pp. 122-123). Some FLSTSA programs may highly emphasize disciplinary learning over intercultural learning, creating a disconnect between the student learning outcomes and the institution's broader internationalization efforts.

To find out if this was the case, Niehaus et al. (2019) analyzed the 663 SLOs and categorized them as disciplinary, intercultural, both, or neither. For SLOs that related to intercultural learning or both disciplinary and intercultural objectives, they further categorized them as focusing on knowledge, skills, attitudes, or simply on gaining experience/exposure to other cultures without necessarily implying specific learning that would take place. Their findings revealed that "55.96% (n=371) of the learning objectives reflected some level of intercultural learning (alone or in combination with disciplinary content), and 71.79% (n=476) reflected some amount of disciplinary content (alone or in combination with intercultural learning)" (Niehaus et al., 2019, p. 128). An analysis of individual syllabi showed that 52% had more of a disciplinary emphasis, 31% had more of an intercultural learning emphasis, and 17% had a very balanced intercultural/disciplinary focus. The researchers also found that 75% of the interculturally-focused SLOs targeted the knowledge component of intercultural competence, including country-specific knowledge and general knowledge about topics such as "cultural competency, cultural humility, diversity, ethnocentrism, and intercultural communication" (Niehaus et al., 2019, p. 129). Forty percent of the interculturally-focused SLOs highlighted the skills development aspect of intercultural competence (e.g., intercultural communication skills, foreign language learning, critical and comparative thinking skills), while only 14% targeted the development of attitudes that are essential for intercultural competence (e.g., respect for differences, cultural self-awareness, openness, empathy) (Niehaus et al., 2019, pp. 130-131). Nine percent of the interculturally-focused SLOs described "exposure" to a culture, people, or experience, but did not necessarily imply that learning was taking place. In addition to the heavy emphasis on knowledge over skills and attitudes, 44% of these syllabi contained SLOs that were *only* related to developing knowledge (Niehaus et al., 2019, p. 131), leaving out the skills and attitudes components that are emphasized in the models.

While culture-specific and culture-general knowledge are important components of intercultural competence, Deardorff's (2006) Process Model also highlights the importance of skills and singles out the attitudes of openness and curiosity as prerequisites for development. Niehaus et al. (2019) suggest that study abroad professionals might help to increase the coverage of intercultural skills and attitudes in FLSTSA courses by providing faculty members with sample SLOs and other forms of training and support while respecting faculty autonomy to determine the content of their programs. They also encourage institutions to not over-rely on FLSTSA programs in their internationalization efforts, but rather as just one component of a broader constellation of efforts (Niehaus et al, 2019). Employing a wide array of initiatives will ensure the inclusion of as many students as possible, even those who cannot study abroad for financial and other reasons.

INTERCULTURAL COMPETENCE DEVELOPMENT IN CAMPUS INTERNATIONALIZATION

Despite the potentially great impact that study abroad can have on student development, intercultural learning should not be seen as something that only happens while abroad. Broader campus internationalization efforts could involve such initiatives as offering workshops that highlight intercultural theories and training, incorporating intercultural learning throughout the curriculum, coursework that enhances the intercultural experiences of international students, and university-wide quality enhancement plans that focus on improving intercultural competence development for the whole student body. Regarding the common campus-wide focus on producing competent global citizens, Gregersen-Hermans (2017) points out that although study abroad continues to be an important component of campus internationalization, many universities increasingly focus on embedding intercultural learning opportunities throughout the curriculum on campus in order to reach all students. The question then becomes how to design and implement these intercultural learning opportunities so that they will have the most impact, as well as how to assess student progress. In accordance with best practices and research on intercultural competence development, Blair (2017) advocates for enriching the learning environment with pedagogical approaches such as Kuh's (2008) high-impact practices and Kolb's (1984) Experiential Learning Cycle. Regarding the assessment of a phenomenon as complex as intercultural competence, Blair proposes taking the broad categories such as knowledge, skills, and attitudes and breaking them down into their constituent parts to develop much more specific outcome statements while limiting assessment ambitions to a few specific elements (Blair, 2017, p. 119). Blair (2017) provides examples of targeted learning outcomes that can be assessed with a combination of the VALUE Rubrics developed by the Association of American Colleges & Universities (AAC&U), such as those created for Intercultural Knowledge and Competence, Global Learning, and Civic Engagement (AAC&U, 2007).

Ideally, targeted intercultural learning should begin early in students' university experience and continue throughout their studies. One strategy is to incorporate intercultural learning in freshman seminars. For example, Binder's (2017) course for first-year undergraduate students at Jacobs University in Bremen, Germany, combined faculty lectures with experiential workshops led by trained peers with the goal of introducing students to intercultural theories, enhancing their understanding of culture-general knowledge, developing their cultural self-awareness, and guiding them in adopting a personal intercultural practice. In addition, Binder's (2017) course introduced students to the personal leadership methodology developed by Schaetti, Ramsey, and Watanabe (2008, 2009) "with its two principles (i.e. mindfulness, creativity) and six practices (i.e. attending to judgment, attending to emotion, attending to physical sensation, cultivating stillness, engaging ambiguity, aligning with vision) as well as its core process of the critical moment dialogue (CMD) which encourages reflection along the six practices" (Binder, 2017, p. 152). Early pedagogical interventions such as these can provide students with the knowledge and tools that they need in order to take advantage of intercultural learning in subsequent coursework and in their personal lives.

Regarding support for both local and international students in campus internationalization efforts, Golubeva (2017) details two variations of a course at the University of Pannonia in Hungary titled "Intercultural Communication for International Mobility," one for local students who plan to study abroad (or are considering it) and one to facilitate the cultural adjustment of international students. Drawing from all five *savoirs* of Byram's (1997) model, as well from Deardorff's (2006) Pyramid Model of Intercultural Competence, the course explores basic concepts of intercultural communication, cultural differences and similarities, the dangers of stereotypes and ethnocentrism, how to navigate culture shock, and developing cultural self-awareness and an ethnorelative view. Students engage in reflective writing on their experiences, analyze cultural incidents, participate in role-playing exercises, and discuss such topics as "1. the emotional dimension of living abroad; 2. the academic experience of studying in a different higher education context; 3. communication and language problems in social contacts with locals" (Golubeva, 2017, p. 188). These types of courses can not only serve local students who are about to go abroad, but also those who have the interest but not the means to do so. Furthermore, offering specialized versions of such courses for international students has the potential to greatly enhance their experience in the host culture.

Addressing the intercultural competence development of the entire student body can also be a worthy goal of campus-wide quality enhancement plans. For example, Togunde and Fall's (2017) case study highlights Spelman College's quality enhancement plan (2011-2017), which was called "Developing Intercultural Competence" or "Spelman Going Global." The overall objective of the plan was to increase student global travel. Based on Deardorff's (2006) Process Model, this initiative's learning outcomes focused on developing the knowledge and attitude components of intercultural competence. Spelman College also developed several curricular innovations related to students' study abroad experiences: a mandatory, one-credit, pre-departure seminar; regular reflective blogging and journaling while abroad; required round-table discussions post-study abroad; and a required reflective essay about the experience in the host country. Students complete program evaluations and self-assess their progress in global knowledge and intercultural understanding both before and after global travel, and their reflective writing prompts are analyzed to gather assessment data. Some notable findings from the initiative include higher graduation rates for students who studied abroad and that "a semester abroad, living with a host family, taking a language course while abroad, being an honor student, and prior enrollment in an internationally focused course are associated with a higher level of intercultural competence" (Togunde & Fall, 2017, p. 273). Regardless of the approaches that are taken, whether they be small-scale workshops or large-scale quality enhancement plans, universities must address the need to increase their students' intercultural awareness and their ability to act as global citizens in an increasingly interconnected and interdependent world.

PEDAGOGICAL APPROACHES AND BEST PRACTICES RELEVANT IN THE CONTEXT OF STUDY ABROAD

In this section, we will offer the readers a panoramic overview of the eight most frequently employed pedagogical approaches by faculty leaders of study abroad programs across various disciplines. Many of these approaches are referenced by the authors in the 11 chapters that follow in Section II of this volume. We hope the readers will recognize that the teaching approaches listed here are to be embedded in the larger framework of curriculum design and implementation guided by the learning theories and conceptual models that pave the way for their practical application during the study abroad program. Our goal here is to provide concise and clear definitions of these pedagogical approaches as cited in previous literature to the extent possible. The eight approaches are identified as the following:

1. Backward design
2. Thematic-based
3. Reflection-based
4. Inquiry-based
5. Problem-based
6. Project-based
7. Performance-based
8. Collaborative learning

Backward Design

This approach places learning outcomes and assessment procedures at the center of the course-planning process (Wiggins & McTighe, 2005). This approach strategically puts focus on the questions and tasks that provide evidence of learning, rather than focusing solely on covering the content from the syllabus. This course design process starts with instructors identifying student learning goals and then designing course content and assessments to help students achieve these goals. Rather than starting with exams or set textbooks, backward design argues that one starts with the end—the desired results (goals or standards) and then derives the curriculum from the evidence of learning (performances) called for by the standard and the teaching needed to equip students to perform (Wiggins & McTighe, 1998).

Thematic-Based

This approach is one where the main topic is divided into a series of stand-alone modules or units that are interrelated to each other by a recurring theme. Tohsaku (2010) defines a thematic unit as an instructional unit that organizes teaching around themes or topics and makes it possible for us to integrate instruction across such areas as language, culture, science, art, literature, and social issues.

Reflection-Based

Reflection refers to the process by which an individual builds meaning by analyzing an experience, evaluating its worth, and conceptualizing its relevance through the synthesis of additional viewpoints and information (Homan, 2006, p. 9). In this approach, students construct meaning or ruminate about experiences rather than regurgitate facts (Savicki & Price, 2018).

Inquiry-Based

Inquiry-based learning is an umbrella term that includes pedagogical strategies such as problem-based learning and case-based learning that prioritizes students exploring, thinking, asking, and answering content questions with peers to acquire new knowledge through a carefully designed activity. Such activities create opportunities for students to authentically engage in and apply the scientific process as researchers rather than following a predetermined protocol (LaForce et. al., 2017; Yew & Goh, 2016). *See also problem-based learning, project-based learning.* According to the University of Buffalo website on Curriculum, Assessment and Teaching Transformation (2022), in an inquiry-based approach, learners formulate questions on the topic of their study and then search for answers based on research and first-hand observations. They seek to find answers to their questions by comparing the newly found information with an already existing body of knowledge. They eventually draw conclusions from their observations and discussions as well as identify paths for future investigations.

Problem-Based

Problem-based learning is a form of student-centered teaching that focuses on having students work through open-ended problems to explore course material. Students are asked to define the problem as part of the process, research content outside of class time, and iterate solutions to arrive at their final response (Nilson, 2016). According to the University of Buffalo website on Curriculum, Assessment and Teaching Transformation (2022), learners acquire knowledge by devising a solution to a problem. Problem-based learning (PBL) activities provide students with real-world problems that require students to work together to devise a solution. As the group works through challenging real-world problems, learners acquire communication and collaboration skills in addition to knowledge. Student groups conduct outside research on student-identified learning issues (unknowns) to devise one or more solutions or resolutions to problems or dilemmas presented in a realistic story or situation; for example, review and critique research studies, work in groups/teams to solve a specific, open-ended problem, and conduct laboratory work.

Project-Based

Project-based learning is a form of student-centered teaching that engages students with course content as they work through a complex project. These projects are typically multifaceted, real-world scenarios. Project-based learning encourages interdisciplinary conversations and group work. Students apply course knowledge to produce something often paired with cooperative learning. They work in groups or teams to design or create something, for example, a piece of equipment, a product or architectural design, a computer code, a multimedia presentation, an artistic or literary work, a website, a research study, and service learning.

Performance-Based

Performance-based learning has students act out roles or improve scripts in a realistic and problematic social or interpersonal situation. Students play out, either in person or virtually, a hypothetical social situation that abstracts key elements from reality. They emulate real-life situations and scenarios, debates, interviews, frame simulations, and so forth.

Collaborative Learning

Collaborative learning is an umbrella term that covers many different methods in which students work together to solve a problem, complete a task, or create a product. Collaborative learning is founded on the concept that learning and knowledge-building are social and require active engagement from students (Smith & MacGregor, 1992). According to the University of Buffalo website on Curriculum, Assessment and Teaching Transformation (2022), students work together in small groups to maximize their own and each other's learning. Cooperative learning differs from typical group work in that it requires interdependence among group members to solve a problem or complete an assignment.

In this chapter, our focus was on presenting an overview of the definitions, learning theories, and conceptual models related to intercultural competence from previous literature. Furthermore, we examined the research literature on the facilitation of intercultural competence in study abroad programs as well as its development as part of campus internationalization efforts in universities around the globe. In Section II of this volume, we present 11 chapters authored by short-term, faculty-led study abroad leaders who provide valuable insights into the design and implementation of study abroad curricula with program activities, tasks, and assignments that purposefully promote intercultural competence among the program participants.

REFERENCES

Association of American Colleges & Universities (AAC&U). (2007). *VALUE rubrics.* Retrieved September 22, 2022, from https://www.aacu.org/initiatives/value-initiative/value-rubrics/

Bennett, J. M. (2008). Transformative training: Designing programs for culture learning. In M. A. Moodian (Ed.), *Contemporary leadership and intercultural competence: Understanding and utilizing cultural diversity to build successful organizations* (pp. 95-110). SAGE Publications.

Bennett, J. M. (2009). Cultivating intercultural competence: A process perspective. In D. K. Deardorff (Ed.), *The SAGE handbook of intercultural competence* (pp. 121-140). SAGE Publications.

Bennett, M. J. (1993). Towards ethnorelativism: A developmental model of intercultural sensitivity. In R. M. Paige (Ed.), *Education for the intercultural experience* (pp. 21-71). Intercultural Press.

Bennett, M. J. (2012). Paradigmatic assumptions and a developmental approach to intercultural learning. In M. Vande Berg, R. M. Paige, and K. H. Lou (Eds.), *Student learning abroad: What our students are learning, what they're not, and what we can do about it* (pp. 90-114). Stylus Publishing.

Bennett, M. J. (2013). *Basic concept of intercultural communication: Paradigms, principles, & practices.* Intercultural Press.

Berger, P., & Luckmann, T. (1966). *The social construction of reality: A treatise in the sociology of knowledge.* Anchor Books.

Binder, N. (2017). Intercultural competence in practice: A peer-learning and reflection-based university course to develop intercultural competence. In D. K. Deardorff & L. A. Arasaratnam-Smith (Eds.), *Intercultural competence in higher education: International approaches, assessment and application* (pp. 151-155). Routledge.

Blair, S. G. (2017). Mapping intercultural competence: Aligning goals, outcomes, evidence, rubrics, and assessment. In D. K. Deardorff & L. A. Arasaratnam-Smith (Eds.), *Intercultural competence in higher education: International approaches, assessment and application* (pp. 110-123). Routledge.

Byram, M. (1997). *Teaching and assessing intercultural communicative competence.* Multilingual Matters.

Byram, M. (2009). Intercultural competence in foreign languages: The intercultural speaker and the pedagogy of foreign language education. In D. K. Deardorff (Ed.), *The SAGE handbook of intercultural competence* (pp. 321-332). SAGE Publications.

Deardorff, D. K. (2006). Identification and assessment of intercultural competence as a student outcome of internationalization. *Journal of Studies in International Education, 10*(3), 241–266. https://doi.org/10.1177/1028315306287002

Deardorff, D. K. (2009). Synthesizing conceptualizations of intercultural competence: A summary and emerging themes. In D. K. Deardorff (Ed.), *The SAGE handbook of intercultural competence* (pp. 264-269). SAGE Publications.

Deardorff, D. K. (2012a). Framework: Intercultural competence model. In K. Berardo & D. K. Deardorff (Eds.), *Building cultural competence: Innovative activities and models* (pp. 45-52). Stylus Publishing.

Deardorff, D. K. (2012b). Framework: Observe, state, explore, evaluate (OSEE) tool. In K. Berardo & D. K. Deardorff (Eds.), *Building cultural competence: Innovative activities and models* (pp. 58-60). Stylus Publishing.

Deardorff, D. K., & Arasaratnam-Smith, L. A. (Eds.). (2017). *Intercultural competence in higher education: International approaches, assessments, and application.* Routledge.

Giovanangeli, A., Oguro, S., & Harbon, L. (2018). Mentoring students' intercultural learning during study abroad. In J. Jackson & S. Oguro (Eds.), *Intercultural interventions in study abroad* (pp. 88-102). Routledge.

Golubeva, I. (2017). Intercultural communication for international mobility. In D. K. Deardorff & L. A. Arasaratnam-Smith (Eds.), *Intercultural competence in higher education: International approaches, assessment and application* (pp. 186-191). Routledge.

Gregersen-Hermans, J. (2017). Intercultural competence development in higher education. In D. K. Deardorff & L. A. Arasaratnam-Smith (Eds.), *Intercultural competence in higher education: International approaches, assessment and application* (pp. 67-82). Routledge.

Hammer, M. R. (2012). The intercultural development inventory: A new frontier in assessment and development of intercultural competence. In M. Vande Berg, R. M. Paige, & K. H. Lou (Eds.), *Student learning abroad: What our students are learning, what they're not, and what we can do about it* (pp. 115-36). Stylus Publishing.

Hammer, M. R. (2009). The intercultural development inventory: An approach for assessing and building intercultural competence. In M. A. Moodian (Ed.), *Contemporary leadership and intercultural competence* (pp. 203-217). SAGE Publications.

Harvey, T. A. (2017). Design and pedagogy for transformative intercultural learning. In B. Kappler Mikk & I. E. Steglitz (Eds.), *Learning across cultures: Locally and globally* (pp. 109-138). NAFSA and Stylus Publishing.

Hawks, S. (2021). Innovative pedagogies for promoting university global engagement in times of crisis. In T. Thurston, K. Lundstrom, & C. González (Eds.), *Resilient pedagogy*. Utah State University. https://ucn.pressbooks.pub/resilientpedagogy/chapter/innovative-pedagogies-for-promoting-university-global-engagement-in-times-of-crisis/

Hepple, E. (2018). Designing and implementing pre-sojourn intercultural workshops in an Australian university. In J. Jackson & S. Oguro (Eds.), *Intercultural interventions in study abroad* (pp. 18-36). Routledge.

Hunter, A. (2008). Transformative learning in international education. In V. Savicki (Ed.), *Developing intercultural competence and transformation: Theory, research, and application in international education* (pp. 92-107). Stylus Publishing.

Homan. A. (2006). *Constructing knowledge through reflection: The Cross Papers issue 9*. League for Innovation in the Community College.

Kelly, G. (1963). *A theory of personality*. Norton Publishing.

Kolb, D. A. (1984). *Experiential learning*. Prentice Hall.

Kuh, G. D. (2008). *High-impact educational practices: What they are, who has access to them, and why they matter*. AAC&U.

Kuhn, T. (1967). *The structure of scientific revolutions*. University of Chicago Press.

LaForce, M., Noble, E., & Blackwell, C. (2017). Problem-based learning (PBL) and student interest in STEM careers: The roles of motivation and ability beliefs. *Education Sciences*, *7*(4), 92. https://doi.org/10.3390/educsci7040092

Lee, L. (2018). Employing telecollaborative exchange to extend intercultural learning after study abroad. In J. Jackson & S. Oguro (Eds.), *Intercultural interventions in study abroad* (pp. 137-154). Routledge.

Mezirow, J. (1991). *Transformative dimensions of adult learning*. Jossey-Bass Publishing.

Mezirow, J. (2000). *Learning as transformation: Critical perspectives on a theory in progress*. Jossey-Bass Publishing.

Nam, K., & Condon, J. (2010). The DIE is cast: The continuing evolution of intercultural communication's favorite classroom exercise. *International Journal of Intercultural Relations*, *34*(1), 81–87. https://doi.org/10.1016/j.ijintrel.2009.09.001

Niehaus, E., Woodman, T. C., Bryan, A., Light, A., & Hill, E. (2019). Student learning objectives: What instructors emphasize in short-term study abroad. *Frontiers: The Interdisciplinary Journal of Study Abroad*, *31*(2), 121–138. https://doi.org/10.36366/frontiers.v31i2.458

Nilson, L. B. (2016). *Teaching at its best: A research-based resource for college instructors* (4th edition). Jossey-Bass.

Paige, R. M. (1993). On the nature of intercultural experiences and intercultural education. In R. M. Paige (Ed.), *Education for the intercultural experience* (pp. 1-19). Intercultural Press.

Paige, R. M. (2013, August 16). *Factors impacting intercultural development in study*. [Paper presentation]. Elon University, Elon, Ohio, United States.

Paige, R. M., & Goode, M. L. (2009). Intercultural competence in international education administration: Cultural mentoring. In D. K. Deardorff (Ed.), *The SAGE handbook of intercultural competence* (pp. 333-349). SAGE Publications.

Passarelli, A., & Kolb, D. A. (2012). Using experiential learning theory to promote student learning and development in programs of education abroad. In M. Vande Berg, R. M. Paige, & K.H. Lou (Eds.), *Student learning abroad: What our students are learning, what they're not, and what we can do about it* (pp. 137-161). Stylus Publishing.

Pasquarelli, S. L. (2018). Defining an academically sound, culturally relevant study abroad curriculum. In S. Pasquarelli, R. Cole., & M. J. Tyson (Eds.), *Passport to change* (pp. 35-59). Stylus Publishing.

Picciano, A. G. (2017). Theories and frameworks for online education: Seeking an integrated model. *Online Learning, 21*(3), 166–190. http://dx.doi.org/10.24059/olj.v21i3.1225

Sanford, N. (1966). *Self and society: Social change and individual development*. Atherton Press.

Savicki, V., & Price, M. V. (2018). Guiding reflection on cultural experience. In S. Pasquarelli, R. Cole., & M. J. Tyson (Eds.), *Passport to change.* (pp. 60-77). Stylus Publishing.

Smith, B., & MacGregor, J. (1992). *What is collaborative learning?* Washington Center Document.

Spitzberg, B. H., & Changnon, G. (2009). Conceptualizing intercultural competence. In D. K. Deardorff (Ed.), *The SAGE handbook of intercultural competence* (pp. 2-52). SAGE Publications.

Strange, H., & Gibson, H. J. (2017). An investigation of experiential and transformative learning in study abroad programs. *Frontiers: The Interdisciplinary Journal of Study Abroad, 29*(1), 85–100. https://doi.org/10.36366/frontiers.v29i1.387

Stuart, D. (2012). Taking stage development theory seriously. In M. Vande Berg, R. M. Paige, & K. H. Lou (Eds.), *Student learning abroad: What our students are learning, what they're not, and what we can do about it.* (pp. 61-89). Stylus Publishing.

Togunde, D. R., & Fall, R. (2017). Developing intercultural competence through international travel experience at Spelman College. In D. K. Deardorff & L. A. Arasaratnam-Smith, (Eds.), *Intercultural competence in higher education: International approaches, assessment and application* (pp. 269-274). Routledge.

Tohsaku. Y. (2010). *Thematic units in Japanese language education* [Lecture handout]. AATJ Language, Culture, and Technology Summer Institute in Japan.

University of Buffalo. (2022). *Office of curriculum, assessment and teaching transformation.* https://www.buffalo.edu/catt/develop/design/teaching-methods.html

Vygotsky, L. S. (1978). *The mind in society*. Harvard University Press.

Weber Bosley, G. (2017). Developing globally prepared students through an experiential constructivist-driven intervention during study abroad. In J. Jackson & S. Oguro (Eds.), *Intercultural interventions in study abroad* (pp. 155-174). Routledge.

Wiggins, G., & McTighe, J. (1998). Backward design. In *Understanding by design* (pp. 13-34). Association for Supervision and Curriculum Development (ASCD).

Wiggins, G., & McTighe, J. (2005). *Understanding by design*. Pearson Education.

Yew, E. H., & Goh, K. (2016). Problem-based learning: An overview of its process and impact on learning. *Health Professions Education, 2*(2), 75–79. https://doi.org/10.1016/j.hpe.2016.01.004

APPENDICES

Appendix 3.1: Intercultural Competence: Self-Reflection

Part 1: The items listed below are invaluable in developing intercultural competence and in interacting effectively and appropriately with people from other cultures. Please rate yourself on the following:

5 = very high 4 = high 3 = average 2 = below average 1 = poor

Intercultural Competence and Rating of 5, 4, 3, 2, or 1					
1. Respect (valuing other cultures)	5	4	3	2	1
2. Openness (to intercultural learning and to people from other cultures)	5	4	3	2	1
3. Tolerance for ambiguity	5	4	3	2	1
4. Flexibility (in using appropriate communication styles and behaviors, in intercultural situations)	5	4	3	2	1
5. Curiosity and discovery	5	4	3	2	1
6. Withholding judgment	5	4	3	2	1
7. Cultural self-awareness/understanding	5	4	3	2	1
8. Understanding others' worldviews	5	4	3	2	1
9. Culture-specific knowledge	5	4	3	2	1
10. Sociolinguistic awareness (awareness of using other languages in social contexts)	5	4	3	2	1
11. Skills to listen, observe, and interpret	5	4	3	2	1
12. Skills to analyze, evaluate, and relate	5	4	3	2	1
13. Empathy (do unto others as you would have others do unto you)	5	4	3	2	1
14. Adaptability (to different communication styles/behaviors, to new cultural environments)	5	4	3	2	1
15. Communication Skills (appropriate and effective communication in intercultural settings)	5	4	3	2	1

Part 2: Reflect on situations requiring intercultural competence—what helped make you more appropriate and effective in your interactions? Now reflect on how you can continue to develop your intercultural competence, especially areas you rated as lower. *Note.* Based on intercultural competence models developed by Deardorff, 2004, "Identification and Assessment of Intercultural Competence as a Student Outcome of Internationalization," by D. K. Deardorff, 2006, *Journal of Studies in International Education, 10*(3), 241–266.

Reproduced from: Darla K. Deardorff, "Framework: Intercultural Competence Model," in *Building Cultural Competence: Innovative Activities and Models*, eds. K. Berardo and D. K. Deardorff (Sterling, VA: Stylus, 2012), 45–52. Used with permission of the publisher.

Section II
Short-Term, Faculty-Led Study Abroad Programs Across Disciplines

Introduction of Case Study Chapters

Priya Ananth and Seok Jeng Jane Lim

Section I introduced foundational knowledge on intercultural competence in study abroad programs. Section II (Chapters 4-14) present unique case study models of short-term, faculty-led study abroad programs. The faculty leaders of each case study demonstrate how intercultural competencies in the areas of knowledge, skills, and attitudes were strategically incorporated into the activities, tasks, and assignments of the study abroad curricula. These intercultural competencies were adapted from Deardorff (2012).

Table Section II Introduction of Intercultural Competencies Used Across the Case Studies

Knowledge	Skills	Attitudes
<ul><li>Cultural self-awareness and understanding</li><li>Understanding others' worldviews</li><li>Culture-specific knowledge</li><li>Academic content knowledge</li></ul>	<ul><li>Creative thinking</li><li>Problem-solving</li><li>Leadership</li><li>Articulation</li><li>Teamwork</li><li>Technology skills</li><li>Listen, observe, interpret</li><li>Analyze, evaluate, relate</li><li>Communication skills</li></ul>	<ul><li>Empathy</li><li>Curiosity and discovery</li><li>Risk-taking</li><li>Withholding judgment</li><li>Open-minded</li><li>Tolerance for ambiguity</li><li>Stepping outside the comfort zone</li><li>Resilience</li><li>Patience</li><li>Respect</li><li>Flexibility</li><li>Adaptability</li></ul>

Section II case study contributors prepared their chapters based on a template that included essential information pertaining to their courses. The materials were organized in a parallel format to increase accessibility of the information for the reader specific to their discipline. Each chapter, therefore, uses the following standardized template:

Introduction
Theoretical Foundations
Course Description
Course History
Course Logistics
Pre-program Activities

Class Activities and Intercultural Competencies
Post-Program and Future Class Activities
Evaluation and Assignments
Student Feedback
Caveats and Reflections
References
Appendices

REFERENCES

Deardorff, D. K. (2012). Framework: Intercultural competence model. In K. Berardo & D. K. Deardorff (Eds.), *Building cultural competence: Innovative activities and models* (pp. 45-52). Stylus Publishing.

Chapter 4

Traveling a Thousand Miles: The Role of Education Diplomacy through Study Abroad in Early Childhood Programs

Seok Jeng Jane Lim and Karen Nourse Reed

Note: Section II includes Chapters 4-14. These chapters use a standardized template to discuss the details of their respective study abroad programs and reference Deardorff's (2012) framework for intercultural competencies. The use of this template and the intercultural competencies framework are described in the Section II introduction. All courses in this section (except for Chapter 6) were taught through Middle Tennessee State University (MTSU), a mid-sized state school located in Murfreesboro, Tennessee (USA).

The short-term study abroad course *Administering Early Childhood Programs* (ECE 4360) is conducted in Singapore during the summer academic term. From 2013-2018, a total of 23 students have participated in the four short-term study abroad programs. A unique aspect of this course is its focus on the administrative, professional, and ethical responsibilities of the educator in early childhood settings in a vibrant international environment. The course emphasizes the development of 21st century skills including important global competency skills that are vital in developing early childhood educators.

THEORETICAL FOUNDATIONS

The growing interest in study abroad programs is a promising development for those who champion education diplomacy. Childhood Education International defines education diplomacy as using "the skills of diplomacy to promote effective cooperation across sectors and among diverse actors to solve education challenges and advance transformational agendas for education" (CE International, n.d.). Teachers who are education diplomats will form strategic partnerships with each other as well as policymakers to support 21st-century skills and global citizenship. To effectively advocate for these practices, a teacher must demonstrate intercultural awareness and appreciation; additionally, they must have a strong knowledge of current professional practices to articulate a vision for curricular progress.

ECE 3460's curriculum is influenced by widely recognized theoretical frameworks. The two theoretical frameworks used are the Global Citizenship Scale developed by Morais and Ogden (2011) and the Experiential Learning Theory developed by Kolb (2015). Global citizenship is a broad concept that encompasses many aspects that one might consider to be synonymous with the term "cosmopolitan": an openness toward other cultures and an awareness of the concerns of others around the world. For the global citizen, this respect for the needs of others can promote "understanding complex issues from multiple vantage points, recognizing sources of global independence... and looking beyond distinctions, at least in one's mind, between insiders and outsiders" (Schattle, 2009, pp. 10-11). To be a global citizen "involves both inward (awareness and commitment) and outward (action) dimensions" (Hanson, 2010, p. 76), and is therefore a complicated concept to impart in a university course. Study abroad programs show great promise in developing global citizenship characteristics among university students (Hanson, 2010; Morais & Ogden, 2011). The Experiential Learning Theory (ELT) developed by Kolb (2015) emphasizes the continual and often circular process the learner takes as they observe, encounter, and undergo circumstances. Kolb (2015) writes that "Ideas are not fixed and immutable elements of thought but are formed and reformed through experience." This manner of learning, therefore, stresses modifying ideas over the memorization of facts or concepts. This approach to learning seemed to be a perfect fit for the experience-rich opportunity of a study abroad course such as ECE 4360.

COURSE DESCRIPTION

Administering Early Childhood Programs is offered in two formats: the traditional on-campus offering and a study abroad version. The course examines diverse early care and educational settings and their influence on child development with an emphasis on program planning and administration in early childhood settings. The purpose of this course is to examine a variety of early childhood settings and public preschool issues. An understanding of state regulations and national standards is required to assist teacher candidates in planning, administering, and teaching in an early childhood program that will enhance the learning process of all involved.

The course focuses on the administrative, professional, and ethical responsibilities of the educator within early childhood settings. The traditional on-campus class is conducted every semester during the academic year on the university campus. A study abroad version was offered during select summer semesters to create an opportunity for students to experience a different culture and diverse setting for their learning.

For the study abroad program, students examined early childhood settings and public preschool issues in a global setting. *Administering Early Childhood Programs* (Study Abroad - Singapore) provided an understanding of the state regulations, standards, and overall framework that impact early care and education in Singapore. It also examined the various preschool settings in Singapore and the importance of being a community of learners in a professional organization. The text used for this course is *Planning and Administering Early Childhood Programs* by Freeman et al. (2017).

Through journals, discussions, observations, question prompts, and group presentations, students bridged their understanding regarding the legal, ethical, and professional responsibilities of an educator. Knowledge gained in this study abroad program was linked to the Tennessee Star Quality Child Care Program and National Association for the Education of Young Children (NAEYC) accreditation of programs for young children, as students compared the different state regulations, preschools, and professional communities that impact the growth and development of a young child.

Course Objectives

- Formulate a working knowledge of the operation of a childcare facility or public preschool classroom.
- Develop an understanding of current issues and trends in early care and education programs including advocacy.
- Develop an understanding of the principles of professionalism regarding high-quality teachers, professional development, and learning communities.
- Examine the criteria and standards required of early childhood facilities and public preschools.
- Compare diverse settings and types of childcare.
- Design a childcare classroom that illustrates a holistic, diverse, and developmentally appropriate philosophy and meets all standards, regulations, and the needs of all students.
- Summarize and demonstrate professional ethics in early childhood education.
- Expand his/her understanding of the needs and strengths of children and families from diverse cultural backgrounds.
- Build a catalyst of coherence in ensuring quality assurance, accountability, and student and leadership achievement.

Course Learning Outcomes

Upon completion of the course, students will be able to:

a. Identify qualities of an excellent early childhood program regarding the curriculum, environment, quality of teachers, and partnership with parents and community.
b. Compare and contrast diverse settings and types of preschool programs.
c. Examine the criteria and standards of Singapore preschool accreditation standards and Tennessee Star Quality Child Care Program and NAEYC accreditation program for young children.
d. Build partnerships with professional organizations both locally and globally in becoming a collaborative educator in the field.
e. Be aware of the impact of diversity and cultural makeup of the family and community that shape the learning and development of a child.
f. Understand developmentally and culturally appropriate practices and approaches to teaching and learning both locally and globally.
g. Become a reflective global professional through observation, documentation, discussion, and partnership.

Study Abroad Course Information

Administering Early Childhood Programs (ECE 4360) is a study abroad course available from Middle Tennessee State University and conducted in Singapore during the summer academic term. Since 2013, a total of four short-term study abroad programs have been completed. The number of students enrolled each summer has historically been very small, from a low of four students in 2013 to a high of eight students in 2016. In all, a total of N=23 students have participated in this program [2013 (N=4); 2014 (N=4); 2016 (N=8); 2018 (N=7)]. Although the course was conducted annually in 2013 and 2014, the initial slow enrollment rate prompted the faculty leader to subsequently move the course to a biennial offering in order to allow for more marketing and promotion of the program. As a result of this change, positive enrollment gains were realized with the 2016 program enrollment increasing to eight. With the 2016 course offering, a minimum of eight students was required for the class to be made available. The positive feedback and response from the students in the 2013 and 2014 cohorts generated excitement and interest for future course offerings that resulted in 2016 enrollment gains. Although the 2018 course offering was also supported by a strong student enrollment, the unfortunate world events of 2020 (including the COVID-19 pandemic and travel restrictions in Singapore) forced the program to halt for a few years.

Teacher Licensure Standards

The course also meets the following teacher licensure standards for PreK-3 (NAEYC, 2019):

> Standard 1: Child Development and Learning in Context (p. 12)
>
> Standard 2: Family-Teacher Partnerships and Community Connections (p. 12)
>
> Standard 3: Child Observation, Documentation, and Assessment (p. 12)
>
> Standard 4: Developmentally, Culturally and Linguistically Appropriate Teaching Practices (p. 13)
>
> Standard 6: Professionalism as an Early Childhood (p. 13)

COURSE HISTORY

The faculty leader for this course is a native citizen of Singapore. When she first joined Middle Tennessee State University in 2012, she realized that many people on campus were not familiar with Singapore, as she was often mistaken as a citizen of China. In addition, some students have never ventured or traveled out of Tennessee; many do not even own a passport. The faculty leader felt a need to educate and share knowledge about this as well as the culture of Singapore. Because of this, she approached the Vice Provost for International Affairs in 2012 for assistance in conducting a study abroad course in Singapore. As there were no students from the College of Education who had participated in prior education abroad programs, the Vice Provost was extremely supportive to make this new Singapore program happen. In addition, consultation with the faculty leader's team of early childhood faculty was crucial in selecting the appropriate course to meet the objectives and licensure requirements. Thus, the study abroad version of the course *Administering Early Childhood Programs* was developed in 2012 and implemented the following summer in 2013.

As a native citizen of Singapore with prior professional connections in the early childhood setting, the faculty leader worked closely with the Association for Early Childhood Educators (Singapore) in planning for the study abroad course. Although the number enrolled in the first study abroad trip to Singapore was below the minimum number required to start a class, the faculty leader proceeded to lead the group without summer pay (with the support of the Vice Provost). Cost was the main barrier for education students to enroll in the study abroad course. The faculty leader actively helped to seek funding and support to make it possible for more education students to study abroad. In 2016, an additional scholarship was provided by the Dean of the College of Education, and an Education Abroad scholarship was started up by the faculty leader and the Dean.

COURSE LOGISTICS

Administering Early Childhood Programs (ECE 4360) is a 3-credit hour upper-division course for students enrolled in the Bachelor of Early Childhood Education degree. This is a major-required course with the prerequisite that students must have been admitted to the teacher education program. Criteria for admission to the teacher education program is rigorous and requires: 45 semester hours of course work, an overall grade point average of 2.75, a background check, three favorable faculty interviews, and successfully passing the Praxis Core Exam (a test for teacher candidates). For the study abroad version of ECE 4360, students who have not been admitted to the teacher education program are allowed to apply with prerequisite permission granted by the faculty leader.

PRE-PROGRAM ACTIVITIES

Several pre-program meetings were scheduled before the trip. The purpose of these meetings was for the students to learn about each other, build a community, and develop a better understanding of the country they would be visiting. As many of the education students had never previously traveled outside of the United States, traveling thousands of miles away for their first international trip was a big adventure. Five pre-program activities were developed to help the students prepare and acclimate to the new country: 1. Knowledge of the country, 2. Building a community, 3. Financial literacy and fundraising, 4. Knowledge of the course, and 5. Pre-departure questionnaire.

1. Knowledge of the Country

This activity utilized a Singapore trivia game. The trivia questions were selected to help students learn aspects of the culture and demographics of Singapore—such as language, mode of transportation, living accommodations, and currency—before arrival. The trivia questions also helped the faculty to pre-assess students for their prior knowledge before departure.

2. Building a Community

This activity utilized a game called Buddy Contract. For this game, students were asked to find a partner with whom to share their likes, dislikes, and personal rituals. The activity also stressed cultural norms as students were asked to write down some of the dos and don'ts in Singapore, teaching them about some acceptable and unacceptable practices. Buddies were made accountable for each other during their study abroad in Singapore, signing a contract stipulating this responsibility before departure. Students were required to place their buddy contracts in a visible spot in their room upon arrival. Each buddy contract differed according to their discussion. In the process of this activity, students developed self-awareness and acceptance of different cultural perspectives.

Below is a sample of the buddy contract:

Dos

- Check in with your buddy
- Stay with the group
- Be respectful of the culture
- Dress professionally and appropriate

Don'ts

- Drink alcohol
- Chew gum
- Go out alone
- Misbehave or be irresponsible

3. Financial Literacy and Fundraising

Because only a limited number of scholarships were available and cost was a major concern for most of the education students, it was important to discuss fundraising ideas prior to departure. Financial literacy, strategies for saving for the study abroad program, and daily expected expenditures were discussed.

4. Knowledge of the Course

Students needed to be aware of the course and assignment requirements before leaving for Singapore. Planning for assignment time and reading time was also discussed. In addition to the required textbook, students were advised to print other required readings as if there was no internet access during the trip.

5. Pre-Departure Questionnaire

A pre-assessment that consisted of seven questions was developed to understand the students' expectations and knowledge of Singapore before the trip. These questions can be seen in Appendix 4.1.

CLASS ACTIVITIES & INTERCULTURAL COMPETENCIES

There were several program activities deployed during the time in Singapore; the goal of these activities was to ensure that the syllabus requirements were met and that students were experiencing the culture of a new country. The program itinerary was arranged with seminars, school visitations, class activities or tasks, and excursions to Singapore sites. Thirteen hours were allocated to school visitations. During these school visits, students were assigned journals/reflections and question prompts to document their expectations, observations, and reflections that promoted the Experiential Learning Theory (Kolb, 2015). Sixteen hours were allocated to in-class activities or seminars. These seminars were assigned alongside an accompanying chapter of the text and often prompted student reflection on the school visitation conducted. These seminars were also held in the dormitory room where the students stayed or in the faculty leader's room. Often during these seminars, students became more self-aware and began to challenge their perceptions of global justice and disparities, as expressed by this student:

> "I am also unsure of the fear that seems so blinding in America. The fear of others seems to create a division within our country that cripples or distracts us from pursuing our dreams and visions as individuals, communities, and as a nation. I question the intentions behind the propagation of such fear, especially in our schools." (Student 1, 2014)

One of the major program activities, "Excursion to Singapore," was an important part of the study abroad for students to know and experience the country and culture. Many of the places visited were suggested by students during the pre-program session. Since Singapore is a multicultural Asian society, the faculty leader intentionally arranged several excursions that reflected this diversity. The range of experiences helped students gain knowledge of the cultural makeup of the family and community of the local children. These excursions were arranged during the day and night, so students had an opportunity to see the community at different times. Places visited included: a zoo, botanical gardens, a duck tour, the Singapore Flyer, a night tour, Sentosa, East Coast Park, and cultural sites such as a museum and Chinatown. Most of the excursions were over the weekend since there were no seminars scheduled during that time. With this arrangement, students could focus on coursework during the week and leisure over the weekend. Grocery shopping and moving around in local transportation were also included in the itinerary. Appendix 4.2 shows a sample itinerary of the study abroad in Singapore.

Seminar Discussion

The seminar discussions took about 16 hours and were held daily except for weekends. The seminars were conducted on the following topics:

a. Singapore preschool accreditation standards, Tennessee Star Quality Child Care Program, and NAEYC accreditation for young children.
b. Comparison of preschool/elementary school visitations.
c. Professional organizations and building partnerships.

The focus was on building content knowledge of Singapore preschool accreditation standards, the Tennessee Star Quality Child Care Program, and NAEYC accreditation for young children. Students were also required to reflect and compare similarities and differences of the school visitations; this activity helped them to learn about different professional organizations, build partnerships, and network. Seminars used an assigned text and a study guide for facilitation and discussion. Case studies incorporating role play and think-pair-share were utilized to generate discussion. Each seminar started with strength-building activities in which each pair of buddies were asked to highlight positive insights; these were followed by questions and reflections on the school visits and the topic of discussion for the day. These seminars encourage intercultural competencies shown in Table 4.1.

Table 4.1. Intercultural Competencies for Seminar Discussion

Knowledge	Skills	Attitudes
• Academic content	• Emerging professionalism • Global transfer	• Critical thinking and reflection

School Visitations

School visitations took about 13 hours total and were conducted almost daily except on weekends. The schools visited included public and private schools as well as professional organizations. During the visit, students were introduced to the school's mission, vision, and schedule; this was followed by assigning the students to different rooms for observation. This activity usually took about 2-3 hours per school. The experience of visiting schools helped in building the students' global competence, which is having an open mind while actively seeking to understand the cultural norms and expectations of others and leveraging this knowledge to interact, communicate, and work effectively outside one's environment (Hanson, 2010; Schattle, 2009). Through school visitations, students could bridge the theory of what they discussed during the seminar to actual practices as well as test their preconceived notions of what they thought the schools would look like. As aptly stated by one student at the end of the trip:

> "I see the world in a whole new light. I see that places I've only dreamed about aren't that different from America. I've found that the typical stereotypes aren't relevant." (Student 2, 2014)

Additional intercultural competencies gained by the students are presented in Table 4.2.

Table 4.2. Intercultural Competencies for School Visitations

Knowledge	Skills	Attitudes
• Academic content • Culturally specific knowledge and understanding host culture's traditions	• Intercultural communications • Interpersonal relationship • Listen and observe	• Emerging professionalism

Tasks

Grocery Shopping and Dining Out

Grocery shopping and dining out allowed the students to learn about the diversity and cultural makeup of the children and families in Singapore. Although this was not part of the syllabus assignment, students gained the most intercultural competency skills and intercultural perspective through these two activities.

On the first day of arrival, students were taken to a nearby grocery store to purchase needed essential items. With this task, students began to use the local currency, compare prices of items to their cost in the United States, and experience new cultural foods they had never previously seen. Although they had already completed the pre-departure discussion on budgeting, students tended to overspend on the first grocery trip. Students needed to be reminded not to overspend as they were often excited to see all the novel items. Dining out in the new cultural setting of Singapore was another new experience for them. Students needed to problem solve to order from the menu and try new foods. The intercultural competencies gained are shown in Table 4.3.

Table 4.3. Intercultural Competencies for Grocery Shopping & Eating Out

Knowledge	Skills	Attitudes
• Global knowledge	• Intercultural communications • Interpersonal relationship • Decision making • Awareness of safety • Problem solving	• Self-discovery • Tolerating and engaging ambiguity

Transportation

Singapore is a small island state, and most people either own a car or use public transportation such as buses, cabs, or the subway known as the Mass Rapid Transport (MRT). During the study abroad program, the faculty leader chartered buses to transport the students to school visitations in order to save time. On the way back to the accommodations, students were divided into groups to take a cab back. During excursions, students were taken on buses so that they could experience the daily life of living in Singapore. Navigating the various places and planning the route to arrive at those places was quite an experience for the students and provided them with an authentic intercultural engagement opportunity since most students had never previously taken public transportation in the United States. Often just naming the destination to the cab driver was a challenge as the names of the areas and venues were in the local dialect, and the students had little prior experience with the language. The faculty leader sometimes witnessed the students practicing hard the night before to ensure the correct pronunciation of the road name. One of the students stated:

"Some challenges I encountered on this trip was the language barrier between myself and locals. Sometimes it was hard to understand what they were saying or what I was saying." (Student 3, 2016)

The intercultural competencies gained for transportation are listed in Table 4.4.

Table 4.4. Intercultural Competencies for Transportation

Knowledge	Skills	Attitudes
- Global knowledge	- Intercultural communications - Interpersonal relationship - Planning and navigation - Sociolinguistic competence	- Self-awareness

POST-PROGRAM AND FUTURE CLASS ACTIVITIES

Post-program activities included a questionnaire as well as video and panel presentations. On the flight back to Tennessee, students were encouraged to complete the post-departure questionnaire consisting of six questions. A week after the students returned, they presented a two-hour panel presentation to invited faculty, students, and family members on the study abroad program at the university. All of the pre-program, program, and post-program activities are presented in Table 4.5.

Table 4.5. Table of Activities for ECE 4360

Pre-Program Activities	Program Activities	Post-Program Activities
- Knowledge of the country: Singapore trivia - Building a community: Buddy contract - Financial literacy and Fundraising - Knowledge of the course - Pre-departure questionnaire	- School visitations (13 hours) - In-class activities/ seminars (16 hours) - Excursion to different multicultural and historical sites in Singapore - Grocery shopping - Local transportation	- Post- departure questionnaire - Video and panel presentation

Future class activities need to focus more on disposition and intercultural competencies. Disposition includes professional competencies such as punctuality, dress code, and posture. Often attitudes and dispositions are not graded as it can be difficult to assign a numerical grade to them, but using a triangulation of data points including self, peer, and faculty evaluations could help in assigning an accurate grade. The evaluation could be assigned during the pre-program, during the program, and after the program. A proposed assignment is found in Appendix 4.3. Another possible assignment would be to involve the students in planning an authentic project during the pre-departure meeting that would build on intercultural competencies.

EVALUATION AND ASSIGNMENTS

Assessment of participant learning is determined through an evaluation of student journals, discussions, observations, reflections and group presentations. At the completion of each study abroad session, students completed their major graded assignment for the course by sharing their new knowledge through a video and panel presentation. This final presentation focused on the impact of the legal, ethical, and professional responsibilities of an educator as the students compared the state regulations, preschools, and professional communities impacting the growth and development of a young child.

The evaluation of the course included both formative and summative assessments. The daily journal and photo documentation and seminar discussions collected the students' observations and reflections in a formative process that was used for their summative final video and panel presentation. All of these assignments were designed with intercultural competencies in mind as the students must work with other individuals, as a group, to build professional connections. The final project had the highest grade weight, as the students demonstrated their competencies by sharing what they learned with an audience who most likely had never been to Singapore. The ability to consider the audience's perspective in this manner was an important development in their professional life as an educator. The evaluation and assignment criteria are listed in Table 4.6.

Table 4.6. Evaluation Breakdown

Learning Activity	Points [% of Grade]	Type of Assessment
Journal/Photo documentation (8 journals)	80 [24%]	Formative
Seminar discussion	60 [18%]	Formative
Interview	30 [9%]	Summative
Video and panel presentation	160 [49%]	Summative
TOTAL Points Possible	330	

Daily Journal/Photo Reflection and Documentation

Students were required to compile a daily journal/photo reflection and documentation describing their expectations of the day, observations, reflections, and one learning point each day (see Appendix 4.4 for assignment description and grading criteria). The photograph taken should support the daily journal content. Specific questions were written to guide the students in their reflections. This was an individual assignment and showcased the self-awareness and growth of the student as the journal progressed from the first entry to the last. One student stated in her journal entry:

> "I was very pleasantly surprised by the state of the center and what materials they did have... It is a government-based program... I honestly thought that we would be going to a center where they had little to nothing in the center. I did not realize how much the government provided in trying to make sure that their children get the best education regardless of what their parents make. This is how it should be; we should give each student an equal chance to succeed in life." (Student 4, 2018)

Intercultural competencies gained for the daily journal/photo reflection is listed in Table 4.7.

Table 4.7. Intercultural Competencies for Daily Journal/ Photo Reflection and Documentation

Knowledge	Skills	Attitudes
• Academic content	• Intercultural communications • Interpersonal relationship • Global transfer	• Emerging professionalism • Self-discovery

Final Group Project: Video and Panel Presentation

The final assignment was group-based and provided opportunities for participants to build a professional learning community as they engaged with the community through their presentations (see Appendix 4.5 for assignment description and grading criteria). In addition, students were required to compile background information on Singapore consisting of its history, geography, demographic makeup, infrastructure, and culture with an emphasis on how these factors impact early childhood education in Singapore. This information was shared during the presentation day as an introduction to the country of Singapore. Students were also required to compile the guest list consisting of family, friends, and faculty and generate an invitation note and a thank you note after the presentation. This assignment helped in preparing the students to become global ambassadors for Singapore in addition to the cultural competencies gained as shown in Table 4.8.

Table 4.8. Intercultural Competencies for Final Group Project

Knowledge	Skills	Attitudes
• Academic content • Global knowledge	• Intercultural communications • Interpersonal relationship • Global interconnectedness • Global competence	• Emerging professionalism

STUDENT FEEDBACK

To understand the collective experience of the study abroad participants, a pre- and post-departure questionnaire was collected. The faculty leader used IRB-approved consent procedures utilizing a convenience sample of 19 students who enrolled in the summer study abroad program in the university's College of Education. Data were collected from three separate years (2014, 2016, and 2018), excluding the first year 2013, where students stayed in Singapore for a duration of 13 days during each study abroad. Of these 19 students consenting to the study, four students were in the 2014 cohort, eight students were in the 2016 cohort, and seven students were in the 2018 cohort. All participants were females in their junior and/or senior year of college. Almost all the students were enrolled in the university's Early Childhood program, with only two participants enrolled in the Child Development and Family Studies program. As for the ethnicity of the participants, there were 14 Caucasians, four African Americans, and one Hispanic student. Of the 19 participants, three were considered non-traditional students, and one was born outside of the United States. Data collected for this study consisted of students' pre- and post-surveys, as well as their completed journals.

From the data, the greatest gains were in the participants' personal and professional growth from the study abroad experiences. Participants in this study abroad learned to build partnerships with schools and professionals from a different culture, thus broadening their perspective and equipping them to later share this information with others in their home country who did not have the opportunity to study abroad in Singapore. The study abroad program helped in building the participants' competencies in both professionalism and as an early childhood educator; it also developed the participants' global citizenship skills of global competency, social responsibility, and global civic engagement. Besides achieving the course goal of improving student knowledge regarding cross-cultural understanding and global citizenship, the study abroad experience boosted the individual students' skill mastery towards professionalism in the early childhood education profession. Some of the students' reflections are included below. Following each quote, the program year and the intercultural competencies gained by the students are listed.

- "The biggest takeaway from this school [is] the focus on dispositions and the idea of embracing multi-racial members of the community. This would be the primary focus of a program I implemented." *(Student 5, 2014, understanding the value of cultural diversity)*
- "This trip…has helped shape and solidify beliefs and aspects within my personal teaching philosophy that I was unaware of. This self-awareness will help me to know

who I am as a teacher instead of trying to emulate teachers I've seen. This trip is an unexpected gift along my path in becoming a teacher (and) lifelong learner." *(Student 6, 2014, cultural self-awareness and capacity for self-assessment)*

CAVEATS AND REFLECTIONS

The major strength of this program was taking the students out of their home country to a brand-new culture and allowing them to immerse themselves in that country while achieving the goals set for the course. Some of the students had never previously traveled out of Tennessee and taking this study abroad program was therefore a big step and challenge for them. Their growth and self-discovery were the major highlights of this course as stated by one student:

> "I loved this trip so much... I learned languages and more about myself. Through the trip I learned that I'm capable of anything I set my mind to. I am willing to try almost anything." (Student 7, 2014)

The major challenge for this program was to meet the minimum class enrollment of eight students, as cost was a major difficulty for the students. Many education students work several jobs to pay for their regular tuition and housing, so paying additional money to enroll in the study abroad course could be difficult. While the pre-departure course on financial literacy was also helpful in teaching students how to save for the trip, additional scholarships and funding would help with this challenge in the future.

Future offerings of the study abroad course must be intentional in focusing on intercultural competencies in order to best prepare our students to be emerging professionals in their future careers. One of the posts shared by a student summarizes the importance of this course to student self-development and intercultural understanding:

> "My goals include expanding my educational perspectives, becoming more aware of cultural diversity by being immersed in a different culture and making professional connections (and) networks that will serve me as a teacher candidate, hopefully lasting a lifetime." (Student 8, 2014)

According to the 2020-2021 MTSU International Affairs annual impact report, the College of Education has one of the lowest rates of student participation in study abroad programs at MTSU, with only 45 Education students participating as compared to 641 students participating from Liberal Arts majors (MTSU Impact Report, 2022, p. 6). Since the faculty leader brought the first study abroad group to Singapore in 2013, there has been a growing interest among other faculty who are interested in starting additional study abroad programs within the College of Education. Study abroad also aligns with the MTSU Quest for Student Success 2025 "Strategic Path 1- enhance the quality of the academic experience" by helping faculty build creative curricula extensively embedded with high-impact learning practices to assist students' achievement (MTSU, n.d.).

The goal of this chapter is to encourage other faculty to take the leap of traveling thousands of miles in conducting faculty-led, short-term study abroad programs. It aligns with many of the institutions' goals while also enabling students to gain global experience and understand a new perspective from beyond the classroom doors.

REFERENCES

Childhood Education International (CE International). (n.d.). *What is education diplomacy?* Retrieved from https://ceinternational1892.org/education-diplomacy/.

Deardorff, D. K. (2006). Identification and assessment of intercultural competence as a student outcome of internationalization. *Journal of Studies in International Education, 10*(2), 241–266. https://doi.org/10.1177/1028315306287002

Deardorff, D. K. (2012). Framework: Intercultural competence model. In K. Berardo & D. K. Deardorff (Eds.), *Building cultural competence: Innovative activities and models* (pp. 45-52). Stylus Publishing.

Freeman, N. K., Decker, C. A., & Decker, J. R. (2017). *Planning and administering early childhood programs* (11th ed.). Pearson.

Hanson, L. (2010). Global citizenship, global health, and the internationalization of curriculum: A study of transformative potential. *Journal of Studies in International Education, 14*(1), 70–88. https://doi.org/10.1177/1028315308323207

Kolb, D. A. (2015). *Experiential learning: Experience as the source of learning and development* (2nd ed.). Pearson Education LTD.

Middle Tennessee State University Office of International Affairs (2022). *Annual impact report 2021-2022.* Retrieved from https://issuu.com/mtsumag/docs/mtsu_ia_annual_report_2021-22.

Middle Tennessee State University (n.d.). *Quest for student success 2025.* Retrieved from https://www.mtsu.edu/quest/.

Morais, D. B., & Ogden, A. C. (2011). Initial development and validation of the global citizenship scale. *Journal of Studies in International Education, 15*(5), 445–466. https://doi.org/10.1177/1028315310375308

National Association for the Education of Young Children (2019). *Professional standards and competencies for early childhood educators.* Retrieved from https://www.naeyc.org/resources/position-statements/professional-standards-competencies.

Schattle, H. (2009). Global citizenship in theory and practice. In R. Lewin (Ed.), *The handbook of practice and research in study abroad: Higher education and the quest for global citizenship* (pp. 3-18). Routledge.

APPENDICES

Appendix 4.1

Pre-departure questionnaire

1. Why did you choose to study abroad for ECE 4360?
2. What are your goals/objectives for this study abroad?
3. What are some possible challenges you might encounter on this program?
4. How do you plan to overcome it?
5. What possible outcome do you think this study abroad might impact upon your college degree and future career?
6. What do you know about Singapore and the culture?
7. How will you share your knowledge with others when you get back to Tennessee? (Only for 2016 & 2018 cohort)
8. Any other comments?

Post-departure questionnaire

1. What is your major highlight of this program?
2. Were your goals/objectives of the program met?
3. Reflect on some challenges you encounter in this program, how did you overcome it?
4. How do you think this study abroad might impact your college and future career?
5. What is your knowledge of Singapore and its culture now?
6. What is something you have learnt as a result of this study abroad to Singapore?
7. How and what will you share with others when you get back to Tennessee? (Only for 2016 & 2018 cohort)
8. Any other comments?

Appendix 4.2

Sample Itinerary for ECE 4360 Administering Early Childhood Programs in Singapore

Days	Itinerary	Instructional Hours
Day 1	Depart from Nashville Airport	
Day 2	On flight	
Day 3	Arrive in Singapore Check into Praisehaven Retreat Centre School visit 1 (12 pm – 3 pm) *Grocery Shopping SEMINAR 1: Overview of Early Childhood Education Program Readings: Chapter 1 (Freeman et al., 2013)	3 hours 2 hours
Day 4	School visit 2 (9 am - 12 pm) Excursion: Jurong Bird Park	3 hours

Days	Itinerary	Instructional Hours
Day 5	SEMINAR 2: Vision, Mission and Program Evaluation Readings: Chapter 2 (Freeman et al., 2013) Excursion: Singapore Zoological Garden	2 hours
Day 6	Visit to local church (11 am) Excursion: Chinatown	
Day 7	School visit 3 (10am-12 pm) Excursion: Singapore Botanical Garden (9 am – 12 pm) Seminar 3: Being a Professional Readings: Chapter 12 & 13 (Freeman et al., 2013)	2 hours 2 hours
Day 8	School visit 4 (9 am - 12 pm) Seminar 4: Accreditation and Policy Readings: Chapters 3 & 4 (Freeman et al., 2013) Excursion: Singapore Night Tour	3 hours 2 hours
Day 9	School visit 5 (10 am- 12 pm) Excursion: National Museum of Singapore Seminar 5: Operationalizing the Early Childhood Program Readings: Chapters 4,5,6,7 (Freeman et al., 2013)	2 hours 2 hours
Day 10	School visit 6 (9 am – 12 pm) Seminar 6: Planning the Program Readings: Chapters 9 & 10 (Freeman et al., 2013)	3 hours 2 hours
Day 11	Seminar 7: Assessment Readings: Chapter 11 (Freeman et al., 2013) Excursion: Duck Tour Excursion: Singapore Flyer	2 hours
Day 12	Excursion: Sentosa Sea Aquarium Excursion: Sentosa Beach	
Day 13	Depart for Nashville HOME SWEET HOME	
Day 15	Video and panel presentation on 10 am – 12pm @ Walker Library –LT&ITC (3rd Floor)	2 hours

Appendix 4.3

Disposition and buddy contract

Students are required to score at least a proficient score according to the performance levels of unsatisfactory, developing, proficient and exemplary for their disposition in all the areas including professional competencies, attitudes, and disposition. In addition, they need to ensure they abide by the buddy contract signed before course departure. The following will be expected during this course:

Attendance, Professionalism, Participation, Collaboration, Dissemination

a. Attend all pre-trip meetings and attend each field experience and all seminars.
b. Conduct yourself professionally, dress appropriately, engage ethically, keep an open mind, and be unbiased.
c. Participate in classroom and school events, participate during seminars and discussions, engage your peers and those with whom we work with in the schools.
d. Collaborate with the group to obtain consensus, cohesion, and unity. Be prepared to step in and step up.
e. Disseminate your learning to the instructors, those in the group, and with others when we return.

Appendix 4.4

Daily Journal/Photo Reflection and Documentation (80 points)

Ten points can be earned by completing a daily journal reflection/ photo documentation on this study abroad . A total of 8 entries will be compiled. Each entry would consist of:
a. Expectations before the day's event
b. Observations
c. Reflections of the day
d. One learning point to implement on program planning and administration in early childhood program
e. Photographs and documentation

The journal/photo documentation will be compiled into a booklet to be submitted and shared during *video/panel presentation day*.

Guiding questions for a) Expectations
- What did you want to know before going to the school?

Guiding questions for b) Observations
- A brief description of the setting; children; culture; teachers; and any other observations.

Guiding questions for c) Reflections
- How is your experience different from what you expected?
- What did you learn about yourself and what changes you plan to make for the next visit?
- What are your strengths?
- What are your challenges?
- What would you do differently the next time?
- What was exciting, surprising, or frustrating about the experience?
- What impacts the way you view the situation/experience?

Guiding questions for d) Learning Point
- What did you learn about the center/ culture/ children/ experience now that you did not know before going? Be specific in your description.

Guiding questions for Final Journal (8th entry)
- Describe your strengths?
- Describe your challenges?
- Which of your skills will you further develop and what will you do to develop them?
- How does this experience bridge what you learned at MTSU?
- What possible outcome do you think this study abroad might impact upon your college degree and future career?
- How will you share your knowledge with others when you get back to Tennessee?

Appendix 4.5

Video and panel presentation on Administering Early Childhood Programs: Study Abroad Singapore (160 points)

The video and panel presentation will focus on the following:
a. Background information of Singapore consisting of its history, geography, demographic makeup, infrastructure, and culture that impact the Early Childhood Education in Singapore.
b. Similarities and differences between Singapore accreditation system to the Tennessee Star Quality Child Care Program and NAEYC accreditation for young children.
c. Comparing different preschools/elementary schools in Singapore.
d. Impact of diversity and culture on the developing child.
e. Design an ideal developmentally and culturally appropriate classroom.
f. Overall personal reflection on this trip.

Chapter 5

Creating Intercultural Learning Opportunities in a Study Abroad Japanese Culture Course

Priya Ananth

Note: Section II includes Chapters 4-14. These chapters use a standardized template to discuss the details of their respective study abroad programs and reference Deardorff's (2012) framework for intercultural competencies. The use of this template and the intercultural competencies framework are described in the Section II introduction. All courses in this section (except for Chapter 6) were taught through Middle Tennessee State University (MTSU), a mid-sized state school located in Murfreesboro, Tennessee (USA).

The *MTSU in Japan* (JAPN 3900) program is a short-term study abroad course that explores the traditional and modern culture of Japan with its primary offshore location at Reitaku University in Minami-Kashiwa in Chiba prefecture of Japan. Chiba prefecture is located on Japan's eastern Pacific coast to the east of Tokyo and is part of the Greater Tokyo Area. The key aspect of this course is the thematic-based pedagogical framework that follows a backward design approach where the learning goals drive the learning activities. This kind of framework enables the students to learn, experience, and reflect on the various theme-based cultural artifacts, practices, and ways of thinking in Japan. Excursions and field trips also cover the surrounding prefectures of Tochigi and Kanagawa, as well as the Tokyo metropolitan area. Four weeks are dedicated to the course, and a few days before and after the course are set aside for travel days. Typically, the program runs from around mid-May to mid-June. The program has been conducted three times so far in 2016, 2017, and 2018, and the number of students in each of those years were 9, 13, and 10 respectively.

THEORETICAL FOUNDATIONS

The main goal of the course is to deepen students' understanding of the cultural complexities of thoughts and values in Japanese society seen from both historical and modern-day perspectives. This goal inevitably requires the students to develop critical and analytical skills to gain knowledge, expand on and articulate their ideas, and monitor their own behaviors, all qualities needed in cross-cultural interactions taking place during study abroad. The course was built on a combination of the experiential learning theory (Kolb, 1984) and the thematic unit-based approach (Tohsaku, 2010) to curriculum building. Kolb's (1984) recursive learning cycle includes the following stages: undergoing concrete experiences, observing and reflecting on the experiences, forming abstract concepts or generalizations about those experiences, and testing those generalizations in new contexts. Based on this model, students are encouraged to actively participate, observe, and reflect on concrete cross-cultural experiences. Students discuss their assumptions in class and then test the implications through purposely designed classroom activities or activities outside of the classroom (Jia, 2019).

A thematic unit-based approach was used to design the curricular structure for this course. This approach is one where the main topic is divided into multiple stand-alone units or modules that are interrelated by a recurring theme. A thematic unit is defined as "an instructional unit that organizes teaching around themes or topics and makes it possible for us to integrate instruction across such areas as language, culture, science, art, literature, and social issues" (Tohsaku, 2010). For this course, the main topic of 'Japanese Culture' was divided into modules such as geography and history, cuisine and fast-food culture, family and work culture, religions and beliefs, popular culture and subcultures, school and college cultures, sports and leisure, and exporting Japan's culture. Excursions, hands-on workshops, lectures, guest speakers, and other activities were integrated around these modules.

While the course curriculum was built on the experiential learning theory and a thematic unit-based approach at the granular level, a backward design approach was adopted to connect the thematic units at the macro level. Rather than starting with the content or set textbooks, backward design argues that one starts with the end—the desired results (goals or standards)—and then derives the curriculum from the evidence of learning (performances) called for by the standard and the teaching needed to equip students to perform (Wiggins & McTighe, 1998). For this course, assessment instruments, evaluation criteria, and learning outcomes were put in place before deciding on the theoretical frameworks, course content, and activities.

COURSE DESCRIPTION

This program offers multiple opportunities for students to explore diverse aspects of traditional and modern Japanese culture. These opportunities enable the students to critically examine, gain first-hand experience, and then reflect upon the myriad of unique cultural artifacts, practices, and ways of thinking they encounter in the everyday life of the Japanese people and their society. While a strong emphasis is placed on learning by examining, doing, and reflecting, the course curriculum also incorporates required texts and readings as a complementary part of this academic course.

There are two required textbooks that students purchase prior to the start of the program: *The Cambridge Companion to Modern Japanese Culture* by Yoshio Sugimoto (2009), and *Introduction to Japanese Culture* by Daniel Sosnoski (1996). The cultural themes chosen for the course follow the topics in the first book, while the second book provides a collection of essays and short articles on specific Japanese cultural artifacts to supplement the first book. Additionally, I also provide other relevant articles, news clippings, website links, and materials as recommended texts that evolve from year to year. The course is taught in English to include all students regardless of their Japanese language background. However, I do include a short

Japanese language lesson at the beginning of each lecture session with the goal of teaching some basic survival Japanese that can be readily used by participants outside of the classroom.

Course Learning Outcomes

There were four primary learning outcomes identified for the course. At the end of this course, the student will be able to:

a. Critically examine a variety of topics related to Japan's traditional and modern-day popular culture and analyze the changes in the ways of thinking of the Japanese people over time as presented in texts, readings, and lectures.

b. Actively participate in experiential activities and excursions to develop firsthand knowledge, skills, and attitudes that are effective and appropriate in interacting with the community outside of class.

c. Reflect upon the similarities and differences between the Japanese culture and their own in a rational and non-judgmental manner.

d. Appropriately articulate facts and opinions and effectively communicate them in both oral and written presentation formats.

COURSE HISTORY

The idea to offer a faculty-led study abroad program to Japan was first proposed by the Vice Provost for International Affairs (IA) at the university. As part of the university's efforts to increase internationalization on campus and to leave our footprints abroad, faculty members were encouraged to propose an MTSU faculty-led signature program. Several faculty members were funded by the IA office to conduct a reconnaissance trip to investigate the logistics and feasibility for putting together a new program. My program would become the first faculty-led program in Japan from my department. After thorough research of content and resources both in Japan and back home, I selected Reitaku University, located in the suburbs of Tokyo, as the program's destination. We already had an exchange partner agreement with the university for the regular semester and year-long programs, so the initial steps of making connections and relationships occurred relatively swiftly. With assistance from the faculty and staff at Reitaku University, and guidance from foreign language colleagues from my home department, I was able to propose and then offer the first program a year later. I successfully conducted this program for three years prior to the onset of the COVID-19 pandemic. My decision to plan, source, budget, and work on all administrative details of the program at MTSU instead of offering it through a consortium or a third-party vendor was driven by a desire to keep the program costs down and to have full autonomy over the curriculum planning.

COURSE LOGISTICS

This 3-credit hour course included 60 hours of in-class lectures in addition to the instruction that occurred during field trips, excursions, and group activities. The course had no prerequisites and could count towards any academic major or minor. Due to the limited available enrollment for the study abroad to Japan, two screening levels were conducted: level 1 was a document review, and level 2 was an in-person interview. For the document review, I included questions mostly on their reasons for participating, how relevant the course would be to their college study, and then logistical questions such as if they had a passport, or if they had previously traveled abroad. For the interview questions, I asked the students more pointed questions about their personal background, including their experience with managing their finances. The purpose of the interview was to see how they behaved in person, if they were suitable for a group setting, and if they came across as thoughtful and empathetic to others. I also encouraged them to share any other issues that they felt comfortable sharing at that point. I decided to include the two-step screening of participants to limit the class size at a maximum of 15 students. For the three years that I ran the program, I did not have to turn away any student after the interview. Following the two screenings, selected students were granted permission to register for the course. Coincidently, there was at least one student every year who had to pull out of the program after registration due to financial or personal reasons. In these cases, I refunded the initial deposits to these students.

PRE-PROGRAM ACTIVITIES

I conducted four pre-departure mandatory orientations that were spread throughout the semester prior to the study abroad semester. These sessions were comprised of information sharing pertaining to the logistics of the course, as well as some introductory lectures on cultural etiquette and appropriate behaviors expected of foreigners in Japan. The main purpose of these sessions was information sharing: both content and logistical, including reminders for dates and deadlines, and offering an informal space for the participants to get to know each other.

CLASS ACTIVITIES & INTERCULTURAL COMPETENCIES

During the program, in-class lectures were scheduled in 3-hour slots and delivered once or twice a day. Out-of-class group activities, field trips, and excursions were designed in half-day, full-day, or weekend slots. Outdoor activities were balanced with the in-class lectures to the maximum extent possible. For example, during the week we discussed traditional Japanese sports, we also watched a live sumo wrestling match. During the in-class lecture for this unit, we invited a guest speaker to give us a lesson about the background history and sumo rules that helped us understand and enjoy various parts of the competition. As part of the history unit, we spent a day in Kamakura, a city in the Kanagawa prefecture that was the center of power for the shoguns, or military generals, from 1185 to 1333, when political power and religious beliefs often conflicted.

Whether it was entering the giant Buddha statue at the Kotoku-in temple in Kamakura or visiting the historical Edo-Tokyo Metropolitan Museum in Tokyo, these experiences made history closer to reality for the students. Performing Zen meditation at the local Buddhist temple, followed by a calligraphy session that involved tracing Buddhist hymns on rice paper in traditional inkstone, was a lesson in how the monks sharpened their concentration skills. Students learned about the rich cuisine culture of Japan through several hands-on workshops, such as making soy sauce at the Kikkoman plant, creating a custom-made cup of ramen noodles by selecting their own ingredients at the Nisshin Cup Noodle Museum, and performing the traditional Japanese tea ceremony in the local teahouse on campus. A visit to the local elementary school provided an opportunity to observe and learn about the teaching and learning styles unique to the Japanese education system. Students also experienced leisure activities, such as karaoke, kabuki theater performance, and an overnight trip to a traditional Japanese hot spring resort in Nikko, a popular town in Tochigi prefecture.

Weekends were free days with optional activities such as a trip to Tokyo Disney Sea, Ghibli Museum, Ueno Zoo, and special events such as the Sailor Moon exhibition. Since the course content involved ten unique cultural topics (such as sports culture, family culture, work culture, school culture, and so forth) based on a common theme centered on Japan, a thematic unit-based pedagogical approach was most suitable to design the curriculum. Each of the ten topics were stand-alone units or modules that were allotted two to three class lecture sessions (usually 4-6 hours per topic) with accompanying activities, field trips, and assignments. Furthermore, the experiential learning theory was purposefully integrated into the curriculum by setting clear expectations about active participation in hands-on activities, outdoor excursions, and various cross-cultural engagements with the local community. It is reassuring to see that the part of the curriculum that was most well-received by the students were the cross-cultural interactions with the local students, whether structured and unstructured. These opportunities were borne out of the guest lectures and collaborative classes where our students actively initiated and engaged in discussions with the Japanese students. The students formed buddy groups, organized periodic meetings and activities, and forged bonds of friendship beyond the classrooms. Refer to a sample program itinerary in Appendix 5.1 for details on the day-by-day breakdown of cultural topics and the interactive activities tied to each of them.

Scavenger Hunt Activity

During the first week of the program, the students were asked to use a campus map and go around the campus and surrounding places to familiarize themselves. The locations included the student cafeteria, main campus gate, supermarket, convenience store, post office, train station, ATM, fast food restaurant, etc. The students were required to take a selfie at the places that they visited, then compile all the photos in a photo diary and label the pictures appropriately. Finally, they were asked to share the link to the photo diary with their family and friends back home via social media. This activity pushed the students to step out of their comfort zone and start developing navigation skills. The activity also provided them an opportunity to connect with family and friends, hence encouraging empathy. The intercultural competencies highlighted in this activity are listed in Table 5.1. Refer to Appendix 5.2 for the guidelines used for this activity.

Table 5.1. Intercultural Competencies for Scavenger Hunt Activity

Knowledge	Skills	Attitudes
• Locations on campus and around	• Map reading • Creating a photo diary • Navigation skills	• Curiosity and discovery • Risk-taking • Stepping out of the comfort zone • Empathy

Elementary School Visit Activity

This activity was a full-day visit to a nearby elementary school and was scheduled in the third week of the program. The day's activities involved class observations, a performative activity that involved conducting a 10-minute mini-lesson on the English language for the Japanese schoolchildren, and participation in after-school club activities. For the mini-lesson, the students started preparing a few days before the day of the visit. They worked in groups of two or three to create interactive lesson plans, teaching materials, and visual aids. The lessons included playing games, using songs, learning English animal sounds, word search quizzes, and role plays. There were six groups in total. They were given time to practice during and after class hours and were provided with feedback from me on their lesson plans. On the day of the visit, we were given a pre-planned schedule by the school authorities with class observations in the morning and afternoon, a mini-lesson during the lunch hour, and optional after-school club activities. The students observed a combination of math, craft, and English language classes. Our student groups were divided into sub-groups during the lunch break, where they actively interacted with the schoolchildren to present their English lessons. The mini-lessons were followed by a cleaning routine (sweeping and mopping of the classrooms and hallways) that the Japanese schoolchildren led with assistance from our students. After school, our students were given the option to attend after-school clubs such as the science club, instrumental music club, etc. The activities during the visit gave our students several opportunities to learn by observing and active listening, to work in groups, and to interact with the local community. This activity provided the students an opportunity to gain intercultural competencies as tabulated in Table 5.2. Refer to Appendix 5.3 for the day's schedule used for this activity.

Table 5.2. Intercultural Competencies for Elementary School Visit Activity

Knowledge	Skills	Attitudes
• Elementary education system of Japan • Teaching English in Japan • Differences in school culture	• Creating lesson plans • Pair/group work • Class management • Observing • Listening	• Open-minded • Stepping outside the comfort zone • Withholding judgment • Resilience • Patience • Tolerance for ambiguity

Inflight Letter Assignment

This was a two-part assignment (at the beginning and at the end of the program) whereby the students wrote a letter to their future self on the onward flight to Japan, and then wrote a reply letter to the first one on the return flight home. The goal of the first letter was to help the students pose at least three questions for which they needed to investigate and come up with answers in Japan. The questions could relate to the course content (that is facts about the Japanese culture they wanted to research), or a reflective question about themselves and their values. The letter assignment was a starting point for reflection on sensitivity to differences, appreciation and respect of diversity, and openness to novelty, acceptance, and flexibility. This assignment was envisioned as a "pause and think" moment that would naturally lead the students to self-reflect while being creative. Students would later have another "pause and think" moment during their return flight when they wrote a reply to their first letter answering the questions they had posed earlier. It was interesting to see that some students added words of praise and self-encouragement in their letters on how much they had learned and how far they had come in four short weeks. In addition to the inflight letter assignment, the students also had to write their daily reflections in an online blog and a final reflection paper assignment at the end of the course. These journaling exercises gave students an insight into their internal readiness toward and awareness of another culture. Intercultural competencies integrated into this activity are summarized in Table 5.3. Refer to Appendix 5.4 for the assignment guidelines.

Table 5.3. Intercultural Competencies for In-Flight Letter Assignment

Knowledge	Skills	Attitudes
<ul><li>Self-awareness</li><li>Awareness about other cultures</li><li>Academic content</li></ul>	<ul><li>Reflective writing</li><li>Creative thinking and problem-solving</li><li>Research</li></ul>	<ul><li>Curiosity and discovery</li><li>Open-minded</li><li>Resilience (to complete assignments on the flight!)</li></ul>

Using Public Transit System Task

Since the program involved extensive local traveling almost daily throughout the length of the program, the students needed to become familiar with and confident in using the public transit system (buses, trains, subways, taxis) in Tokyo. While Tokyo's transit system is one of the most efficient in the world, it can also be overwhelming for an inexperienced traveler. Figuring out the train and subway maps and purchasing the appropriate fare ticket can be a skill category by itself. There are other challenges as well. For example, it is rare to find direct connections between places, and one is often required to make multiple transfers between trains or modes of transport. Another challenge (less in Tokyo city) is to find romanization of station names or English translations of train announcements.

To get the students to understand the transit system and use it independently, I designed a task in which 2-3 students were made in charge of navigating the rest of the group to an assigned destination. They had to research all possible routes and fares to get to the destination on time. On my part, I introduced them to a couple of English language Japanese travel apps and gave them the station names for the start and endpoint. For example, the navigation leaders for the trip to Ghibli Museum used the travel app to decide the best route, with minimum transfers, within a reasonable amount of time, and well before our scheduled entry time. I would do the exact search on my end, and the student leaders and I would compare notes. The best route would be agreed upon by consensus and then shared with the rest of the class to have the same information. On the day of the trip, the navigators would lead the group giving clear directions about the platform number, train transfer, fare for each transfer, etc. In effect, the navigators were responsible for getting the whole group safely and on time to the destination. They would also then lead the way on our return. Since there were numerous places to visit in our itinerary, all students got at least one opportunity to be the group navigator. Students often picked their favorite destination to be the navigator for the day. However, some preferred not to volunteer more than once.

Towards the latter half of the program, students felt comfortable venturing out independently during free time and weekends. This task was immensely beneficial in helping students hone their navigation skills, step out of their comfort zone, and develop leadership skills. This task offered an opportunity where students were pushed into trying something unfamiliar and learned that making mistakes is part of the process. Also since this was a group task, the students always had peer support and were never completely out of their comfort zones. This task allowed the students to focus on intercultural competencies listed in Table 5.4. Refer to Appendix 5.5 for examples of travel apps and travel plans for this task.

Table 5.4. Intercultural Competencies for Using Public Transit System Task

Knowledge	Skills	Attitudes
<ul><li>Locations in Tokyo and suburbs</li><li>The public transit system in Tokyo</li><li>Differences in transportation cultures</li></ul>	<ul><li>Map reading</li><li>Using travel apps</li><li>Research and critical thinking</li><li>Leadership</li><li>Decision making</li><li>Teamwork</li></ul>	<ul><li>Patience</li><li>Risk-taking</li><li>Stepping outside the comfort zone</li><li>Withholding judgment</li><li>Empathy</li><li>Tolerance for ambiguity</li></ul>

Class Presentations Assignment

Besides assigning written research papers and reflection papers, I had students do in-class presentations at various points in the program as part of their evaluated assignments. There were mainly two types of in-class presentations. The first type was a presentation on a topic from within the content area. Each student had to present one topic of their choice from a list of ten that were relevant to the course. For example, in the unit on leisure culture, a student prepared a presentation on *onsen,* or traditional Japanese spa. This unit was timed immediately before going on a weekend trip to a Japanese *onsen* resort in a location four hours north of Tokyo. For the presentation, the student was asked to include the rules about using a public *onsen*. In the unit on work culture, a student was assigned a presentation on exchanging business cards in Japan. The students then followed up by creating their own business cards in Japanese and role-playing with appropriate bowing etiquette and the proper way of exchanging cards. In the unit on Japanese popular culture, all students made presentations on introducing one of their favorite works and a character from any of the popular culture genres: manga, anime, video games, JPop, and so forth.

The second type of presentation was for the final group project. For this one, each student group had to research a topic of their collective interest related to Japanese culture (traditional or modern) and then make an interactive final oral presentation that would be teachable to their classmates. One group, for example, inspired by the amulets and charms sold at Japanese temples and shrines, researched and presented on this topic. For the interactive activity, they had their classmates make an origami amulet. Another group focused on introducing the New Year festivities of Japan and taught the class three kinds of communal games traditionally played in Japanese homes during the New Year holidays. A third group worked on the housing culture and landscape patterns of modern Japanese homes. For the interactive activity, everyone designed a house floor plan with the characteristics of an eco-friendly Japanese home. Another group worked on Japanese cuisine culture and shared a Japanese recipe prepared in the dorm kitchen for their final presentation. The assignment required students to make their presentations teachable and interactive, which compelled them to be creative, think out of the box, work in teams, and be empathetic and mindful of each other and their audience. This assignment helped the students develop intercultural competencies as shown in Table 5.5. Refer to Appendix 5.6 for the assignment prompt

Table 5.5. Intercultural Competencies for Class Presentations Assignment

Knowledge	Skills	Attitudes
• Academic content area • Awareness of other cultures • Differences with own culture	• Creative thinking and problem-solving • Teamwork • Articulation • Oral presentation • Leadership	• Open-minded • Empathy • Risk-taking • Patience • Tolerance for ambiguity

Partnerships with Local Students

Both structured and unstructured student interactions in partnership with the local students were built into the program throughout the four weeks. The students evaluated these interactions as the most memorable and enjoyable experiences of the entire program. Group interactions included the following:

a. Student volunteers from the host university led the effort and organized structured buddy group meetings three times in the program. They organized introductions and games at the first meeting, watched anime followed by discussions in their second meeting, and then set up a kimono-wearing activity at the third meeting.

b. Our students were invited to participate in a weekly English language table on campus, where they played a variety of creative games learning fun Japanese words and phrases while also helping the host students practice English conversation.

c. Students on both sides participated in collaborative lectures organized by the faculty. They then kept up the communication by meeting up over the weekends to go for movies, pizza parties, karaoke, and trips to Pokémon Center, Owl Café, Cat Café, Sanrio Store, and more.

These student partnerships led to forming strong bonds of friendship at a very personal level for those students who chose to maintain these friendships even after returning to the United States. It became clear that the program's curricular structure, with its focus on community interaction, directly impacted the students' ability to develop intercultural competence. Through these partnerships, the students could gain intercultural competencies as listed in Table 5.6.

Table 5.6. Intercultural Competencies for Partnerships with Local Students

Knowledge	Skills	Attitudes
• Awareness of self • Awareness of other cultures	• Teamwork • Articulation • Observing • Listening	• Open-minded • Withholding judgment • Patience • Tolerance for ambiguity • Respect • Adaptability • Flexibility • Empathy

POST-PROGRAM AND FUTURE CLASS ACTIVITIES

There was one mandatory group meeting in the week immediately after our return. Additionally, one optional information panel session was held in the following semester as part of International Education Week, where students shared their experiences and reflections with the university community.

On the next iteration of the MTSU in Japan program, I would like to incorporate a few different ideas. First, there is still potential to experiment with hands-on class activities and assignments that could help students gain intercultural skills and attitudes: for example, assignments that will require the students to conduct onsite interviews with the local community and collect survey data on various sociocultural phenomena such as the use of English words in Japanese, linguistic code-switching (shifting between a language or dialect), use of personal pronouns, and such. This activity will not only add to their knowledge domain but will result in increased gains in confidence and articulation skills. Given the favorable student feedback on the cross-cultural interactions with the local people, it may be worthwhile to investigate the possibility of arranging home-visit experiences, even if for a weekend. Second, I would like to add practical tasks to the itinerary that require students to use more than just their map-reading and navigational skills. For example, I can have student groups take the initiative to plan and create a full itinerary for a day trip. This would require them to first conduct their own research to select a suitable destination, check out the various modes of transportation available, places to eat, things to do, time management, and budgeting. The preparation for this activity would span over several weeks and can be assigned for deployment during one of the several free weekends. Third, the online photo album assignments could be swapped out with a few shorter, low-stake extra credit assignments using social media to keep the students engaged and motivated. Finally, as many of the past participants have been Japanese majors and minors, it would be useful to increase the number of optional opportunities for casual conversations with local speakers. Such experiences would be excellent occasions for students to improve their Japanese language proficiency.

EVALUATION AND ASSIGNMENTS

The evaluation criterion for this course was based on the following components;

1. Attendance and Class Participation   15%
2. Chapter summaries   5%
3. In-flight letter assignment   5%
4. Presentations   10%
5. Photo diaries   20%
6. Daily online blog   20%
7. Final group project   15%
8. Reflection paper   5%
9. Discipline   5%

    I measured the daily and weekly progress made by the students through formative assessments, such as class participation, chapter summaries, in-flight letter assignment, daily online journaling blog, photo diaries, and presentations for each of the topic sets. These formative assessment tools assisted me in periodically gauging the amount of material learned by the students. The summative assessment included the final group project and the reflection paper assignment that helped me evaluate how much the students had learned throughout this program. The ultimate goal of using the formative and summative assessment tools was to see how much of the students' learning outcomes had been attained.

    In addition, I assigned 5% of the overall grade to soft skills such as politeness, respect for others, active listening and engagement, and teamwork. At the beginning of the course, it was made clear that there would be no tolerance for behaviors related to tardiness, disruptions, disrespect towards others, and lack of discipline. I had the students sign a contract that spelled out the program policies, rules, and regulations at both institutions and consequences for violations. I included several items in the contract that directly referred to the targeted soft skills. Refer to Appendix 5.7 for a sample of the contract agreement for this course.

STUDENT FEEDBACK

The reflection papers that students submitted at the end of the course yielded encouraging responses specific to gains in intercultural competencies during the three years of the *MTSU in Japan* program. Below are three direct quotes taken from the student reflection papers. Following each quote, the program year and the intercultural competencies gained by the students are listed.

1. "For me, personally, the greatest impact of the program was a sense of inspiration and determination…Before the program, I was uncertain of how comfortable I would be living and working in Japan. After this past month, I am absolutely sure that I would be thrilled to live the rest of my life there. Furthermore, I have witnessed firsthand how my current skill set and education stack up against the necessities of Japanese life, and that translates into a very clear goal for my continued studies." *(Student 1, 2017, determination, taking risks, Japanese language skills)*

2. "The best takeaway from this trip is the appreciation of two cultures: Japan and home. I found myself comparing a lot of things I experienced here to America. It's important to have a chance to step back and reflect on one's own too. Because many of us have lived our lives in one place, we can ignore and take for granted our own culture. Our culture is our norm and our everyday, so we can't see it from an outside perspective. Having a chance to go to a country on the opposite side of the world than mine was a perfect opportunity to do that… This trip gave me more confidence than I previously had about studying abroad for a year in Japan." *(Student 2, 2017, appreciation of other cultures, comparing and analyzing, reflection, confidence)*

3. "I would recommend this program to another student because of just how much can be gained from the experience. I feel like a changed person; I feel compelled to be nicer to those around me, more appreciative of what others do for me, and more respectful of nature and the products we consume. I feel happier and like that my life has been much more enriched by this experience. For those who are going into a field that has the potential to touch international audiences, I believe a study abroad experience, especially to Japan, is almost necessary so that you can become sensitive to world views and another culture that is so different than our own." *(Student 3, 2018, appreciative of others, respectful, intercultural sensitivity, observing differences)*

To summarize these quotes, the students themselves experienced transformation in more than one way. Even in this short-term program, they saw a visible growth in their own intercultural competency skills (compare, analyze, reflect, etc.) and attitudes (empathy, adaptability, open-mindedness, etc.). As a faculty leader, it is extremely gratifying to see such outcomes, especially when articulated by the participants themselves.

CAVEATS AND REFLECTIONS

Although the *MTSU in Japan* program has only been offered three times as of August 2023, I think it has been able to achieve its purpose of introducing diverse aspects of the Japanese culture to our students in ways that would not have been possible with an on-campus iteration of the same course. In addition to providing the content knowledge, this course also effectively integrated key intercultural competencies by intentionally weaving them into the class activities, tasks, and assignments. The experiential activities and tasks involving cross-cultural interactions provided the most opportunity to integrate intercultural competency skills and attitudes. As a faculty leader, it is encouraging to see that the intercultural competency-infused activities and interactions led some students to make important life decisions, such as going for an extended second study abroad and applying for jobs to teach English in Japanese schools after graduation.

In future programs, it might be helpful to add a few more opportunities for students to come together for reflections in the post-program stage of the cycle. Although some of the students continued to communicate through social media, those post-program activities gradually declined as time went by. It might also be helpful to talk to students about what intercultural competencies are and encourage them to always be mindful of those. Including the intercultural competency elements in the assessment rubrics would also be one way to make their importance visible to the students. Faculty leaders must intentionally introduce the students to the benefits of developing intercultural competencies starting as early as possible, even during the recruitment stage. With some creativity, the ideas presented in this chapter can be effectively adapted to any other short-term, faculty-led study abroad program regardless of the discipline.

REFERENCES

Deardorff, D. K. (2012). Framework: Intercultural competence model. In K. Berardo & D. K. Deardorff (Eds.), *Building cultural competence: Innovative activities and models* (pp. 45-52). Stylus Publishing.

Jia, J. (2019). Understanding Chinese behavioral culture through cross-cultural communication. In P. Ananth & L. T. Lyons (Eds.), *Incorporating foreign language content in humanities courses* (pp. 124-132). Routledge.

Kolb, D. (1984). *Experiential learning: Experience as the source of learning and development.* Prentice Hall.

Sosnoski, D. (1996). *Introduction to Japanese culture.* Tuttle Publishing.

Sugimoto, Y. (2009). *The Cambridge companion to modern Japanese culture.* Cambridge University Press.

Tohsaku. Y. (2010). *Thematic units in Japanese language education* [Lecture handout]. AATJ Language, Culture, and Technology Summer Institute in Japan.

Wiggins, G., & McTighe, J. (1998). *Understanding by design.* Association for Supervision and Curriculum Development.

APPENDICES

Appendix 5.1: Sample Itinerary

Appendix 5.1: Sample Itinerary for Japan Program

Date	Morning	Afternoon
May 10	Depart Nashville	
May 11		Arrive Tokyo
May 12	Campus orientation	
May 13		Tokyo Tower evening tour
May 14	Course Introduction	Lecture 1 (introduction) Evening: Welcome party
May 15	Lecture 2 (sports culture)	Sumo guest lecture Buddy Group Meeting #1
May 16	Edo Tokyo Museum	Sumo Tournament
May 17	Lecture 3 (food culture)	Lecture 3 continued (food culture) Traditional sit-down dinner
May 18	Kamakura	Kamakura
May 19	Free day	Optional: Meiji Jingu, Harajuku, Shibuya
May 20	Free day	Optional: Asakusa
May 21	Lecture 4 (family culture)	Lecture 5 (religions)
May 22	Kikkoman Shoyu Sauce Museum	Guest lecture (Japanese religions)
May 23	Lecture 6 (work culture)	Lecture 6 continued (work culture)
May 24	Kabuki Museum	Kabuki Performance
May 25	Lecture 7 (pop culture)	Lecture 7 continued (pop culture) Buddy Group Meeting #2
May 26	Free day	Optional: Sumida River cruise, Odaiba
May 27	Nikko onsen	Nikko onsen
May 28	Nikko onsen	Nikko onsen
May 29	Cross cultural communication guest lecture	Lecture 8 (school culture) Temple Visit for Zazen
May 30	Elementary school visit	Elementary school visit
May 31	Toshiba Museum	Free time
June 1	Transfer to YMCA in Tokyo city	Tokyo tour
June 2	Yokohama: Nisshin Cup Museum	Ramen Museum
June 3	Free day	Optional: Akihabara, Nezu
June 4	Free day	
June 5	Return to Reitaku campus	Lecture 9 (leisure culture) Tea Ceremony on campus
June 6	Ghibli Studio Visit	

Date	Morning	Afternoon
June 7	Lecture 10 (exporting Japanese culture)	Wrap up (final projects prep)
June 8	Final Projects	Final Projects Buddy Group Meeting #3
June 9	Free day	Optional: Karaoke
June 10	Free day	Optional: Tokyo Disney
June 11	Free day	packing and post office
June 12	Depart Tokyo	Arrive Nashville

Appendix 5.2: Reitaku Scavenger Hunt Guidelines

Objectives: Getting to know the Reitaku University campus and surroundings

Directions:
1. Go to the following destinations on foot and take a picture.
2. Create a "Reitaku Scavenger Hunt" PhotoPeach album. Label your pictures.
3. Upload the link as part of your daily blog for May 26.

Destinations:

a. Hiiragi Café (with a Reitaku student)
b. Main Gate or Side Gate entry to campus (with a guard man)
c. Rose Garden (smelling the roses)
d. Yamazaki convenience store (with your favorite snack)
e. "Reitaku Daigaku Mae" Bus stop (going towards the station)
f. Post Office (closest to campus)
g. Seven-Eleven ATM
h. Okaasan supermarket
i. Lawson convenience store
j. Your favorite restaurant around campus

Appendix 5.3: Elementary School Visit Schedule

Appendix 5.3: Elementary School Visit Schedule

Start Time	Activity
9:00-10:30	Lecture/Prep at CMSE Classroom
10:50	Leave campus
11:00	Arrive at school, explanation, school tour, etc.
11:20	4th class period observation
12:05	Lunch (bring your lunch)
12:40-12:50	Mini Lesson
12:50	Break
13:15-13:35	Cleaning activity
13:40	5th class period observation
14:25	Wrap up meeting
14:45	Club activities observation
15:30	Return to campus

Appendix 5.4: Inflight Letter Assignment Guidelines

You will be required to write a letter to your future self during the onward flight posing three (3) questions that you would like to know about Japan. On the return flight, you will reply to this letter while answering those questions. To answer the questions, you will need to investigate the questions during your time in Japan. There will be two (2) letter assignments in total.

Guidelines

Write a letter addressed to your future self, formatted with an opening, main body, and closing. In the main body, compose three (3) questions related to the theme of this course (Japanese traditional and modern culture) that you would like to explore in Japan. While in Japan, investigate the answers to these questions.

You will write a reply addressed to yourself following the same format (opening, main body, closing) on your return flight. In the main body, you will be answering the questions you had posed in the first letter. Keep the answers to each question brief, 150-200 words at minimum for each answer.

Appendix 5.5: Public Transportation Sample Plan

Japanese Travel Apps
https://www.hyperdia.com/
https://world.jorudan.co.jp/mln/en/?sub_lang=ja

Sample Travel Plan to Ghibli Museum
Start Point: Minami-Kashiwa
Destination: Mitaka
Total time: 76 minutes
Total fare: 910 Yens
Number of Transfers: One

Table 5.7: Travel details to go from Minami-Kashiwa to Mitaka

From	Via	To	Notes
Minami-Kashiwa	Ayase (non-stop)	Shin Ochanomizu	Takes 22 minutes and costs 510 Yens using the JR Joban Line Local that changes to Tokyo Metro Chiyoda Line for Mukougaoka Yuen
Shin Ochanomizu	Ochanomizu	Mitaka	Walk 6 minutes to the JR Special Rapid for Takao which takes 27 minutes and costs 400 Yens

Appendix 5.6: Final Class Presentation Guidelines

The final group project will be an interactive class presentation on a topic related to Japanese culture. Each group consisting of 2-3 students will make a 30-minute presentation on the final day. All members of the group must contribute equally to get a fair grade for this project. Detailed guidelines are given below:

The final project will be an interactive group project involving a topic of your choice. Each group must follow the criteria given below:

a. Choose any topic that interests your group or has not been covered in this class.

b. Your presentation must include a compare and contrast element of that topic with American culture. You may present the pros and cons of each culture, looking at why they are different in those ways.

c. You will need to make the presentation interactive with the audience by way of teaching them through your research something that they did not know.

d. Structure your presentation to include title, introduction, main content, conclusion, references. Include activities such as short skits, pop quizzes, games -- be creative!

e. Prepare a brief outline for the project (include title, intro, main body, conclusion) and get it approved by me by Friday, May 25

f. The length of the presentation will be 30 minutes per group.

Appendix 5.7: Participant Contract Agreement Sample

- ☐ I will attend all class sessions and all events that are a part of the program itinerary (my grades will be affected adversely should I not adhere to the attendance policy).
- ☐ I will be punctual to all class sessions as well as group events and will not make excuses for tardiness. (*Tardiness will NOT be tolerated as group events are coordinated with the help of many individuals*).
- ☐ I understand that I serve as an ambassador for both MTSU and the United States, and I will uphold the highest standard of student conduct and behavior.
- ☐ I will refrain from certain behaviors and activities that carry unacceptable risk both to myself and others.
- ☐ I will agree to use the 3-3-4-4 (*san-san-yon-yon*) buddy system at all times during our travels.
- ☐ I understand that this is an academic experience and that academic responsibilities take priority.
- ☐ If there is a medical emergency, I will contact my program faculty/leaders immediately.
- ☐ I will read, understand, and abide by the laws of Reitaku University and Scholars Dorm (read p.2).
- ☐ I will not travel overnight without faculty supervision. I agree to the curfew time of 10 pm on all weekdays and weekends.
- ☐ I will strive to
  - Being polite and listen to one another
  - Participate and engage with the group
  - Respect other students, leaders, and local people affiliated with the program
- ☐ I understand MTSU policy prohibits alcohol (even if you are of drinking age) or drug use as this is an MTSU-sponsored program.

Consequences for Violation
    1. Verbal warning, 2. Written warning, 3. Dismissal

By signing this document, you agree to the above contract details.
Student Name (printed):
Student Name (signed) and Dated:
Student cell phone #:

Chapter 6

Developing Learner Autonomy Through a Three-Week Learning Trip in Japan

Mako Nozu

Note: Section II includes Chapters 4-14. These chapters use a standardized template to discuss the details of their respective study abroad programs and reference Deardorff's (2012) framework for intercultural competencies. The use of this template and the intercultural competencies framework are described in the Section II introduction. All courses in this section (except for Chapter 6) were taught through Middle Tennessee State University (MTSU), a mid-sized state school located in Murfreesboro, Tennessee (USA). The program in Chapter 6 was conducted through the University of South Florida in Tampa, Florida (USA).

USF Japan: Culture, History, and Society is a summer program offered through the University of South Florida (USF). During this program, 20 participants visit nine different cities in Japan, traveling from western Japan to eastern Japan in mid-May to early June during the summer session at USF. The following cities are visited: Fukuoka, Nagasaki, Beppu, Hiroshima, Kyoto, Osaka, Nara, Tokyo, and Yokohama. A unique feature of this program is the attention on nurturing learner autonomy and on the role of the faculty as a facilitator. Various activities, tasks, and assignments were designed keeping these features in mind.

THEORETICAL FOUNDATIONS

When designing this course, three different theoretical foundations were considered: a constructivist approach; an experiential learning-based approach; and a collaborative approach. Creating student-centered learning environments and developing learner autonomy were the main approaches for the learning trip in Japan. Thus, in designing the course, a constructivist approach was considered because learning is a social activity through interaction with others (Dewey, 1938). In the constructivist approach, it is believed that people actively construct their own knowledge and that they build new knowledge upon the foundation of previous learning (Elliott et al., 2000; Phillips, 1995). For that, learners need to become aware of their own process of making meaning and appreciate how other people make meaning in different ways (Harvey, 2017). Through this approach, participants may construct their knowledge of Japan and Japanese culture rather than being passive participants (McLeod, 2019; University of Buffalo, 2022). Therefore, the faculty leader designed the course by creating activities that facilitated the construction of knowledge and experience. During the pre-departure phase, the participants read about various topics on general Japanese concepts that underlie the Japanese daily code of conduct related to their learning trip. The participants then reinforce the information learned from reading by experiencing it firsthand during the learning trip. The participants also reflect on their learning and experiences during the post-trip phase. These three phases, pre-departure, learning trip, and post-trip, allow the participants to transform their experience into learning through reflection and conceptualization. The phases were implemented into the course to facilitate an experiential learning-based approach for participants.

The second theoretical foundation used was the experiential learning-based approach that involves hands-on experiences in learning. Moreover, in an experiential learning-based approach, learners need concrete experiences, reflection on those experiences, and connection with concepts and other experiences in order to make meaning (Harvey, 2017). Through the learning cycle of experiencing, reflecting, thinking, and acting, they apply what they have learned to a new concrete experience (Harvey, 2017; Kolb, 1984). In this course, the participants experience the cycle of input and discussion, experience, and reflection for their effective learning to occur. Effective learning varies individually, so the curriculum must be adapted accordingly.

There is a need for the course theme to be general or flexible due to the participants' various backgrounds since students from various disciplines can apply for the course. For that purpose, the faculty leader's role should be interactive as a facilitator. Additionally, throughout the learning trip in Japan, the participants work in groups, collaborating and cooperating with each other in a variety of hands-on activities, which also leads to the third theoretical foundation, collaborative approach. A collaborative approach involves teamwork, pools in different abilities of learners, and allows differentiated teaching practices with different groups (Yadav, 2021). Throughout the course, especially during the learning trip in Japan, teamwork and collaboration are essential elements for the successful completion of the study abroad program.

COURSE DESCRIPTION

The course was designed to facilitate a successful knowledge base of Japan, and participation is open to students from any disciplines or background. The course seeks to nurture the participants' multicultural awareness needed to successfully navigate today's society and to investigate general concepts of Japanese culture, history, and society.

This course aims to give the participants an overall understanding of Japan and its culture through firsthand experiences in Japan. It also aims to nurture learner autonomy and enhance adaptability and flexibility through a variety of hands-on experiences, as well as to step out of their comfort zones. Students will develop a broad understanding of Japanese society and culture through readings and field trips. Through the course, the participants will be able to learn about another country, compare cultural differences with their own, and broaden their perspectives.

In this course, the participants engage in activities where they read and learn about the basics of Japan's culture, history, and society. There is no core textbook for the course; however, the participants read chapters from *The Japanese Mind: Understanding Contemporary*

Japanese Culture (Davies & Ikeno, 2011), *Understanding Japanese Society* (Hendry, 2012), *Wabi Sabi: The Japanese Art of Impermanence* (Juniper, 2011), and *Japanese Rinzai Zen Buddhism* (Borup, 2008). Through these readings, they gain general knowledge about Japanese society and culture before their trip to Japan. Additionally, students obtain firsthand personal experiences in Japan, analyze their learning experiences, and discuss cultural differences for further understanding. Finally, the students identify and demonstrate knowledge attained about the different elements of Japanese culture, history, and society.

Moreover, the participants focus on one of the following topics (but not limited to them) throughout the program:

1. People in general
2. Daily food
3. Community
4. Culture
5. Religious practices
6. Urban planning and neighborhood

Course Learning Outcomes

Upon completion of the program, the participants will be able to:

a. Differentiate Japanese culture and society from their own.
b. Express appreciation of cultural differences.
c. Report a deeper understanding of Japanese culture and society.
d. Present certain significant aspects of Japanese culture and/or society by creating a picture portfolio.

COURSE HISTORY

The course was originally designed as a geo-perspective course for the USF Honors College in 2014. The course served as an introductory course about Japan to the Honors College students, where they learned about Japanese society. In its first year, it had two-week in-classroom sessions before the two-week learning trip in Japan. Since it gained popularity among non-Honors College students, especially among the students in the Japanese program, it was modified to the current course style (JPT4957) after submitting the course proposal to the Florida State Board of Education. Until 2019, for five consecutive years, USF Japan was one of the most popular summer programs at USF. After a brief pause starting in 2020 due to the COVID-19 pandemic's travel restrictions, the program resumed in the summer of 2023.

COURSE LOGISTICS

The study abroad applications open on the USF Education Abroad website at the beginning of the new academic year in August of every year, with rolling admission. The Japan program usually becomes full by the end of November. No prerequisite courses are required to take part in this summer program in Japan; any students at USF or any other institutions who are interested in Japanese culture and society can apply for the program with or without prior Japanese language knowledge. It is not a required course for World Languages majors with an East Asian Languages concentration, but it can be an elective course. Often, students take this course because of their interests. Once 20 students are accepted and committed, the Education Abroad office enrolls the participants in *JPT4957 Japan Study Program: Culture, History* and in the summer A term, which is a three-credit hour course. There is no formal in-class instruction during the course session; however, the participants and the faculty leader start meeting informally during the spring semester for pre-departure activities.

PRE-PROGRAM ACTIVITIES

Even though the primary focus of the course is the three-week learning trip to Japan, during the pre-departure phase, the students gather for at least three meetings and become familiar with fellow participants and the faculty leader. A constructivist approach and collaborative approach are strongly taken into consideration in this phase. The purposes of these meetings are to create a student-centered environment, promote learner autonomy, and encourage teamwork among students. They are also assigned a series of reading materials designed to impart the basic knowledge of Japanese culture and history and to provide a foundation for the three-week learning experience in Japan. The reading assignments are mainly from books titled *The Japanese Mind: Understanding Contemporary Japanese Culture* (Davies & Ikeno, 2011) and *Understanding Japanese Society* (Hendry, 2012). Students also learn about Japanese Zen Buddhism and Shintoism, a religion that originated in Japan, from the assigned readings. A few topics from the texts are assigned before each meeting, and the participants discuss and share their opinions about the topics in small group settings to deepen and expand their understanding, and eventually narrow down their primary focus of observation and learning during their stay in Japan.

Additionally, some of the topics are taken up for discussion by the whole class. At the end of each meeting, a quick formative verbal assessment is conducted with a few review questions about keywords and concepts. The faculty leader acts as a facilitator for discussions to encourage learner autonomy. At the end of each meeting, the groups verbally review the discussion topics together, which serves as a quick formative assessment of their understanding. As a final component of the pre-program activities, the participants submit an expectation essay of at least 1,000-words regarding what they would focus on observing and what they expect to gain in Japan before their departure to Japan. Furthermore, depending on the participants' backgrounds with the Japanese language, the faculty leader provides a summary of the language and the basic and useful phrases for those with no prior knowledge of the language. Participants with higher Japanese proficiency sometimes act as mentor teachers and offer quick and simple Japanese lessons to others.

CLASS ACTIVITIES & INTERCULTURAL COMPETENCIES

During the three-week learning trip to Japan, there is no classroom instruction provided. An experiential learning-based approach is the main approach in this phase, where the participants visit various locations to learn through observations and firsthand personal experiences. They travel from Kyushu, in the western part of Japan, to Tokyo, in the eastern part of Japan. As the participants travel through the learning trip, they rely on the public transportation systems in Japan including buses, subways, trains, and bullet trains, and become familiar with navigating around the country. The participants learn a lot about Japan through their hands-on experiences in this learning trip phase. Collaboration, cooperation, and teamwork, as well as harmony, are essential during the learning trip since all the participants travel around the country together. For the complete schedule summary, see Appendix 6.1.

The three-week learning trip in Japan consists of a variety of hands-on activities. The core intercultural competencies that emerged as a result of these activities were flexibility, adaptability, stepping out of the comfort zone, and awareness of self and other cultures. The following are examples of the activities, tasks, and assignments.

Activities

Through the course activities, the participants developed teamwork, collaboration, adaptability, and observation skills as demonstrated through the following activities.

Presentations at National Institute of Technology, Oita College

During the pre-departure phase, the participants were divided into five small groups (four students in each group) that prepared a seven-minute slide presentation in simple English. They selected their presentation topics on the introduction of 1. USF, 2. Florida and Tampa, 3. Theme Parks in Florida, 4. Famous sightseeing spots in the United States, and 5. Popular food in the United States.

These presentations were given to a college English class at the National Institute of Technology, Oita College. USF students set up five presentation stations in a lecture room. The Japanese students were also divided into five small groups. USF students remained at their own station while Japanese students rotated in groups to a different station every ten minutes (seven-minute presentation and three-minute Q&A). In this way, USF students repeated their presentations five times to different audiences. As they repeated, they gradually adapted themselves for better and more efficient presentation deliveries; they adjusted themselves more toward their audience. Many of them started bending over or kneeling on the floor so that they could maintain eye contact on the same level with their audience on a chair instead of standing in front of them. They also started using more body movements and hand gestures to express their messages. Some mixed the Japanese language when the audience had some difficulty understanding English. By the time they repeated their presentations five times, they had improved their presentation skills dramatically and gained self-confidence in delivering their messages to the audience. They also brought gifts from USF and Florida and snack samples for the Japanese students to taste. This activity provides the students an opportunity to gain the intercultural competencies identified in Table 6.1.

Table 6.1. Intercultural Competencies for Presentations at Oita College

Knowledge	Skills	Attitude
• Awareness about self and other culture	• Teamwork • Collaboration • Critical thinking • Technology skills • Observing • Decision making • Learning through interaction – communication skills	• Flexibility • Adaptability • Stepping out of the comfort zone

Taiko Drum Lesson

In the 2019 program, the participants learned how to play the Japanese Taiko Drum by receiving an hour-long lesson from professional Taiko performers in Tokyo. Participants first learned how to hold the Taiko drumsticks and stand properly in front of the drum, and then how to hit the drum. They were divided into 4 groups by rows and started with simple hits and gradually learned how to hit harmoniously. They were encouraged to shout out loud in Japanese as they were instructed. In the beginning, participants felt shy but eventually stepped out of their comfort zone to try speaking louder and harder. They repeatedly practiced the same rhythm until their drumbeats sounded in harmony. At the end of the lesson, their performance synchronized as a complete piece of music, and the participants' smiles were sparkling with a sense of accomplishment and confidence. Intercultural competencies gained by the participants through this task are shown in Table 6.2.

Table 6.2. Intercultural Competencies for Taiko Drum Lesson

Knowledge	Skills	Attitude
• Culture-specific knowledge, e.g., Taiko	• Teamwork • Collaboration • Harmony • Learning through interaction • Observing	• Curiosity • Discovery • Stepping out of the comfort zone • Open-minded • Adaptability • Flexibility

Tasks

Through the tasks, the participants developed decision-making, navigation, map reading, and judgment skills.

Meeting with the Faculty Leader at the Hotel Lobby in Fukuoka

The participants were to travel to the first destination by themselves since many of them had a preferred itinerary to travel to Japan; each participant decided when and how to travel to the first destination instead of traveling as a whole class. They were also given the choice to travel with the faculty leader to Japan and were encouraged to travel with other participants in groups. Through the pre-departure meetings and group chats, the participants became familiar with each other and most of them decided to travel together as a group. They were provided with detailed instructions on how to transit at international airports in Japan, how to get to the subway station at the airport, how to buy a subway ticket and take a subway, and how to get to the hotel from the subway exit (see Appendix 6.2). Ultimately, their very first task in the learning trip was to arrive safely at the hotel in Fukuoka by the predetermined date and time. Thus far, all the participants have managed to arrive at the hotel on time.

Witnessing their proud and relieved smiles upon arrival is priceless every single time. Participants gain confidence through this "survival" task since this is the first time traveling abroad and taking the subway for many of the participants. Even though detailed instructions have been provided by the faculty leader, participants often use their own strategies to accomplish the task. In previous years, some participants asked strangers to help them out with directions and arrived at the hotel accompanied by a Japanese person. Some used Google maps, and one even took a taxi on their own from the airport. Intercultural competencies integrated into this activity are summarized in Table 6.3.

Table 6.3. Intercultural Competencies for Meeting with the Faculty Leader in Fukuoka

Knowledge	Skills	Attitude
• Awareness about other cultures	• Critical thinking • Decision making • Navigation skills • Map Reading • Planning • Observing • Interacting independently with the local people and system - Communication skills	• Making judgment • Stepping out of the comfort zone • Risk-taking • Tolerance for ambiguity • Flexibility

Climbing Mountains – Mt. Misen and Mt. Inari

Since there are no mountains in Florida, many students at USF are not accustomed to seeing mountains in their daily life nor climbing them. Thus, we have decided to incorporate mountain climbing experiences into the program. We have two events related to mountains: one at Mt. Misen on Miyajima Island in Hiroshima and the other at Mt. Inari at the Fushimi Inari Shrine in Kyoto. These are not mandatory activities; depending on the participants' health and physical conditions, they can choose whether to opt-out or complete the tasks.

Mt. Misen is a 535m high (1755 ft) mountain. A ropeway leads up the mountain from the town, and we must climb the rest of the way to the peak, which is another 100m higher (328 ft) from the upper ropeway station. The participants can choose to enjoy the scenery at the observatory near the ropeway station and wait for others who hike up the mountain peak to come back. Those who prefer a challenge can trek up to the peak on unpaved hiking paths and enjoy the spectacular view of the Seto Inland Sea. There are numerous Buddhist structures near the peak to stop by while hiking. They can always return to the ropeway station in the middle of hiking depending on their physical conditions. The whole group unites at the upper ropeway station about two hours after hiking.

Mt. Inari is located behind the Fushimi Inari Shrine, which enshrines Inari, the god of the rice harvest, commerce, and business. The mountain is 233m high (764 ft), and there is a pilgrimage circle with paved stairs around the shrines. There are thousands of red *torii* (Shinto Shrine gates) along the hiking paths. Upon arrival at Fushimi Inari Shrine, the participants are to look freely around the main shrine areas and climb up the mountain and meet back at the entrance of the shrine at a set time in about two hours.

Through these mountain climbing tasks, according to the interviews with the participants after the activity, they have developed self-confidence and a sense of accomplishment. The faculty leader witnessed that the students encouraged one another to keep up with their fellow participants while hiking. Some students have also built leadership skills in navigating through the hiking trails. Intercultural competencies observed in this activity are identified in Table 6.4.

Table 6.4. Intercultural Competencies for Climbing Mountains

Knowledge	Skills	Attitude
• Awareness of self	• Navigation skills • Map reading	• Making judgment • Decision making • Stepping out of the comfort zone • Risk-taking • Hardworking

POST-PROGRAM AND FUTURE ACTIVITIES

After the learning trip to Japan, the participants think back and reflect on their experiences in Japan. This functions as the reflection and thinking phases of Kolb's learning cycle in the experiential learning-based approach (Harvey, 2017; Kolb, 1984). Participants connect to the acting phase of the learning cycle by incorporating the values and behaviors that they have learned in this course into their daily lives. They submit a 1,000-word reflection essay that highlights their experience in Japan. In this essay, they look back on their trip and identify the most influential or eye-opening moments for them. In addition, participants consider how they can apply their cross-cultural experiences to their lives as a global citizen. Based on their reflections, the participants have discussions about what they have learned through the course.

The comparisons of the expectation and reflection essays are remarkable. In their expectation essays, many participants state their concerns that their unconscious behaviors as foreign visitors may offend Japanese people or that they may accidentally do something rude in Japan. They express more concern than excitement before their trip. In their reflection essay, on the other hand, they state that they should be more considerate of others and what they should do in the United States to improve their society. Examples of actions they mentioned in the essays are lining up while waiting for a bus or train, walking on one side on walkways, and standing on one side of escalators instead of standing in the middle so those who are in a hurry can pass on the other side. Many students stated that they now observe the society of the United States more objectively and show a sense of confidence in their reflection essay.

In addition to the essay, the students select five photos of significance from the trip, with at least a two-sentence caption that explains why each photo was chosen and why it was of significance to the trip. During the following fall semester, the participants are encouraged to present their experiences in Japanese courses, USF Japanese Culture Club meetings, and Education Abroad information sessions.

Upon reflection of this trip, there could be improvements to future activities. During the trip, the participants have limited interaction with Japanese people in their age group. Thus, we would like to include visits to more schools during the trip. It could be a high school or a college/technical school. Ideally, we would visit one school in western Japan and another school in the Tokyo area. The faculty leader is working on arranging one visit with her former colleague who currently works at a technical school in Japan. In addition, when planning for future study abroad, students in both schools can begin with virtual language and cultural exchanges on Microsoft Teams during the academic year before the summer. These virtual exchanges will serve as pre-trip activities in which the students get to know each other. In the summer, the participants will visit the technical school in Japan for in-person activities for a day.

Another possible activity is food education. Participants visit a farm in Kyoto, where they help harvest vegetables and learn about nutrition and how to cook them since many enjoy Japanese cuisine and are interested in learning about Japanese food. Through the process of harvesting and cooking the vegetables, the participants are required to interact with the farmers to deepen their knowledge of the food that they consume daily.

Through these interactions with local people, participants can enhance their understanding of others' worldviews and culture-specific knowledge. Moreover, since most of the participants may not be very familiar with farming in general, they would learn how vegetables are grown and processed before going on the market. Furthermore, the farmers may not speak much English; some of the participants with higher Japanese proficiency may need to play the role of a translator, which will be a great opportunity to improve their Japanese language and leadership capabilities.

EVALUATION AND ASSIGNMENTS

Grades are issued based on the total points earned for the pre-departure preparation for the trip, the trip participation, and the completion of the assignments. Table 6.5 shows the grading distributions which have been used for the course:

Table 6.5. Evaluation Breakdown

Phase of Course	Assignments	Point Value
Pre-departure Phase	Reading and Discussions	10
	Expectation Essay	10
Learning Trip	Participation in Daily Activities	60
Post-trip Phase	Reflection Essay	10
	Significant Photos with a Caption	10
Total Point Value		100

The pre-departure assignments are used as formative assessments to evaluate how the participants are learning through reading and discussions. During the learning trip, the faculty leader observes the individual students for their participation in daily activities. If a participant has a problem following the program itinerary, the faculty leader would privately follow up with the individual. In that sense, formative assessments are used throughout the learning trip. The post-trip assignments are used for summative assessments to evaluate how much the participants have learned throughout the course. Since the participants are from different disciplines, the scope of the assignment topics are set broadly depending on the students' purposes and interests.

Expectation Essay

During the pre-departure phase, the participants meet with the faculty leader at least three times and discuss Japanese culture and society based on their previous knowledge, experience, and reading assignments. We also ask previous participants to join the meetings and share their experiences and advice. Before their departure to Japan in May, the participants are asked to submit an expectation essay (at least 1,000 words) regarding what they want to gain from the trip, what they want to focus on observing and learning, etc. Since the participants' majors and backgrounds vary, they have autonomy in their learning focus. This assignment allowed the students to focus on the intercultural competencies listed in Table 6.6.

Table 6.6. Intercultural Competencies for Expectation Essay

Knowledge	Skills	Attitude
• Awareness of self	• Articulation in writing	• Autonomy • Curiosity

Reflection Essay and Five Photos of Significance

Upon their return to the United States, the participants start working on a reflection essay (at least 1,000 words). In this essay, students reflect on their trip and identify what were the most influential or eye-opening experiences. In addition, students would consider how they can apply their cross-cultural experiences to their lives as a global citizen. Based on the reflections, the students discuss what they learned through the course. In addition to the essay, they select five photos of significance from the trip, with at least a two-sentence caption that explains choice selection and why it is significant to them (see Appendix 6.3 for assignment details). Students submit the essay and photos two weeks after the program ends in Tokyo. This assignment allowed the students to focus on the intercultural competencies identified in Table 6.7.

Table 6.7 Intercultural Competencies for Reflection Essay and Photos of Significance

Knowledge	Skills	Attitude
• Awareness of self • Understanding others' worldviews • Deeper knowledge and understanding of culture	• Articulation	• Open-minded • Reflection • Discovery

STUDENT FEEDBACK

The score on the student course evaluations in 2019 was 4.96 out of 5.00. The only category that received "very good" rather than "excellent" was the "expression of expectation for performance" category in the USF course evaluation. Upon reflection, the faculty leader should have articulated clearer explanations and expectations to the participants in the pre-departure phase. Despite the ambiguity in expectation for performance, however, the participants seemed to gain intercultural competencies as seen in the following students' comments regarding the school visit at Oita Kosen. After each quote, the intercultural competencies gained by the students are listed.

"I liked interacting with students at Oita Kosen because of the exposure to other perspectives and ways of thinking that these experiences provided, as well as practicing my ability to speak the language." (*Student 1, awareness of other perspectives; Japanese language communication skills*)

"Oita Kosen and speaking with students was such a unique experience. I have forgotten why I even wanted to become a teacher and these students, as well as the faculty, have reminded me why. It was great to see how the students reacted to learning about Florida. It was great to see the students break the mold and come over to socialize with us despite our language barriers. It was great to learn about so many social-related cultural aspects of Japanese culture. Every aspect of the day, while nerve wracking at first, is something I will always cherish into the future." (*Student 2, cultural self-awareness/understanding, awareness of other perspectives, learning through interaction – communication skills, stepping outside the comfort zone, open-minded, respect*)

According to the comments above, the participants have developed intercultural competency characteristics mainly in attitudes, such as respect, flexibility, adaptability, open-mindedness, and the ability to learn from other people's perspectives. Participants have also improved their communication skills by interacting with Japanese students. Their comments illustrate the concept of understanding others' worldviews.

CAVEATS AND REFLECTIONS

The strength of the course is that the participants can immerse themselves into Japanese society. Participants learn firsthand the lifestyle of the Japanese, such as taking public transportation and buying meals at restaurants and convenience stores, which are quite different from the lifestyle of the participants. Moreover, traveling abroad is a first-time experience for many of the participants, and even going through immigration and customs are significant experiences that make them step outside their comfort zone and broaden their horizons. As one of the students stated in their comments, the participants learned not only about Japanese culture but also important life lessons that will last a lifetime. A student commented in the course evaluation that, "Zen Meditation was a very relaxing activity and it taught me a few valuable lessons in life. I hope to continue to meditate when I return to the States."

Since college is preparation for life in the global society, educators should make sure that the students gain intercultural experiences and competencies through college courses by incorporating student-centered learning and learner autonomy into a course. Educators should integrate activities that require teamwork, creative and critical thinking, and problem-solving skills into lesson plans. Moreover, educators should encourage students to step outside of their comfort zone and respect others through their teaching. By doing so, students will gain intercultural experiences through collaboration, communication, and interaction with others. They will develop intercultural competency characteristics in all categories: knowledge, skills, and attitudes. Another benefit of this course is that it serves as an introduction to Japan for the participants. After participating in this program, many students have intentions to return to Japan by applying for semester abroad programs, graduate schools, the JET (Japan Exchange and Teaching) Program, or job positions in Japan.

One of the challenges we consistently face is the program cost. The faculty leader tries to keep the cost as low as possible by finding less expensive accommodations and activities, but the program cost increases every year. The group used to stay at business hotels with buffet-style breakfasts, but the prices at these hotels have increased dramatically over the last few years. Since there were many students who did not take advantage of the hotel breakfast, the accommodation plans without breakfast will be adopted for future summer programs, which will save about $200 per student, even if the participants are to buy breakfast at convenience stores every day. Considering the current inflation worldwide, a further increase in the program's cost is expected in the coming years. Although there are several scholarships available through the education abroad office and student loans specifically for study abroad are available from USF Credit Union, only select participants would benefit from this financial aid. Therefore, other accommodation options such as youth hostels, dormitories, and weekly apartments will also be taken into consideration for future trips.

Despite the increase in the program cost the USF Japan program maintains its popularity among students. Even before the program applications are available each year, the faculty leader receives quite a few inquiries about the program. Some are interested in taking part in the program as non-degree-seeking students even though they have already graduated from USF. Over 20 students started their online applications within two days after the application opened for summer 2023. The education abroad advisor was astonished at the level of student interest and remarked that he had never witnessed such a popular program in his career as an advisor. The faculty leader believes that the reputation and popularity of the program were primarily built through word-of-mouth recommendations from past participants rather than extensive marketing efforts by the faculty. This indicates that the program has delivered valuable intercultural experiences and competencies to the students, which they long to experience and highly appreciate. By participating in this program, students develop intercultural competency characteristics to become global citizens who are equipped to thrive in today's society. These skills are essential in navigating an interconnected world where cross-cultural understanding and adaptability are highly valued.

REFERENCES

Borup, J. (2008). *Japanese Rinzai Zen Buddhism: Myoshinji, a living religion*. Brill.

Davies, R., & Ikeno, O. (2011). *The Japanese mind: Understanding contemporary Japanese culture*. Tuttle Publishing.

Deardorff, D. K. (2012). Framework: Intercultural competence model. In K. Berardo & D. K. Deardorff (Eds.), *Building cultural competence: Innovative activities and models* (pp. 45-52). Stylus Publishing.

Dewey, J. (1938) *Experience and education*. Collier Books.

Elliott, S. N., Kratochwill, T. R., Littlefield Cook, J., & Travers, J. (2000). *Educational psychology: Effective teaching, effective learning* (3rd ed.). McGraw.

Harvey, T. A. (2017). Design and pedagogy for transformative intercultural learning. In B. Kappler Mikk & I. Steglitz (Eds.), *Learning across cultures: Locally and globally* (3rd ed., pp. 109-138). NAFSA: Association of International Educators/Stylus.

Heine, S., & Wright, D. S. (2006). *Zen classics: Formative texts in the history of Zen Buddhism*. Oxford University Press.

Hendry, J. (2012). *Understanding Japanese society*. Taylor and Francis.

Juniper, A. (2011). *Wabi Sabi: The Japanese art of impermanence*. Tuttle Publishing.

Kolb, D. A. (1984). *Experiential learning: Experience as the source of learning and development.* Prentice Hall.

McLeod, S. (2019). *Constructivism as a theory for teaching and learning.* Simply Psychology. https://www.simplypsychology.org/constructivism.html

Phillips, D. C. (1995). The good, the bad, and the ugly: The many faces of constructivism. *Educational Researcher, 24*(7), 5–12. https://doi.org/10.3102/0013189X024007005

University of Buffalo (2022). *Curriculum, assessment and teaching transformation.* https://www.buffalo.edu/catt/develop/theory/constructivism.html

Yadav, K. (2021). *Pedagogy as a tool of effective teaching and learning.* https://www.evelynlearning.com/pedagogy-as-a-tool-of-effective-teaching-and-learning/

APPENDICES

Appendix 6.1: Japan Trip Schedule

Day	Morning	Afternoon
Day 1	Depart from Tampa-Fukuoka	
Day 2		Arrive in Fukuoka 9:00 Meeting at the hotel lobby
Day 3	9:00 Meet at the hotel lobby 10:30-11:30 Disaster Prevention Center	12:30 Group Lunch Dazaifu
Day 4	8:40 Meet at the hotel lobby 9:20-10:30 Asahi Beer Factory Tour	Hakata Furusato Kan Temple tour
Day 5	6:45 Meet at the hotel lobby Train to Nagasaki Peace Dome and Museum, Chinatown, Suwa Shrine, and Glover Garden Train to Hakata	
Day 6	8:15 Hotel Check out - pack for two nights in Beppu Train to Beppu	Takasaki Mountain –Monkey Park Beppu
Day 7	8:30 Meet at the hotel lobby Beppu Hills	
Day 8	8:00 Hotel Check-out; Visit Oita Kosen; Train to Hakata	
Day 9	8:00 Hotel Check-out Bullet Train to Hiroshima	Peace Memorial Museum/Park Hiroshima Castle
Day 10	9:00 Meet at the hotel lobby Miyajima/Misen Mountain Climbing	
Day 11	7:30 Hotel Check-out Bullet Train to Kyoto	1:00 Kanji Museum 3:30-6:30 Samurai Kenbu Experience 7:00 Group Dinner
Day 12	8:00 Meet at the hotel lobby 9:00-10:30 Wagashi making	Sanjusangendo Kiyomizu

Day 13	8:00 Meet at the hotel lobby 9:00 Kyo-Yuzen dye experience Nijo-Castle	Kinkakuji
Day 14	6:00 Nishi-Honganji Morning Service (optional) 9:00 Meet at the hotel lobby Visit Nara – Todaiji, Nara Park, Kasuga Shrine	
Day 15	8:45 Meet at the hotel lobby 10:00-11:30 Zen Meditation @ Taizo-in	Arashiyama bamboo forests River Cruise Trolley Train
Day 16	8:30 Meet at the hotel lobby Fushimi Inari	7:00 Group Dinner
Day 17	8:30 Meet at the hotel lobby Visit Osaka – Osaka Castle 13:30 Osaka Aquarium	
Day 18	7:45 Hotel Check-out Bullet Train to Tokyo	3:30-4:30 Taiko Drum Experience 7:30 Team Lab Planets
Day 19	9:20 Meet at the hotel lobby Train to Yokohama 11:00 Cup Noodle Museum 11:45 Chicken Ramen Factory	Yokohama Free
Day 20	9:00 Meet at the hotel lobby 9:30 Tokyo Metropolitan Government Building Observatories	Harajuku/Akihabara
Day 21	10:00 Program dismissed in the hotel lobby	

Appendix 6.2: Airport Transits & Directions to the Hotel

Note: This is an example for reference only. Airport transits, directions, and currency amounts may change.

Arrival at Narita Airport

If you are flying with **Delta** or **United**, you will arrive at **Terminal 1** (Delta-North Wing, United-South Wing). Your connection flight to Fukuoka is by **ANA (NH)**. When you get to the arrival lobby, go toward the right. The ANA domestic check-in counter is located at the far end of the building. You re-check your luggage and go upstairs for security.

If you are flying with **American** or **Japan Airlines**, you will arrive in **Terminal 2**. Your connection flight to Fukuoka is by **JAL (JL)**. When you get to the arrival lobby, go toward the left. The JAL domestic check-in is located at the far end of the main building. You re-check your luggage and go upstairs for security.

If you are flying with **Jetstar** to Fukuoka, you will need to go to **Terminal 3**. You need to take a shuttle bus to Terminal 3. From Terminal 1 arrival floor, go outside and look for **BUS STOP #6**, which will be between the North Wing and the South Wing. It will be a 10-minute ride.

Arrival at Haneda Airport

You will arrive at the International Terminal. At the arrival lobby, go toward the right and look for the domestic connecting flight baggage check-in counter. After re-checking in, proceed to the domestic connecting security check area. Then, an airline connecting bus will take you to the domestic terminal.

Or go downstairs for the free shuttle bus to the domestic terminals. Look for **bus stop Number 0** on the first floor (outside).

Remember the following:

- If your flight to Fukuoka is by **JAL (JL)** or **SKY**, you need to go to **Terminal 1**.
- If your flight to Fukuoka is by **ANA (NH)**, you need to go to **Terminal 2**.

JAL & SKY – You get off the bus at **Terminal 1 (bus stop #8) (red terminal)**. Go upstairs.

If you are taking **SKY**, go to the North Wing and look for the **SKY (スカイマーク)** counter and check-in.

If you are taking **JAL**, go to the **South Wing JAL** counter and check-in.

ANA – You get off the bus at **Terminal 2 (bus stop #9) (blue terminal)**. Go upstairs.

Go to one of the check-in counters and check-in your luggage.

Arrival at Nagoya – Chubu Kokusai Airport

You will arrive on the **second floor**. Go to the **third floor** and look for **ANA check-in counter (K~P)**.

How to get to Comfort Hotel in Hataka, Fukuoka

When you arrive at Fukuoka Airport (*Domestic* from Tokyo/Nagoya/Osaka), you will be on the first floor. Look for the Subway (Chika-tetsu in Japanese) sign and go to the basement.

If you are arriving at Fukuoka on an *international flight,* take a shuttle bus to the domestic terminal and get off the bus at the last stop (domestic terminal south – Kokunai-sen terminal Minami) and follow the Subway sign and go downstairs.

Then, do the following:

1. At the Subway station, purchase a **260-yen** ticket at one of the machines (CASH ONLY! Make sure you have some Japanese yen). You can insert money and push the 260-yen button. The machine should take bills as well as coins.
2. Put the ticket in the ticket gate (Kaisatsu) and take it as you go through the gate. DO NOT FORGET TO GRAB the ticket when you enter the station to the tracks.
3. Our destination is **Hakata Station (K11)**, and it is just two stations away from Fukuoka Airport (Kuukoo) **(K13)** and takes only 5 minutes on the orange line.
4. When you get off the train at Hakata Station, follow the ticket gate sign. Again, you insert the ticket into the gate and go through. This time, the ticket WILL NOT come out; you just keep walking without the ticket.

5. Then, look for the **WEST 8 Exit** (you will still be on the underground level); when you take the stairs up at the WEST 8 Exit, the hotel will be just around the corner.
(OR you can take the WEST 9 Exit to the ground level and cross the street at the traffic signal.)
The hotel is just across from the station; it should be just a few-minute walk.
There is a Seven-Eleven convenience store next door.

Appendix 6.3: Reflection Essay and Five (5) Photos of Significance

Upon your return to Tampa, please start working on your reflection essay (at least 1,000 words) and choose five (5) most important pictures that you have taken in Japan. In this essay you look back at the trip and identify what was the most influential or eye-opening to you. In addition, you should consider how to apply your cross-cultural experiences to your life as a global citizen. Moreover, please select five (5) photos of significance from the trip, with at least a two-sentence caption that explains why each photo was chosen and why it is of significance for you during the trip. Both the essay and the photos are to be submitted by June 18.

Chapter 7

This Isn't What I Expected in Cuba: Challenging the Imaginative Geographies of Students Through Study Abroad

James Chaney

Note: Section II includes Chapters 4-14. These chapters use a standardized template to discuss the details of their respective study abroad programs and reference Deardorff's (2012) framework for intercultural competencies. The use of this template and the intercultural competencies framework are described in the Section II introduction. All courses in this section (except for Chapter 6) were taught through Middle Tennessee State University (MTSU), a mid-sized state school located in Murfreesboro, Tennessee (USA).

This chapter covers the short-term study abroad course *Global Studies: Special Problems and Topics—Cuba in the 21st Century* (GS 3200). The main goal of this program is to challenge the imaginative geographies of students in a study abroad context. A unique aspect of this course is its development in different academic subjects (e.g., geography, political science), which casts a wider net for recruitment. The program's curriculum is designed around service learning, place-based education, and active learning activities. This 12-day study abroad program includes the cities of Havana, Viñales, Trinidad, Santa Clara, and Varadero (the itinerary is listed in Appendix 7.1). The program ran in January 2016 and 2017 and again in June 2018 with a total of 44 participants.

THEORETICAL FOUNDATIONS

In both research and pedagogy, geographers emphasize firsthand experience through fieldwork. Accordingly, going abroad presents a variety of experiential opportunities for geographers to educate students about other societies, places, and ways of life. Study abroad programs that require frequent interactions with the local denizens in another country encourage students to challenge their preconceived notions about the world, appreciate cultural differences, and enhance their understanding of global processes and outcomes (Jokisch, 2009). Furthermore, programs that prioritize immersion activities involving casual, day-to-day activities of host community members give students a unique frame of reference regarding the routines and challenges of everyday people in societies outside the United States (Keese, 2013).

Geographers often approach the presumptions that one society holds about other societies through the concept of imaginative geographies (or imagined geographies). Imaginative geographies refer to how humans perceive and represent other places, peoples, cultures, and landscapes that, "articulate [their] desires, fantasies, and fears...and the grids of power between them and their "Others"" (Gregory et al., 2009, p. 370). The origin of the concept can be traced to Said's (1978) seminal critique of Western society's depiction of the "Orient," which referred to the lands and cultures located east/southeast of Europe. Said's work on imaginative geographies was pivotal in the establishment of postcolonialism as a focus of study and has been re-conceptualized to analyze a wider range of geopolitical relationships and issues. As Beech (2014) interprets it, "imaginative geographies arise from perceived power relations between two nations or regions, where the more dominant of the two produces representations of the 'Other'" (p. 174). Thus contextually, imaginative geographies can operate asymmetrically within an "us versus them" perspective, where one society or members of a society compare what they understand as familiar or "normal" regarding their culture or ways of life with the norms, politics, or customs of another society, which they see as exotic, different, or even undeveloped and unsophisticated. Since Cuba has long held a prominent place in the imaginative geographies of U.S. society, it affords students the perfect study abroad location to question, analyze, and rework these deeply embedded misconceptions based on unequal power relations and sociocultural differences.

While the pedagogical framework of this program covers a host of topics and issues to give students a broad understanding of the development, character, and struggles of the Cuban people, my focus in this chapter is to elaborate on the experiential learning activities and critical reflection assignments we employ during and after our trip to promote cross-cultural understanding, hone intercultural skills, and develop global awareness. Our strategy to achieve this utilizes an instructional methodology that challenges the imaginative geographies which U.S. citizens often have of Cuban society. That is, we set out to encourage students to critically think about their preconceptions of, and assumptions about life in Cuba. Additionally, we encourage students to consider how the dominant narratives about Cuba, which have been and still are being constructed and conveyed in U.S. media and politics, influence their perceptions. Our method is twofold. First, we have students participate in different types of experiential learning practices as identified by Wurdinger and Carlson (2010), such as service learning, place-based education, and active learning. Second, we require critical reflection discussions and exercises that take different forms during and after the program. For example, after each day's activities in Cuba, we debrief as a group to discuss our experiences and perspectives.

COURSE DESCRIPTION

The purpose of this course is to explore contemporary Cuba, delve further into the challenges and changes taking place on the island, and critically engage the imaginative geographies that U.S. society holds about Cuba. As such, the pedagogical framework of this program is designed to cover a host of topics and issues to give students a comprehensive understanding of the development, character, and struggles of the Cuban people. This requires an understanding of the historical context and uniqueness of the problems the country faces. The program combines experiential learning activities (visits to museums and historic sites, landscape interpretation, local guest speakers, volunteering with a community-based organization) with readings, discussions, and research before and after the field experience. The two required texts are

Cuban Landscapes: Heritage, Memory, and Place by Joseph L. Scarpaci and Armando H. Portela (2009) and *Cuba: What Everyone Needs to Know* by Julia E. Sweig (2016). These predeparture readings provide a comprehensive knowledge base needed to understand and appreciate the places we visit and issues we engage with while on the island. Homestays and engagement with local Cubans in urban and rural communities are fundamental components of this program as they give students a unique frame of reference regarding the daily routines and challenges of everyday people in societies outside the United States. These types of encounters broaden a student's worldview and enlighten their perception of "other" people(s) and places.

Course Learning Outcomes

At the end of this course, the students will:

a. Be able to read cultural landscapes and understand the sociocultural, economic, and political processes that form them.
b. Understand the complexity of other societies in relation to geopolitics, history, geography, economics, and culture.
c. Understand the role media and popular culture play in the construction and maintenance of national and cultural identities.
d. Be able to recognize, analyze, and reflect on the impact of one's culture and society on one's values, assumptions, perceptions, expectations, and behavior.

COURSE HISTORY

Cuba: Perhaps no other country in Latin America shares such a long, complex, and often contentious relationship with the United States. Since its days as a colonial possession of Spain until the present, Cuban society has been influenced by the geopolitical and economic interests of the mainland United States (Chomsky et al., 2019). During the first half of the 20th century, Cuba developed into a popular tourist destination for Americans, while U.S. companies gained control of much of the island's economy. However, following Cuba's 1959 Revolution and its geopolitical pivot towards the Soviet Union, U.S.-Cuba relations deteriorated. In response, U.S. media and political discourse about Cuba turned negative, altering public perceptions about Cuban society. And, as U.S. sentiments soured, misconceptions and uninformed opinions developed about the island nation and its people (Chomsky et al., 2019). For these reasons, Cuba is a compelling destination for any educational endeavor concerning international politics, intercultural understanding, and global awareness.

My interest in Cuba originated in 2007 when I began working on a book project that explored the historical, cultural, and migratory ties between Cuba and New Orleans. As travel restrictions between Cuba and the United States loosened during the Obama administration (2009-2017), I traveled to the island for research purposes. During my three-week stay there, I made several important contacts and started contemplating a short-term study abroad that would include both excursions to well-known sites and interactions with Cubans in places outside of the typical tourist's gaze. As a cultural geographer who specializes in Latin America, my objective for this program was to explore the sociocultural fabric of the island and to interpret how it is represented in historical and current landscapes. Yet, Cuba is well-suited for a myriad of didactic foci, and any educational excursion to the island aiming to examine its society should include a political component in its curriculum. Simply put, political and economic interests are so deeply entwined throughout Cuba's colonial and post-colonial history that they cannot be excluded from any contemporary analysis of the nation and its people. For that reason, I asked a political scientist from my university to co-lead the program. This colleague conducts research on Latin American politics and was particularly interested in creating a course that looked at the impact that Cuba's 1959 Revolution had on its identity. This idea complemented the program's theme and was easy to integrate into its course of study. Furthermore, it facilitated an interdepartmental and interdisciplinary collaboration in the creation of the course used in the program.

We were awarded money from MTSU's Office of International Affairs to travel to Cuba for a site evaluation during the summer of 2015. On our preliminary visit, we met with several of my contacts to discuss our objectives for the trip, which included understanding the geopolitical situation of Cuba and how it affects the livelihoods of everyday Cubans. Our method to achieve this was through immersion, utilizing homestays, service and place-based learning activities, landscape analysis during excursions, and free time to explore non-tourist places and spaces in the locations we visit. My primary contact in Havana serves as a coordinator for Candela Tours, a U.S.-based tour operator run by a geography professor at Texas State University. Candela Tours was our third-party provider and handled our logistics (including flights between Fort Lauderdale and Havana), visas, lodging, excursions, and some meals. Since Candela Tours is run by another academic, our pedagogical approaches were easy to implement into the program's itinerary. Candela Tours utilized the "People-to-People" category, which was one of the authorized travel options to Cuba through the U.S. Department of Treasury before being restricted in 2019 (Aguilera, 2019).

COURSE LOGISTICS

Although I had initially planned to offer this course under a geography designation, I opted to use a 3-credit hour *Global Studies: Special Problems and Topics* (GS 3200) course and titled it "Cuba in the 21st Century." This designation meets the upper-division course requirements for all majors and minors in my department and allows me to attract more students. My colleague and I have cross-listed the course with a political science course titled *Advanced Studies in Comparative Politics* (PS 4850) to meet the requirements of political science and international relations majors and minors. We also work with a Spanish professor at our university who offers Spanish majors and minors participating in our program a 3-credit hour upper division independent study course. Therefore, certain students can earn a total of 6 university credit hours. This also allows us to cast a wider net for recruitment. The program's course requirements include readings, participant observation, reflection assignments, and three post-trip meetings.

PRE-PROGRAM ACTIVITIES

For the first two years of this program, the trip took place in January before the spring semester started. As a result of this scheduling, other than a predeparture orientation, we were unable to assign in-person activities before the trip. We also followed this schedule during the third year, though this took place in June. Our predeparture meeting covers the program's itinerary, planning for a service-learning activity, how to pack, common etiquette with host families, how to convert currency, and what to expect in Cuba. Students are required to purchase two texts before the trip: *Cuban Landscapes: Heritage, Memory, and Place* (Scarpaci & Portela, 2009) and *Cuba: What Everyone Needs to Know* (Sweig, 2016). The first book examines the human-environmental relationship between Cuba and its people. More importantly for this course, the book's authors lay out how identity and politics are displayed in landscapes. This text was a great companion for students as many of the places we visited were discussed in its chapters. The second book focuses on the geopolitical history between Cuba and the United States. Both books serve as necessary primers for the program and give students a foundation for many of the themes we engage with during and after the trip. In their formative journal entries and summative research paper, students must include citations and information from both texts.

We also require students to watch the documentary *Black in Latin America: Cuba, The Next Revolution* (Pollack et al., 2011) before departure. This documentary investigates how the concept of race is/was constructed in Cuban society and how Cuba has tried to mitigate racism since the 1959 Revolution. This documentary is found on the course's D2L page (the learning management platform used at our university) along with instructions for keeping a journal in Cuba and the final essay assignment. The final essay assignment is a research paper involving a geopolitical, sociocultural, environmental, or economic issue affecting contemporary Cuban society. Students have the freedom to choose whatever topic they wish to research; however, it must be approved by the program's instructors and based on questions from assigned materials and field observations.

CLASS ACTIVITIES & INTERCULTURAL COMPETENCIES

Homestays

Homestays are an important component of the program's experiential, place-based learning process. While studying abroad gives students the opportunity to learn about local customs and practice a language with native speakers, Cuban homestays also enable students to experience firsthand the significant impact that the U.S. embargo has had on the day-to-day activities of regular Cubans. The 60-year-old embargo restricts almost all U.S.-owned or majority-owned businesses from trading with or operating in Cuba (Sweig, 2016). As a result, Cuba has been isolated from global commerce and suffered from continual shortages in products such as basic foodstuffs, building materials, machine and automobile parts, and so on. Likewise, the embargo makes it harder for Cuba to access international financial resources, which, in turn, significantly stifles the island's economic development. Since students stay in the homes of native Cubans, they directly observe how international sanctions complicate the daily lives of their hosts and the human toll of the embargo on Cuban society.

Students report that staying with host families gives them a unique perspective on how Cubans overcome challenges brought on by shortages and economic hardship. Some students accompany their hosts on errands, helping them find daily essentials such as toilet paper, food, or shampoo by visiting state-run stores in Havana or by buying products on Cuba's informal market. Participating in these activities teaches students adaptation skills, empathy, and cultural understanding. The intercultural competencies gained by the students through this activity are listed in Table 7.1.

Table 7.1. Intercultural Competencies for Homestays

Knowledge	Skills	Attitudes
• Cultural self-awareness/understanding • Understanding other's worldviews	• Communication • Listen, observe, & evaluate	• Empathy • Adaptability • Patience • Withholding judgment

Navigating Havana

With over two million inhabitants, Havana is the largest city in Cuba. Like other urban areas in Latin America, the city is compact and designed in an orthogonal grid-like pattern with narrow streets, alleyways, and plazas. Yet, while seemingly organized, Havana can be disorienting to first-time visitors. For that reason, one of the first activities for students is to walk the neighborhood of Vedado with me and learn about the different transportation options, as well as the locations of Havana's Wi-Fi zones. The main transportation options in Havana are coco taxis, private taxis, *almendrones* (ridesharing taxis), state-run public taxis (Cubataxis), public buses, and city tour buses that follow a very limited route. Each transportation option has advantages; however, destinations and budgets must be considered when choosing how to move around the city. For example, metro buses are inexpensive (10 pesos or $.40). Yet, they are crowded, and deciphering bus routes is confusing. Cubataxis are nicer vehicles with air conditioning that can take passengers anywhere in the city, but they are expensive. Coco taxis charge between $3 to $5 to travel between neighborhoods and their main station is a few blocks from our homestays.

While showing students the different transportation options in Havana, I explain how to access the internet. Most homestays do not have access to the internet, and, because of the embargo, U.S. cellular plans do not cover Cuba. Therefore, students must use Cuba's public Wi-Fi platform which can only be accessed in certain public locations and hotels. To access the internet, students must use a Nauta card that can be purchased at any Telecommunications Company of Cuba (ETECSA) offices. I walk with students to an ETECSA office and help them buy their first card.

Most MTSU students participating in this program are unfamiliar with public transportation; thus, relying on Havana's public transportation options is an immersive problem-solving activity that requires figuring out how to be mobile in an unfamiliar city. Likewise, students must also engage with Cubans to both buy Nauta cards and find Wi-Fi zones which are rarely marked. These tasks promote information gathering and cognitive flexibility in a new environment as described in Table 7.2.

Table 7.2. Intercultural Competencies for Navigating Havana

Knowledge	Skills	Attitudes
• Culture-specific knowledge	• Problem-solving • Communication	• Risk-taking • Cognitive flexibility • Stepping out of one's comfort zone

Service Learning through Volunteer Work

Kaye (2004) states that a service-learning activity requires three components: 1) planning to assist in filling a community need, 2) action, and 3) reflection on experience and outcome. We incorporate these three components into our volunteer activity restoring a school in Havana with the nonprofit organization Proyecto Espiral. In the program's predeparture meeting, we discuss the activity, what it entails, and what supplies we can contribute from the United States. Considering that certain supplies (e.g., paint brushes, latex gloves, tools) are not readily available in Cuba, students are asked to plan among themselves what supplies they will bring. We meet with local Espiral volunteers at a school in the morning and begin working on the restoration project. Later, we eat lunch with the volunteers. This gives students a chance to converse informally with Espiral members—most of whom are of the same age.

This is one of the most popular activities of the program. During debriefing sessions in Cuba and the in-class seminars after returning to the United States, students regularly convey that they enjoyed getting to help with a community project and working alongside local volunteers. Some students exchange contact information to stay in touch with the Cuban volunteers, and they often plan to meet up with them during their free time in Havana. This activity is designed to develop intercultural competencies such as relationship building, teamwork with people of a different culture, empathy, and conversing in another language since most of the volunteers do not speak English. The intercultural competencies from this task are listed in Table 7.3.

Table 7.3. Intercultural Competencies for Service Learning through Volunteer Work

Knowledge	Skills	Attitudes
• Understanding other worldviews • Academic content knowledge	• Teamwork • Communication • Listen, observe, & evaluate	• Respect • Empathy

Voluntary Outings with Locals

We purposely organized the program to give students free time at night and on some afternoons to encourage them to explore Cuba on their own. Although this is not an assigned task, students must venture out on their own to buy food or personal items or for entertainment options not included in the program. Because Cuba is generally a safe country, students (in pairs or groups) are relatively safe to go out without a faculty leader (Sweig, 2016). In fact, students often make friends with the Cubans we interact with during the program activities or with members of their host families. The Cubans we meet are often open to inviting students to see and experience Cuba outside the program's itinerary, like concerts, salsa dancing, or spending time on the Malecon (Havana's famous boardwalk). Thus, students get the chance to plan their own cultural activities that fit their specific interests while interacting leisurely with local Cubans.

This non-programmed task is empowering for students in that they are free to decide what they want to do. These types of engagements help develop curiosity, discovery, and risk-taking by making students step outside their comfort zone. Likewise, students must utilize their language skills to successfully interact with Cubans while on their own. The specific intercultural competencies acquired through voluntary outings are listed in Table 7.4.

Table 7.4. Intercultural Competencies for Voluntary Outings with Locals

Knowledge	Skills	Attitudes
<ul><li>Cultural-specific knowledge</li><li>Cultural self-awareness/understanding</li></ul>	<ul><li>Communication</li></ul>	<ul><li>Curiosity</li><li>Discovery</li><li>Risk-taking</li><li>Stepping out of one's comfort zone</li></ul>

Place-Based Learning in Viñales

During our first full day in Viñales, students spend the afternoon with a family on their tobacco farm learning about tobacco cultivation and cigar production. That evening, the family prepares dinner, and we eat with them at their home. Before arriving at the farm, students are required to read from their assigned texts about tobacco landscapes and farming and to prepare questions to ask family members about their farm, profession, and life in general. Students also are asked to observe how life in rural Cuba differs from that in Havana. This activity allows students to juxtapose urban and rural life on the island. Students note how their conversations with residents in Viñales are different from those they have in Havana, suggesting that perspectives seem more relaxed. Yet students observe that life in a Cuban farm community is hard work. For example, tobacco farmers are mandated to sell 90% of their tobacco crop to the government for a set low price. The remaining 10% is sold to tourists and is an important source of additional income (Chomsky et al. 2019) . Consequently, farmers are reliant on tourism and must develop ways to market their product, which is usually in the form of cigars. This activity teaches students specific knowledge about agriculture in Cuba and gives them a cultural understanding of rural life on the island. Table 7.5 outlines the intercultural competencies gained while visiting a tobacco farm in Viñales.

Table 7.5. Intercultural Competencies for Place-based Learning in Viñales

Knowledge	Skills	Attitudes
• Academic content knowledge • Cultural-specific knowledge • Understanding others' worldviews	• Communication • Observe, listen, & evaluate • Analyze, interpret, & relate	• Respect • Empathy • Withhold judgment

POST-PROGRAM ACTIVITIES AND ASSIGNMENTS

Study abroad programs should be conceptualized as an immersive and introspective undertaking where students apply a critical perspective to what they observe, encounter, and participate in while abroad and, upon their return, reflect deeply on their experiences (Keese, 2013). For this reason, post-program reflection activities are fundamental for the meaning-making process after returning from abroad because they obligate students to draw comparisons from their experiences abroad with their lives in the United States. In doing so, students contemplate, question, and often alter their prior presumptions and attitudes about the societies they return from (Sharma et al., 2011). This is a crucial step in deconstructing the imaginative geographies held by students before departing and replacing those preconceived notions with a more comprehensive and factual interpretation of the culture(s) and society they encounter during their time abroad.

This program utilizes post-program activities to not only help students examine (and challenge) their preconceptions about and observations in Cuba but also consider the role that geopolitics—particularly U.S. foreign diplomacy—has played in the shaping of Cuban society as well as how Cuba is portrayed in U.S. media. We want students to contemplate and share their experiences in a group setting so that they can listen to other points of view and perspectives regarding what they observed during the program. To achieve this, we require students to attend three in-person, post-trip seminars on campus. The seminars are student-led. My colleague and I guide the discussions with pre-selected topics, but students drive the conversations based on their interests, impressions, and opinions derived from their readings, assignments, and experiences in Cuba.

In the first seminar, students discuss their predeparture assumptions about Cuba and explain how their experiences in Cuba challenged these preconceptions. They must give three examples that they have included in their journals. While many of these experiences have been touched on during the daily debriefings in Cuba, students are asked to flesh out their thoughts on these experiences and share how they have internalized different observations and encounters while abroad. This approach encourages students to think critically about their prior beliefs concerning Cuban society and contrast them with what they experienced during the trip. Likewise, students share how they learned to navigate (socially, economically, and geographically) in another culture. This includes examples of what students did outside of the program's scheduled itinerary, such as going out at night, shopping in local stores, or conversing with host families or other Cubans they met. Students often mention how venturing out on their own or having conversations with Cubans in their free time helped them build the confidence to operate in a different culture. Finally, at the end of the first seminar, students must identify a research topic for their final essay.

For the second seminar, students write a précis on the documentary *Black in Latin America: Cuba: The Next Revolution* (Pollack, 2011) and include their own thoughts regarding how Cuban society has handled racism as compared to U.S. society. The video demonstrated how racial polemics on the island are entangled with politics—both past and present. We discuss things that we observed about race and racial categories while in Cuba and juxtapose those observations to themes presented in the documentary. We also consider what U.S. society could learn from Cuba about mitigating racism as students return from the island with a deeper understanding of the fluidity of racial conceptualizations in other societies and cultures outside of the United States.

In the final seminar, students briefly discuss the research they have conducted for their essay assignment. We talk about why each student became interested in their topic and how/if researching that topic changed their opinion about Cuban society or the United States' policies towards Cuba. While the themes that students choose to research vary widely from topics about cigar production to gender roles in tourism, this exercise gives students the opportunity to develop culture-specific knowledge about Cuban society and convey what they have learned. Students are expected to finish their essays by the end of the spring semester and upload them to the online learning management system.

On the next trip, I plan to lengthen our time in rural areas and have students volunteer in local farming communities we visit to learn more about horticulture practices in less-developed countries. This would give students service-learning opportunities in urban and rural settings, allowing them to better juxtapose different ways of life in Cuba. An activity we are tentatively planning for our next program is an excursion to the coffee farming communities in the Sierra Maestra Mountains of eastern Cuba. Since this program primarily runs in January, students will be able to work with Cuban farmers during the harvest season and learn about one of Cuba's emerging lucrative exports. This type of experiential learning activity would further enhance the intercultural competence development of students not only through exposure to new cultural environments and practices but also through active participation. We expect this exercise to build skills in listening and observing as well as to promote openness towards adapting to different intercultural communication and learning preferences, thus increasing intercultural awareness and expanding understanding of different worldviews.

EVALUATION AND ASSIGNMENTS

The criteria for participation and the research essay are discussed earlier. Participation is a formative assessment of the learning outcomes that takes place in the field and during our debriefing sessions on the island, as well as in post-program seminars (refer to Appendix 7.2).

The research essay serves as a summative assessment that, while focusing on a particular issue, requires students to incorporate and analyze how different sociocultural, economic, geopolitical, and geographic processes affect their paper's theme. Journals are a formative assessment that allows us to evaluate students' intercultural competencies acquisition. Journal entries must include accounts of the students' experiences, reactions to these experiences, new/old perceptions about Cuban society, and critical reflections about their own imaginative geographies. Thus, journals primarily evaluate the course's learning outcomes, particularly objectives C and D shared previously. The course's percentage scheme and assignment instructions are listed in Appendix 7.2.

STUDENT FEEDBACK

The standard university evaluations of the course(s) and instructors demonstrate that students generally have positive opinions about the program. Of course, journals and discussion sessions provide much richer, more nuanced descriptions of students' views of the trip. Unsurprisingly, each student's experience is different, so what is meaningful varies per individual. While excursions are popular, the excursions students prefer vary not only by student but also by group. Nevertheless, most students state that the most impactful activities were interactions with Cubans either during a planned event or in their free time. This includes visits to farms in Viñales, our hike in the mountains, volunteering, time spent with homestay host families, or venturing out on their own time. The following anonymized quotes from student journals illustrate the positive reaction students had when engaging directly with Cubans which exhibit some of the intercultural competencies gained through these experiences. After each quote, the program year and the intercultural competencies gained by the students are listed.

> "Although there was a small language barrier [with the Espiral volunteers], because we were so eager to learn more from people our age—and vice versa—this was not an obstacle. It was thrilling to learn about the history of the Afro-Cuban religion, the most popular religion on the island, as it was created after the freeing of the first slaves. All and all, today was a great experience that gave us insight into the lives of Cubans that like us were college students eager to learn more about another culture." *(Student 1, service-learning project, Havana, 2016, cultural self-awareness/understanding; cultural-specific knowledge; academic content knowledge; curiosity)*

> [After touring the farm] "we walked to a small outbuilding near the dining area to watch real Cuban cigars being handcrafted by a third-generation tobacco farmer. This was a wonderful experience of education, conversation, and laughter." (*Student 2, Tobacco farm tour, Viñales, 2017, cultural-specific knowledge; academic content knowledge; listen, observe, and interpret; communication skills*)

> "In Santa Clara, we talked to our host dad and he told us to ask him anything we wanted to know about Cuba. I asked him what changes he has seen in his life in Cuba and he talked for a couple of hours about it! It was really amazing to hear from a Cuban what he thought." (*Student 3, conversation with host family, Santa Clara, 2018, understanding others' worldviews; curiosity; communication skills*)

> "This study abroad not only helped my Spanish-speaking skills, but it also helped me to feel more comfortable in an environment where everyone has a culture and language

different from mine." (*Student 4, upon return, 2017, adaptability; communication skills; tolerance for ambiguity*)

During seminar sessions, we asked students which locations they enjoyed the most. Two discernable opinions emerged regarding urban and rural destinations. Many students stated that they would like more opportunities to visit rural locations and engage with people in those communities. Others indicate that they would prefer to spend most of the program in Havana to gain a deeper immersive experience in one place.

CAVEATS AND REFLECTIONS

Overall, this program has been a success. Its objectives align with the mission of the Global Studies and Human Geography Department, which includes the development of critical thinking, communication, and complex analysis skills that enable students to work effectively across cultures—all of which are skills needed to work and thrive in multicultural societies. Many of our majors are interested in Latin America and improving their Spanish. This program gives them a unique opportunity to engage both educational goals. Furthermore, partnering with political science and Spanish professors permits more students to earn credits applicable to their majors/minors and allows us to cast a wider net for recruitment. Working with professors from other disciplines also facilitates academic synergy which strengthens the program and enhances the pedagogy.

One major concern for this program is the lack of assignments before the trip and a need for more predeparture meetings. As aforementioned, the original dates for the program prohibited formal course meetings, so students were expected to read material on their own before departure. Root and Ngampornchai (2012) posit that to fully develop intercultural competence through study abroad programs, predeparture training is necessary to effectively leverage the experiential benefits of being in another culture. Certainly, frequent meetings before departure to discuss themes and issues pertaining to the trip would make the program more effective and impactful for students. A potential remedy for this is to implement mandatory predeparture meetings using a video conferencing platform, such as Zoom or Microsoft Teams, or simply to run the program during dates that allow sufficient time for in-person predeparture meetings.

Another concern is the precariousness of being able to conduct a study abroad program in Cuba. Because of the contentious geopolitical relationship between the U.S. and Cuba, the program was put on hold in 2019. This uncertainty complicates the planning, recruitment, and execution of the program. Nevertheless, the precarity of travel to Cuba is the allure for many students, as it stokes their imaginative geographies of a place that they see as off-limits. As such, a well-orchestrated study abroad program on the island can effectively challenge students' misconceptions about Cuba, demystify their beliefs about Cuban society, and foster fundamental intercultural skills they will need in an ever-globalizing world.

As student participation in short-term study abroad programs continues to grow in the United States, it is increasingly important for program directors to consider innovative ways to encourage students to not merely visit sites but rather meaningfully engage with the people, places, and cultures they encounter while abroad. This chapter describes five on-site activities that require students to learn about Cuban society through interactive experiences. Post-trip seminars allow students to critically examine, reflect upon, and share their observations, thoughts, and viewpoints of modern Cuba. This approach can serve as a framework for other short-term study abroad programs that seek to enhance students' intercultural understanding and competence, while challenging the imaginative geographies they held predeparture.

REFERENCES

Aguilera, J. (2019). *It just got a lot harder for Americans to travel to Cuba. Here's what to know.* Time. Retrieved June 26, 2023, from https://time.com/5601203/us-cuba-travel-cruise-restrictions.

Beech, S. (2014). Why place matters: Imaginative geography and international student mobility. *Area, 46*(2), 170–177. https://doi.org/10.1111/area.12096

Berger, K. C. (2004). *A complete guide to service learning.* Free Spirit Publishing.

Chomsky, A., Carr, B., Prieto, A., & Smorkaloff, P. M. (Eds). (2019). *The Cuba reader: History, culture, politics* (2nd ed.). Duke University Press Book. https://doi.org/10.1515/9781478004561

Deardorff, D. K. (2012). Framework: Intercultural competence model. In K. Berardo & D. K. Deardorff (Eds.), *Building cultural competence: Innovative activities and models* (pp. 45-52). Stylus Publishing.

Gregory, G., Johnston, R., Pratt, G., Watts, M., & Whatmore, S. (2009). *The dictionary of human geography.* Blackwell Publishing.

Jokisch, B. (2009). Making a traditional study-abroad program geographic: A theoretically informed regional approach. *Journal of Geography, 108*(3), 105–111. https://doi.org/10.1080/00221340903103318

Kaye, C. B. (2004). *The complete guide to service learning: Proven, practical ways to engage students in civic responsibility, academic curriculum, and social action.* Free Spirit Publishing Inc.

Keese, J. (2013). Study abroad: Geography does it better. *Yearbook of the Association of Pacific Coast Geographers, 75,* 15–27. https://doi.org/10.1353/pcg.2013.0005

Pollack, R. (Director). (2011). *Black in Latin America: Cuba, the next revolution.* [Film; television]. Inkwell Films; Wall to Wall Media LTD; and THIRTEEN.

Root, E., & Ngampornchai, A. (2012). "I came back as a new human being": Student descriptions of intercultural competence acquired through education abroad experiences. *Journal of Studies in International Education, 17*(5), 513–532. https://doi.org/10.1177/1028315312468008

Said, E. (1978). *Orientalism.* Pantheon.

Scarpaci, J. L., & Portela, A. H. (2009). *Cuban landscapes: Heritage, memory, and place.* Guilford Press.

Sharma, S., Phillon, J., & Malewski, E. (2011). Examining the practice of critical reflection of developing pre-service teachers' multicultural competencies: Findings from a study abroad program in Honduras. *Issues in Teacher Education, 20*(2), 9–22. https://files.eric.ed.gov/fulltext/EJ954551.pdf

Sweig, J. E. (2016). *Cuba: What everyone needs to know* (3rd ed.). Oxford.

Wurdinger, S., & Carlson, J. A. (2018). *Teaching for experiential learning: Five approaches that work.* Rowman & Littlefield.

APPENDICES

Appendix 7.1: Program Itinerary June 5–17, 2018

Date and Location	Morning Activities	Afternoon and Evening Activities
Tuesday, June 5 Ft. Lauderdale to Havana	Meet at Ft. Lauderdale Airport to check in/receive visa for flight to Havana – program begins	Arrive at Jose Marti International Airport in Havana; Meet host families; Tour Vedado Neighborhood and welcome dinner
Wednesday, June 6 Havana	Meet at Coco taxi station Tour of Old Havana – on foot and by bus with Cuban architect/urban planner, overview of the growth and development of the city	Afternoon – late lunch in state-run restaurant Evening – debrief and free time.
Thursday, June 7 Havana	Take public transportation to Museum of the Revolution. Lecture on Revolution	Afternoon – excursion to Hemmingway's countryside residence. Evening – return to Havana and tour El Hotel National Debrief and free time
Friday, June 8 Havana	Visit to U.S. Embassy Lunch with host families or on your own	Afternoon – pool party at country home, salsa lessons, lecture on Cuba's healthcare system from local medical doctor Evening – debrief in Havana and free time
Saturday, June 9 Havana	Lecture on Cuban educational system, service activity (renovating public school) with community members from Proyecto Espiral.	Afternoon – debrief Evening – optional cultural activity (modern dance or other musical performance) and/or free time
Sunday, June 10 Viñales	Depart for Viñales Visit Soroa waterfall, Las Terrazas bioreserve, and botanical garden	Afternoon – meet host families and tour organic farm Evening – dinner at organic farm and debrief
Monday, June 11 Viñales	Hike through karst topography of Viñales and lecture on physical geography Debrief during lunch	Afternoon/Evening – visit to tobacco farm and have dinner with family

Tuesday, June 12 Trinidad	Depart for Trinidad Stop at Playa Girón (Bay of Pigs) to visit museum and have lunch	Afternoon – arrive in Trinidad, meet host families in Trinidad Debrief
Wednesday, June 13 Trinidad	Walking tour of colonial Trinidad, accompanied by city historian.	Afternoon – visit to sugar mill and colonial plantation Optional snorkeling in Trinidad Debrief in Historical town plaza
Thursday, June 14 Santa Clara	Depart for Santa Clara Lunch at Laguna de Guanaroca and lecture on Mangroves	Afternoon – Che Memorial, visit with Cuban official to explain Cuban political system Evening – debrief and meet host families
Friday, June 15 Varadero	Depart for Varadero Walking tour of the Varadero tourist complex	Afternoon/Evening – meet host families and free time
Saturday, June 16 Havana	Free time in Varadero Return to Havana, tour of Soviet-style housing community (Alamar)	Afternoon – Lunch with Cuban family in Alamar apartment Meet with members of CDRs (Committees in Defense of the Revolution) Evening – debrief and Farewell dinner in Sancho Panza restaurant
Sunday, June 17 Havana to Ft. Lauderdale	Depart for Jose Marti International Airport in Havana – program ends	Arrive at Ft. Lauderdale Airport.

Appendix 7.2: Assignments

Percentage Scheme for Participation and Assignments

The percentage scheme for this course is determined by two assignments and student participation during the program:

    Participation: 35%
    Research Essay: 30 %
    Journal: 35%

Note: Participation includes field activities and participation in group discussions.

Assignment Instructions for Participation

Participation: Each student will be evaluated on their level of participation and engagement during the program. That is, students will be expected to participate in all outings and activities while in Cuba. Missing excursions or service-learning activities will result in a lower participation grade.

Assignment Instructions for Research Essay

Research Essay: Each student will focus on a particular topic during the course and work one-on-one with one of the instructors to produce a short 5–6-page essay. The essay should describe a particular challenge facing contemporary Cuba, lay out the historical context, analyze recent developments, and discuss the many implications. This essay should draw on supplemental readings and research.

Assignment Instructions for Journal

Students are expected to maintain a study abroad journal recording notes, ideas, commentary, insights, observations, etc. We will have informal debriefing meetings almost daily to discuss insights, reflections, and interpretations.

Chapter 8

Cultural Immersion in France

Nancy Sloan Goldberg

Note: Section II includes Chapters 4-14. These chapters use a standardized template to discuss the details of their respective study abroad programs and reference Deardorff's (2012) framework for intercultural competencies. The use of this template and the intercultural competencies framework are described in the Section II introduction. All courses in this section (except for Chapter 6) were taught through Middle Tennessee State University (MTSU), a mid-sized state school located in Murfreesboro, Tennessee (USA).

The *MTSU Summer Normandy*, a French immersion program (2005-2019), changed names and sites three times during its fourteen-year tenure: MTSU-Cherbourg IUT Summer Program (2005-2009), MTSU-IUT Cherbourg-Manche (2010-2015) and MTSU Summer in Normandy Program (2016-2019). The Institut Universitaire de Technologie (IUT) is the community college system in France. The four-week (later three-week) program was housed in university buildings in the small cities of Cherbourg-Octeville, Saint-Lô, and Caen, all in Normandy, France. The uniqueness of this program is its dual focus on expanding students' linguistic and cultural competencies in the backdrop of French historical events. Students created deeper connections with the people as well as the history of France through various immersion activities. The program takes place during the month of June and included 9-19 students each summer with an average of 12 students. The program has run 14 times since its inauguration in 2005.

THEORETICAL FOUNDATIONS

Foundational elements to the course include experiential learning, a functional/notional syllabus, and standards-based oral proficiencies. Both the Common European Framework of Reference for Languages (CEFR) and the American Council on the Teaching of Foreign Languages (ACTFL) focus on the fundamental values of culture, communication, and comparison to develop transparent and comprehensive syllabi. This focus is needed to design integrated teaching and learning materials and create assessments that help students progress independently. These standard theories draw many of their current values from previous research. Kolb's (1984) cycle of experiential learning remains an invaluable source on the principles of the integration of knowledge, activity, and reflection. The Boston Center for Teaching and Learning highlights four broad categories of student engagement that are mutually dependent: active experimentation, during which learners test new ideas and enhance their skills in a new experience; concrete experience, where learners engage in an authentic situation; reflective observation, which provides space for the learner to discern new events and relate it to past experiences; and abstract conceptualization, in which the learner separates the concrete experiences into new, abstract concepts (Boston University, n.d.). Moore (2010) focuses on practical examples of experiential learning outside the classroom, including study abroad, service learning, and student teaching.

According to the Experiential Learning guide published by Boston University, during the experiential learning process, "the learner is actively engaged in posing questions, investigating, experimenting, being curious, solving problems, assuming responsibility, being creative, and constructing meaning." Further, the faculty leader's roles include selecting suitable experiences, posing problems, setting boundaries, supporting learners, ensuring physical and emotional safety, and facilitating the learning process (Boston University, n.d.). For an extensive inventory of best practices for successful experiential education, with emphasis on the relationships between the learner and the educator, risk taking, and the possibility to learn from successes to misunderstandings, refer to Gass et al. (2012).

In keeping with these standards of best practices, I filled the roles of both program director and teacher, conducted all classes and evaluations, and was with the students for the entire nine hours each day. All activities, homework, and group projects were conducted in French. Regardless of venue, attendance was required for all events, both in and outside the classroom. In order to accommodate different student learning preferences, I categorized all activities according to the VARK modalities. Fleming and Mills (1992) used the acronym VARK to define learners' preferences as Visual, Aural/Auditory, Read/wRite, Kinesthetic/Hands-on, and Multimodality.

Another pillar of the course was the individual homestay. This important aspect enhanced the immersion experience and emphasized the everyday cultural aspects of living in France. Moreover, in keeping with the CEFR/ACTFL goals as stated above, the students engaged in reflection on cultural differences and were encouraged to analyze and compare the worldview of the host family with their own. There were ample opportunities for this type of individual connection. Each student lived with a different host family and shared all meals (except for midweek lunch), evenings, and weekends as part of the homestay experience. The homestay provided an informal, family-oriented, and non-judgmental space to speak French and experience what normal life was like in a French home. Both the classroom space and the family space were areas that were familiar to students, affording them a comfortable atmosphere in which to acquire new vocabulary, discover new applications, and combine these elements to successfully develop new language competencies.

In all these activities, students produced language comprehensible to their peers but also to native speakers not accustomed to speaking with foreign students. The students applied new language elements with new-found poise to engage with native speakers of all ages. Activities enabled the students to communicate confidently at every level of formality, such as with local officials or a Holocaust survivor, to less formal situations, such as Sunday dinners, and tasks outside the classroom. MTSU students also organized and created Service-Learning Projects to provide local French elementary school teachers with American cultural detail to enhance their

English classes. These days were spent with the French children, many of whom were from our homestay families.

COURSE DESCRIPTION

The course enabled second- and third-year French language students at MTSU to spend four (later three) weeks in an immersive study in France. From 2005 to 2015, the course also included a six-day stay in Paris. The program featured nine or more instructional hours per weekday organized and taught by me and evenings and weekends with French host families. The language requirement for this program included two semesters of college-level French with a grade of C or better.

The course's theme was the culture and people of Normandy. The main course objective was to build confidence in each student's oral and aural skills while engaging directly with the people and culture of Normandy in the French language. Further objectives included replacing cultural preconceptions with lived experiences and learning to use the French language with different audiences in varied settings. Rather than use a traditional text, students explored realia obtained on-site and interviewed and conversed with native speakers. The students also had access to online resources unique to Normandy. I supplied materials, new vocabulary, and the necessary historical background.

Course Learning Outcomes

At the end of the course, students will:

a. Participate in learning practices that are 90% experiential and 10% academic.
b. Demonstrate effective skills in communication in French, engagement with French culture, the community in Normandy, and the comparison of French and American cultures.
c. Understand the causal relationship that connects and determines cultural artifacts with language use and will examine and appraise similarities and differences with their own culture.
d. Convey these new interpretations and other recent perceptions in narratives they construct, using different time registers (past, present, future).
e. Engage in everyday communicative functions in French, such as using public transportation to go from the homestay site to the classroom and return home and purchasing food in the university cafeteria.
f. Indicate knowledge of the province of Normandy, especially its economy and agriculture, and will analyze the important role that the towns of Cherbourg, Saint-Lô, and Caen had in French history, especially during World War II and the medieval period.
g. Apply current and long-standing language structures independently in public settings outside the classroom, such as the train station, shops, and with homestay families.
h. Work collaboratively to successfully communicate in more complicated public settings, especially in the museum portion of the program in Paris.
i. Engage in tasks designed to develop soft skills, such as problem-solving, diplomacy, planning, organizing, and expressing emotions.

j. Demonstrate their comprehension of the knowledge acquired during the program in a culminating activity with the homestay families. Students will write, compose, or otherwise construct an original skit, piece of music, poem, artwork, or other creative product and will present their projects to all the extended homestay families.

COURSE HISTORY

The course was a reformulation of the summer program operated by MTSU and the Université de Picardie Jules Verne, which I directed in 2004. This program included about 100 French language American students from MTSU and other universities outside Tennessee. All students lived together in an unsupervised residence hall, and the faculty shared an apartment about five miles away. In the 2004 program model, local French high school teachers were recruited to teach and evaluate the American students. There was no input invited from the American faculty whose role was minimized to being mere chaperones. This model was problematic and none of my American colleagues at that time agreed to continue without substantial changes. These circumstances led me to make major alterations to the program structure and execution that was maintained in the future iterations of the program from 2005 until 2019.

COURSE LOGISTICS

The reformulated course carried six credit hours at Middle Tennessee State University. Students had required course responsibilities seven days a week, including class activities from 9 am to 5 pm Monday through Friday and during the evening hours and weekends with their host families. Students were either in class with me or were with members of their French family, and thus were able to obtain a high level of immersion.

The large number of contact hours (120+) justified six hours of credit and allowed the students to qualify for financial aid. Staying with host families and eating lunch in the university dining hall made the program extremely cost-effective, an important incentive for MTSU students. This was also cost-effective for the university, as minimal financial support was needed since the students paid their own expenses. Students were recruited from our own MTSU classes, and many friends signed up together. MTSU students were eligible to participate, regardless of major or minor, if they had studied French for at least two years at the college level.

PRE-PROGRAM ACTIVITIES

Most students who participated in the program represented various skills in French and had almost no experience going abroad. Through interactions with the students, I realized they not only see me as their teacher, but also as a role model while abroad. This aspect as well as the physical security and emotional health of our students informed the organizational structure of the program, as students were unaccustomed to navigating a foreign culture. The students understood the priorities: first, safety, and second, speaking French while having fun. The course organization was built on the prior relationship between the students and me, as I had taught many of them before the summer, recruited them from my classes, and conducted pre-departure orientations and placement tests. This established relationship created a level of trust and comfort between the students and me in the new setting and served to reduce the anxiety and negative affect inherent with native speaker faculty.

Pre-program activities had two major components: a language proficiency assessment and four hours of group orientation with additional individual sessions. The skills measurement was important in the placement of students with their host families, some of whom spoke no English and would not be able to secure the student's safety in an emergency. I conducted the ACTFL Oral Proficiency Interview (OPI) with each student both before leaving for France and at the end of the program. This exit interview included additional questions designed to evaluate the summer program as a whole and was one of the tools used for the final assessment and grading.

The four hours of group orientation were lively sessions on the MTSU campus with both serious and lighthearted moments that grounded the group and helped them bond in a shared experience. We discussed minute details of the program, including buying air tickets, navigating the airport to find the group meeting place, and the types of clothes needed for Normandy. The clothing issue was important because American students dress more informally than French students their age, and our students needed to know that short shorts and plunging necklines were considered proper only for the beach. We analyzed cultural differences between French and American families to help students understand what to expect in their respective homes. Water and power conservation remain central concerns for French families, and our students understood the use of minute timers, short showers, less food waste, and spending quality time interacting personally with their French parents. The safety of the students was paramount, and we discussed ways to minimize unwanted encounters. This included an interactive workshop on personal safety conducted by a certified RAD (Rape Aggression Defense) system instructor.

CLASS ACTIVITIES & INTERCULTURAL COMPETENCIES

Program activities encompassed a conscious design of experiences in French where cognitive strategies increased critical speaking and listening skills, provided opportunities for reflection, and served to create community among the students (ACTFL, n.d.; Boston University, n.d.; Council of Europe, n.d.; Gass et al., 2012; Fleming & Mills, 1992; Kolb, 1984). Accordingly, both class activities and outside modules led learners to acquire cultural knowledge as well as increase communicative proficiency. These integrated cultural subjects combine aspects of French culture with speaking and listening, all within the format of VARK (Visual, Aural/Auditory, Read/wRite, Kinesthetic) learning preferences. These principles applied to all activities whether they took place inside or outside the classroom, and during field trips or workshops. For example, in blending a cultural artifact (e.g., buying fruit at an open market), learners can observe the importance of the weekly market in France (VRK), learn how to make a purchase (AK), and handle money (VK). As the students advanced in their confidence and knowledge, so did the complexity of the activities. For example, during the morning warm-up, each student narrated a summary of the entire previous evening in the past tense with emphasis on the family's conversation with the learner and others (VAK). This content was recycled and extended through role plays and imagined conversations in the future or conditional tenses (AR) and also by reflecting on each person's or family member's possible thoughts and concerns (VARK). Individually or in teams, students then competed with others in the class to match up the statements with the correct person (VARK).

These same theoretical guidelines informed the selection of the field trips according to their cultural and historical content, their opportunities for interactive communication, and the ability to provide prospects for comprehensive, holistic activities. Assignments incorporated a cohesive and layered approach to integrating all four language skills with cultural content, such as daily life and local history. Students used French exclusively to engage in preparatory activities and assignments before each day trip, to share what they had learned, and finally to observe, record, and evaluate their impressions. For a tabulated program itinerary and list of course activities, see Appendix 8.1. Some representative activities included in the list are classroom cheese tasting, an art museum visit, and an outdoor market activity. Refer to Appendix 8.2 for guidelines and prompts on these activities.

Following the theoretical guidelines used in the design of the course as stated earlier, every activity, task, and assignment integrated proficiencies in language and culture. Many of these undertakings also featured the development of the skills, knowledge, and attitudes inherent in intercultural competencies. Learners gained culture-specific knowledge and self-awareness, honed their communication skills with native French speakers of all ages, and learned to adapt to new and even uncomfortable situations while remaining polite and respectful. In each of these activities, the students designed their own interactions, articulating their observations and interpretations in a journal that they later used as a springboard for peer discussion and further analysis (see Appendix 8.3 for guidelines given to the students specifically about intercultural competency).

Homestay Program

The individual homestay provided consistent and sustained immersion in the French language and everyday cultural aspects of family life in France. Learners developed intercultural competencies through adaptation to a totally unknown situation, and, consequently, they understood the need for flexibility and a tolerant attitude. Everyday situations, such as using the family washing machine, required tact, thoughtful consideration of the price of water and electricity in France, and withholding judgment concerning the condition of the appliance. Having meals with the family provided the opportunity for sharing ideas and opinions on important issues like education and immigration but also less serious subjects like the famous Eurovision Song Contest. The host families and students developed a deep emotional bond, and most kept in touch with each other for years after. One family even came to Tennessee the next year for the wedding of their American student. This activity reinforced the intercultural competencies listed in Table 8.1.

Table 8.1: Intercultural Competencies in Homestay Program Activity

Knowledge	Skills	Attitudes
• Understanding others' worldviews • Culture-specific knowledge	• Observe • Listen • Problem-solving • Interpret and analyze	• Flexibility • Withholding judgment • Respect • Stepping outside the comfort zone

Formal French Meal

A local restaurant owner and chef conducted an all-day interactive workshop on all aspects of a traditional French meal. Students learned how to arrange flowers, set a table, and plan, prepare, and present a four-course meal. More importantly, their collaboration with the chef, who was not accustomed to foreign students, brought an appreciation of the significance of food and food preparation in French culture and the reverence French people have for their cuisine. In a restaurant style fashion, the students were organized into groups and received orders from the chef. Students solved these tasks with teamwork and observation of the chef himself, and the results earned praise from him. Through this activity, the students gained invaluable intercultural competencies as listed in Table 8.2.

Table 8.2: Intercultural Competencies in Formal French Meal Activity

Knowledge	Skills	Attitudes
• Culture-specific knowledge	• Teamwork • Communication skills; listen and observe	• Curiosity, discovery • Adaptability • Stepping outside the comfort zone

Culminating Activity

Student achievement and success were showcased in a culminating activity described earlier, during which the students wrote an original skit, performed a poem or a piece of music, or displayed imaginative artwork. Prepared for a talent show, many students had musical instruments with them, and they researched and patiently learned by heart a piece by a French composer. Those with musical talents sang or performed newly acquired French folk songs, and the actors found and interpreted well-known poems. These were performed in front an audience of host families, their children, and friends. The audience welcomed this display of hard work and creativity which they understood to be an expression of affection for them and their culture. The potluck meal was an opportunity for French families to discover a bit of American culture, as this type of communal meal is uncommon in France. Parents often commented that their judgment of American society had changed through participating in this event and through interactions with the students in general. Intercultural competencies emphasized in the culminating activity are listed in Table 8.3.

Table 8.3: Intercultural Competencies in Culminating Activity

Knowledge	Skills	Attitudes
- Cultural self-awareness - Culture-specific knowledge - Academic content knowledge	- Creative thinking - Teamwork - Articulation - Technology skills	- Stepping outside the comfort zone - Risk-taking - Patience - Respect

Sunday Dinner

Most French families live in proximity to each other, and it is common to find three and four generations living within short driving distances. Eating Sunday dinner at the home of the eldest grandparent or even great-grandparent is a long-standing French tradition. Guests from outside the family do not generally attend, so it was a special honor for our students to be invited to participate each week. This formal meal usually lasts from 3-4 hours, with many courses, including pauses for stories and songs. The students welcomed the opportunity to communicate with members of the extended French family and to hear diverse views from cousins, aunts, and uncles on everyday matters. However, the length of time at the table, the new and unusual foods, and being the focus of the family's attention as a special guest, seemed all very challenging to the American students. Students worked together to identify skills (such as active listening, observing, and relating) that would allow them to adapt to this novel cultural experience while remaining open-minded and respectful. The intercultural competencies integrated into this activity are highlighted in Table 8.4.

Table 8.4: Intercultural Competencies in Sunday Dinner Activity

Knowledge	Skills	Attitudes
- Understanding others' worldviews - Culture-specific knowledge	- Communication skills; listen; observe; relate	- Empathy - Open-mindedness - Adaptability - Stepping outside the comfort zone

Holocaust Survivor

In preparation for the visit to the D-Day (the day when the Allied forces launched an invasion on Nazi-occupied France during WWII) Beaches in the area, a historian and/or a local researcher gave lectures to the students on the events leading up to and including all aspects of

World War II. After these traditional classroom presentations a Holocaust survivor spoke to the students about his experiences from the age of 14 to 18, when he was liberated from the Dachau concentration camp. Despite his advanced age (he passed away in 2015), he stood for nearly two hours and recounted the cruelty, barbarity, and violence of what he had endured. The students were at first shocked and uncomfortable, and many realized that they had little knowledge of any part of the war, and thus voiced feelings of guilt. Students responded to the survivor with many tears, but also empathy and warmth, and they welcomed the appeal for tolerance and peace that ended his presentation. The students formulated questions for him about his life after the war and wondered if they would have had the same strength and courage as he showed. See Appendix 8.2 for sample prompts for this activity. Intercultural competencies targeted in this activity are listed in Table 8.5.

Table 8.5: Intercultural Competencies in Holocaust Survivor Activity

Knowledge	Skills	Attitudes
• Culture-specific knowledge • Academic content knowledge	• Listen; observe; evaluate; interpret	• Empathy • Discovery • Respect • Stepping outside the comfort zone

Service Learning in French Schools

Since many of the homestay parents had children in the local public schools, it was natural that the American students be invited to visit the classrooms. The local teachers formalized these visits into a mini-course on American culture, where the MTSU students taught games and songs and tutored the students in the English classes. The American students adapted well to the impromptu nature of many of the sessions, improvising contests, demonstrating baseball, and reading stories to the French children. The MTSU students were also asked to observe and evaluate the English classes themselves, and they solved this potentially awkward situation by withholding an outright verbal judgment and instead emphasizing the enthusiasm of the teacher and students. This activity allowed the students to develop the intercultural competencies listed in Table 8.6.

Table 8.6: Intercultural Competencies in Service Learning in French Schools Activity

Knowledge	Skills	Attitudes
• Cultural self-awareness • Understanding others' cultural attitudes	• Creative thinking • Problem-solving • Leadership • Teamwork • Communication skills	• Risk-taking • Resilience • Patience • Adaptability • Open-minded • Respect

Six Days in Paris

Students visited museums and other cultural and historical sites, navigated the city on public transportation, and ate in restaurants in groups or on their own. Learners observed and analyzed famous examples of French art and culture. They became adept at interpreting the highly automated systems, asking for directions, and making small talk with French people. They expressed pride in their progress in French. In this activity, the students gained the intercultural competencies listed in Table 8.7.

Table 8.7: Intercultural Competencies in Six Days in Paris Activity

Knowledge	Skills	Attitudes
• Culture-specific knowledge • Academic content knowledge	• Problem-solving • Articulation • Teamwork • Communication skills	• Curiosity • Discovery • Open-minded • Adaptability

POST-PROGRAM AND FUTURE CLASS ACTIVITIES

Students typically had many commitments to meet after returning to the United States, especially summer jobs and additional summer courses. After devoting every minute to the summer program for four weeks, they needed to resume other activities and family obligations. However, students enrolled in the Honors College later offered presentations to the Honors faculty and students.

The summer program ended in 2020 because of COVID-19 and has not restarted. The partner school has also eliminated its summer program. In 2018, I tentatively planned to expand our MTSU students' interaction with IUT students. Casual meetups were not practical because the French students did not have adequate experience with non-native French learners. I thought it might work better to match up student learners of English with ours. Sadly, we did not get a chance to implement this new feature because of COVID-19.

EVALUATION AND ASSIGNMENTS

The formative evaluation was based solely on my assessment of each student's effort, participation, and cooperation. The grading system for the course was pass/fail with an 80% positive achievement rate on all activities, tasks, and assignments, including intercultural competencies, required for a grade of P, with 100% attendance. The evaluation was recorded every day and communicated to each student at the end of the week. The summary evaluation was based on grades from the culminating activity and the individual post-test. Since the culminating activity was a group effort, with ample class time to prepare, the grades generally reflected the fun atmosphere at the end of the course. See Appendix 8.4 for the grading scale used for this course.

STUDENT FEEDBACK

Formal evaluations were rare in the early years of this program. Later, when the MTSU summer programs were institutionalized, the Office of Education Abroad conducted student evaluations after the students returned to campus. Since none of the results were shared with me, I relied on the comments made to me by individual students. Students had grown close to their host families and appreciated the intercultural experiences that caused them to reflect on shared commonalities with French people, as well as new and even surprising ways of doing things. They expressed a new awareness of seeing the world as French people envisioned it. They were also proud of the advances they made in their mastery of the French language and proudly used the informal vocabulary taught to them by the teenage members of the family. Several of the students wrote notes to me, some even in French, and shared below. Following each quote, the program year and the intercultural competencies gained by the students are listed.

> "There are not enough words in the dictionary to express the life changing experience that was our trip to France. My appreciation for the world, as well as my country now embody complete meaning." (*Student 1, 2006, understanding others' world views, cultural self-awareness, respect*)

> "I've learned so much, both technically and culturally. I learned a lot of French, the grammar and the culture! It was an unbelievable experience!" (*Student 2, 2015, stepping outside of comfort zones, communication, and technology skills*)

> "I have had the most life changing experience. Aside from improving my French speaking and listening abilities, I feel more confident about my beliefs and also I feel more sure of what I want in life. I have gained new insight of the person I am and the person I want to grow to be." (*Student 3, 2018, risk-taking, adaptability, open-mindedness*)

Students Survey Pre/Post Data

I administered the ACTFL Oral Proficiency Interview (OPI) to each student as a pretest before leaving for France to gain an understanding of their language level. The OPI consists of Novice, Intermediate, and Advanced, with most of the program learners testing at the Intermediate-Low level, which meant that they could speak on simple topics in two to three sentences. A few students were at the Novice level, meaning that their speech was limited to rote phrases and lists. The Summary OPI administered at the end of the program showed a marked increase in French proficiency, with most students achieving the Intermediate-High level, a leap of two levels. Even those students at the Novice Level improved by two steps and could speak for longer periods on topics they had experienced. All students successfully used the past tense, and some chose to use the future and the subjunctive in their answers. Most importantly, the students responded in a self-assured and confident manner, with few hesitations and less searching for their words. Students were eager to give their opinions in French, and most seemed to forget they were in a (somewhat) formal test situation.

CAVEATS AND REFLECTIONS

The motivation of the students to experience French culture directly through language was the strength of the program. Their dedication to this goal, their open-mindedness, and their flexibility were important keys to their success. The warm support of their host families nurtured student growth on the weekends, making the homestay an irreplaceable foundation of the program. Further, the very full daily schedule and assignments during the week left little time for questionable or risky behavior. It was important that the 10-12 students and I both knew each other to some degree before the trip. The course was one of the first of its kind at MTSU and served as a model for other summer programs that sought to internationalize the curriculum.

The following practical suggestions are for faculty leaders and program coordinators:

1. One director/teacher in charge of all aspects of the program, including curriculum design, teaching, implementation of activities, and program budget (the program was self-funded from student fees);
2. Keep the number of students small, no more than 14;
3. Get to know the students well before leaving campus;
4. Create activities that meet program goals and are enjoyable and unique to the program ;
5. Use local events and sites as learning spaces, such as municipal locations that are free;
6. Require homestay with one student per family including weekends;
7. An on-site program partner is needed to recruit families well in advance. There should be a contract so the hosts know what is expected in terms of meals provided, curfew times, etc.;
8. Create a full seven-day-per-week program with no opportunity for questionable behavior;
9. Include a culminating activity that doubles as a farewell party; encourage student creativity.

The *Summer in Normandy* program was successfully conducted for 15 years due to its dual pedagogical focus on developing students' French language proficiency as well as their intercultural competencies. The organizational pillars of the course were the classroom and the homestay families, and the discussions, activities, and assignments situated within the two overlapping spheres. The curriculum sought to engage the imagination of the students to make deeper connections with the French people, their history, and their modern everyday culture. The ideas and tips presented in this chapter can be replicated in other faculty-led programs that aim to focus on increasing foreign language proficiency in tandem with growing cultural competency.

REFERENCES

ACTFL: Oral Proficiency Interview (OPI) Description. (n.d.). Retrieved June 15, 2022, from https://www.actfl.org/assessment-research-and-development/actfl-assessments/actfl-postsecondary-assessments/oral-proficiency-interview-opi

Boston University. (n.d.). *Experiential learning.* Center for Teaching Learning RSS. Retrieved June 15, 2022, from https://www.bu.edu/ctl/guides/experiential-learning/

Council of Europe. (n.d.). *Common European framework of reference for languages: Learning, teaching, assessment (CEFR).* Common European Framework of Reference for Languages (CEFR). Retrieved June 15, 2022, from https://www.coe.int/en/web/common-european-framework-reference-languages

Deardorff, D. K. (2012). Framework: Intercultural competence model. In K. Berardo & D. K. Deardorff (Eds.), *Building cultural competence: Innovative activities and models* (pp. 45-52). Stylus Publishing.

Fleming, N. D., & Mills, C. (1992). Not another inventory, rather a catalyst for reflection. *To Improve the Academy, 11,* 137–155. https://digitalcommons.unl.edu/podimproveacad/246?utm_source=digitalcommons.unl.edu%2Fpodimproveacad%2F246&utm_medium=PDF&utm_campaign=PDFCoverPages

Gass, M., Gillis, H. L., & Russell, K. C. (2012). *Adventure therapy: Theory research and practice.* Routledge.

Kolb, D. (1984). *Experiential learning: Experience as the source of learning and development.* Prentice Hall.

Moore, D. T. (2010). Forms and issues in experiential learning. In D. M. Qualters (Ed.), *New directions for teaching and learning* (pp. 3-13). Wiley.

APPENDICES

Appendix 8.1: Program Itinerary and Course Activities

Note: This itinerary was used in Caen (2016) where all activities were in the target language.

Day	Morning	Afternoon
1	Arrival in Paris; meet students and accompany them to program site.	Host families and French liaison meet us at program site.
2	Students remain with hosts all day to get to know them and recover from jet lag	
3	In-class topic: ACTFL oral interview (pretest) Getting around, asking directions, politeness; describing oneself Research and read about the life of Guillaume le Conquérant in Caen and Falaise	Walk together to the pedestrian shopping street; exchange money if needed. Students buy bus passes in TL Follow the "Trail of Guillaume" in the city center, including the cathedral and the two Abbeys. Homework for tomorrow: 10 observations of the day

Day	Morning	Afternoon
4	In-class topics: various activities on house, garden, 10 observations	Prepare for trip and activity at Mont-Saint-Michel
5	Travel by bus to and spend day at Mont-Saint-Michel	Visit to the manuscript museum in Avranches Homework for tomorrow: 10 observations of the day
6	In-class topics: various activities on health, pharmacy, hair stylist Prepare art museum activity	Art museum activity Homework for tomorrow: 10 observations of the day
7-8	Weekend with host family	
9	In-class topic: prepare for service learning	Service learning in French schools
10	In-class topic: discuss service-learning experience Prepare visit to the Bayeux Tapestry Museum including history, impact of Guillaume's victory	Documentary film on local farmer Free time
11	Travel by train to Bayeux; visit the Museum of the Tapestry and the Cathedral	Visit to the Museum Baron Gérard Homework for tomorrow: 10 observations of the day
12	In-class topics: trades and professions; weather, the dairy industry	Visit to the Museum of Normandy (19th century social history) Homework for tomorrow: 10 observations of the day
13	Travel by bus to Livarot (cheese factory) and the automaton museum at Falaise	Visit to the interactive Chateau at Falaise, the birthplace of Guillaume
14-15	Weekend with host family	
16	In class topics: cuisine, table arts, food and restaurants Documentary French film on WWII (part one); prepare questions for afternoon speaker	Guest speaker: events leading up to WWII in France and in Germany; Holocaust Survivor: life in the concentration camps and post-war difficulties in France

Day	Morning	Afternoon
17	In-class topics: clothing, humor Open grammar topic (practice and discussion) Documentary French film on WWII (part two)	Visit to the Mémorial, WWII museum Homework for tomorrow: 10 observations of the day
18	In-class topics: D-Day and the Battle of Normandy Begin preparation for culminating project	Prepare site visits for tomorrow
19	Travel by bus to sites important for the D-Day landings: the Airborne Museum, the German battery at Azeville, Pointe du Hoc, Utah Beach and Omaha Beach	Visit to the extensive orientation center at the American Cemetery at Omaha Beach Guided visit of the cemetery with participation in the ceremonial lowering of the American flag before closing Homework for tomorrow: 10 observations of the day
20	In-class: ACTFL oral interview (posttest) Finish culminating project	Finish culminating project 7PM: presentation of culminating project to host parents and friends Pot-luck supper
21	Weekend with host family	Official end of the summer program
22	Departure for airport for US	
23-28	Some years: travel by train to Paris	Spend 6 days in Paris visiting sites and museums. Students write observations and discuss them each morning at breakfast

Class Activities, Tasks, Assignments

The activities, tasks, and assignments summarized below merge communicative and intercultural themes according to the theoretical framework. Learners fulfilled the assignments orally, through in-class writing assignments, or in personal journals. It is important to note that there are many connections among the competencies sought, and the activities are easily adaptable to changing situations and new opportunities. The activities took place both inside and outside the classroom, thus creating a learning space without walls. The tasks and assignments listed below often rotated from year to year. Students performed the following:

1. Narrated the previous evening's events, answering questions from their peers and hypothesizing about the future.
2. Recycled previous learning by responding to situation cards ("Explain to the waiter in an expensive restaurant in Paris that you forgot your wallet") both individually and with partners.
3. Studied visual images of homes, related new vocabulary to the images, and described each room in the host family's home.
4. Reviewed vocabulary needed for map reading, applied the words by drawing a map with a partner, then blindfolded learners followed their partner's directions; followed by a walk to the city center to apply orientation and map terms.
5. Created a story based on freely chosen images, narrated it to the class verbally or through actions, class recycled content with questions or hypotheses.
6. Daily assessment and discussion of sentiments and emotions.
7. Reviewed physical and emotional descriptors, then described themselves and compared those portrayals with their host family and American family.
8. Reviewed vocabulary of professions in France, applied new words in a Password style game.
9. Presentation of local cheeses and cheesemaking, with formal tasting protocol and analysis.
10. Food preparation and meals with host family; topics of conversation among family members and with the student; the family's evening activities
11. Comparison of French family's daily life with student's life in the US
12. Organization of French homes and disposition of furniture and bathroom fixtures, comparison with American toilets and showers.
13. Ways French and Americans express emotion.
14. Analysis of the dairy industry as a vital part of the economy in Normandy.
15. Individually or in teams, viewed visual images and heard interviews introducing the concepts, vocabulary, and historical context of the site visit for that afternoon, e.g. horse breeding facility, cheese factory, and museums. Learners kept journals and/or lists of their observations and impressions which were presented to the class the next day.
16. Walk to *Musée du Bocage Normand*, a regional agricultural museum highlighting the history, ethnography, economy, and agriculture of Normandy; learners investigated farm animal culture of Normandy, local crop raising practices in the cultivation of linen and other fibers for cloth; hands-on interaction with 19th-century farm equipment, clothing and other everyday artifacts from a typical rural Norman farm (observations/impressions).
17. Guided visit to the *Musée de la Glacerie*, history of the glass and mirror factory that produced the mirrors for Versailles and fueled the local Norman economy for decades; the evolution of roofing in the area; clothing of 19th-century residents, especially handmade lace headdresses and typical trousseau items (observations/impressions).
18. Guided visit to *Musée des beaux-arts*, learners viewed and analyzed the works of artists they had prepared during the morning session and presented their appraisals to the class; students asked questions.
19. Scrutinized the long history and construction of Mont Saint-Michel through visual images and film; students then visited the site, including the basilica and the village (observations/impressions).

20. Visit to the *Mémorial Museum* on the battle of Normandy and war in the 20th century; students researched and learned about World War II through film and the presentations of guest speakers, including a Holocaust survivor; students furthered their knowledge by engaging in free-style questioning and interviewing; learners applied this new information to the visit to the museum (observations/impressions).
21. Visit to a medieval Scriptorium; students engaged in an interactive and hands-on history of vellum, papyrus, and ink; reflected on the process of manuscript writing and illumination in the Middle Ages, applied new understanding in their close observation of a collection of medieval manuscripts (observations/impressions).
22. Visit to a working cider production facility, where students learned the history, procedures, and cider making's central importance to regional life, customs, and importance to the local economy (observations/impressions).
23. Participated in an all-day hands-on workshop on the formal traditional French table, including flower arrangements, table settings, preparation, and presentation of local cuisine (meal included).
24. Participated in a chocolate sculpting workshop, learned the importance of gastronomy and cuisine competitions in French culture and the history of chocolate and techniques of chocolate sculpting (tasting included).
25. Visited the memorial to Major James Howie and understood the importance of the US 29th Division in the Battle of Normandy during WWII (observations/impressions).
26. Visited the regional historical archives, viewed ancient maps, manuscripts, genealogy scrolls, and other rare documents (observations/impressions).
27. Visited *La Cité de la Mer*; a research center and aquarium; students learned how nuclear energy works in France through an examination of a retired atomic submarine (observations/impressions)
28. Participated in a workshop on making traditional Norman bobbin lace and executed simple designs using bobbins, pins, and threads of this time-honored regional craft.
29. Participated in a workshop taught by a regional Folklore group; learners performed traditional Norman folk dances and tried out 19th-century instruments.
30. Attended sessions at a local circus school; students learned and performed partner acrobatics, juggling, tumbling, and rope tricks.
31. Went individually to a traditional local outdoor market, bought items for lunch, recorded the prices, and presented the results to the class before eating together.
32. Played a hidden objects game in the shopping area of Cherbourg; learners read signs, asked local residents for directions, and bought small items to arrive at the next clue.
33. Bought a one-week ticket to ride the subway in Paris; students learned to overcome adverse conditions, such as noise and impatient commuters.
34. Navigated the complex Paris Museum map and ticket structure and were able to use the voucher to its maximum advantage.
35. Engaged directly in authentic listening situations with adult native speakers.
36. Visited and read interactive panels at sites important to the D-Day Landings, especially the American Beaches and the American Cemetery; they applied what they had previously learned about World War II, they reflected on the events of June 6, 1944, and imagined themselves in that situation and shared their emotions; they collected sand and participated in the lowering of the American flag at the cemetery at Omaha Beach (observations/impressions).

37. Visited Giverny, the home and gardens of Claude Monet; learners explored the gardens and related real-life nature to the paintings of Monet.
38. Visited an interactive museum to view the Bayeux Tapestry; learners analyzed its construction, the meaning of the panels, and its symbols; they understood the tapestry's more than 1000-year-old history and the efforts necessary to protect this priceless work of art; students also visited the Musée Baron Gérard, an art and history museum with collections of paintings and ceramics from antiquity to the present.
39. Visited the city and harbor of Saint-Malo; students explored the walled ramparts and understood the importance of the location of the port to merchants, pirates, and explorers, such as Jacques Cartier, who set sail for Canada from Saint-Malo in 1534.

Appendix 8.2: Sample Prompts

Classroom Cheese Tasting
In class before the activity, students learn the importance of cheese to French culture, how it is manufactured, the kinds of milk used to make the 349 types of cheese, and the cheese specific to each region, including Normandy. Students sample at least five kinds of cheese, according to traditional French protocol, and discuss and rate each cheese using as many new words as possible. Students write a summary report of their tastes and opinions.

Art Museum Visit
In class before the visit, students research the museum's collection, choose one artist each, and learn about the life, works, and styles of that artist. The student prepares a list of general questions to answer through research. At the museum, each student locates the work and presents it to the class; other students ask questions based on their own research.

Outdoor Market Activity
In class before the activity, students acquire a vocabulary of French food and products likely to be at the market; students make a list of what they intend to buy; and roleplay merchant and buyer with student-generated questions in French. At the market, students write down the prices and names of what they bought; the class meets up, and each student describes what they bought, how many, and the price before eating.

Presentation and Conversation with a Holocaust Survivor
Before the session, students spend considerable time at a local World War II Museum, learning about the war, the D-Day invasion, and the Holocaust. Students prepare a list of possible questions for the speaker. At the session, they listen to the speaker, take notes, and ask him questions. The students also participate in a discussion about the post-war period and the possibilities for world peace. Students write in their journals about this experience, recording what impressed and/or shocked them.

Appendix 8.3: Intercultural Competency General Guidelines

These guidelines are given to the students pre-departure.
1. Remember you are in a foreign country and people will see you as representatives of the United States. You are not invisible.

2. Treat your homestay families like your grandparents, not your parents.
3. Staring at strangers is not considered rude in France; neither is getting too close to people in crowds.
4. French people do not normally smile at everyone the way Americans do, so don't assume they are angry.
5. When speaking, think about what you want to say first and express yourself simply. Your level in French is not the same as it is in English; don't worry about accuracy.

Appendix 8.4: Grading Scale

The grading system for the course was pass/fail, and in order to pass, learners needed to achieve an average of 80% on all activities, tasks, and assignments, including intercultural competencies. Perfect attendance was required. Student progress was measured using an assessment scale of 0 to 4 informed by guidelines from the American Council for the Teaching of Foreign Languages (ACTFL), where 0=0; 1=25%; 2=50%; 3=75% and 4=100%. These daily grades alerted the students to any problems, and regular conferences enabled students to make adjustments to any aspect of their participation. Achievement was high and enthusiastic, even though everyone knew that no one had ever failed the course.

Chapter 9

The Historic Preservation Approach: The Importance of Place and 'Boots on the Ground'

Stacey Graham

Note: Section II includes Chapters 4-14. These chapters use a standardized template to discuss the details of their respective study abroad programs and reference Deardorff's (2012) framework for intercultural competencies. The use of this template and the intercultural competencies framework are described in the Section II introduction. All courses in this section (except for Chapter 6) were taught through Middle Tennessee State University (MTSU), a mid-sized state school located in Murfreesboro, Tennessee (USA).

The *MTSU in Scotland* program centers on a history course, *International Historic Preservation* (HIST 3075/6940), at both the undergraduate and graduate student levels. Students spend three weeks in July living, working, and exploring Scotland in the United Kingdom. The world-famous city of Edinburgh, a UNESCO World Heritage Site, is the homebase for this program. A unique aspect of this course is its "boots on the ground" approach (experiential learning framework) in which students, like the practitioners of historic preservation projects, engage with historic places, talk with community members, and work to create an experience that is meaningful to both community stakeholders and visitors to the site. Due to its site-oriented approach this course is ideally taught in a study abroad format. A small group of students works best for the program goals; ten students participated in 2016, eight in 2019, and six in 2022.

THEORETICAL FOUNDATIONS

While the course is offered through the History Department, my staff position is with the Center for Historic Preservation (CHP), a Center for Excellence at MTSU with a four-decades-long institutional track record of community-driven preservation projects throughout Tennessee and the Southern U.S. My study abroad course is therefore based on a framework of experiential learning that we at the Center normally refer to as "boots on the ground" (MTSU Center for Historic Preservation, 2015; Weiler et al., 2022). This approach conveys the CHP's philosophy that the best way to learn about a historic site is to show up in person, listen to community partners and stakeholders, determine what their values and priorities are, and shape preservation plans in response that are useful for the community, while still adhering to sound historical research and best practices in historic preservation. Even though a short-term study abroad (STSA) program does not have adequate time to create actual preservation plans, students still learn the skills of identifying and listening to community partners and determining site significance (Niehaus et al., 2019). These skills together determine "why this place matters," which is an essential part of preservation best practices in both the U.S. and other countries.

This place-based learning approach is based on the idea that places are primary sources for learning and the local community is a hands-on classroom that allows teachers to engage students with real-world problems while also satisfying content standards (Smith & Sobel, 2010). Most study abroad programs are by nature place-based, but the Scotland program takes that further by centering places as the basis for learning, rather than as mere backdrops for other related content. Any townscape, countryside, historic site, or museum we visit is open to analysis and inquiry. This also reflects a thematic approach to study abroad, wherein students learn to view each site they visit through the lens of historic preservation-themed questions.

COURSE DESCRIPTION

By visiting museums and historic sites, including the National Museum of Scotland, Greyfriars Kirkyard, Culloden Battlefield, the Isle of Skye, the Royal Mile, etc., students learn how to analyze and evaluate historic sites, material culture, and cultural landscapes. Students participate in hands-on preservation by taking part in local archaeological and conservation projects led by experts. Students also learn about how heritage organizations, such as Historic Environment Scotland, the National Trust, and the UNESCO World Heritage Center, address the preservation and public interpretation of their properties. These experiences are complemented by a variety of readings, from recent online news articles to excerpts from scholarly publications, to provide historical context and a basis for discussion (see Appendix 9.1 for a list of readings). In addition to academic work, students learn how to conduct everyday activities and interact with strangers in a foreign environment, and they learn how to be good ambassadors for their university and their country.

Course Learning Outcomes

As a result of participating in this program, students will:

a. Learn to examine historic sites and objects and understand the different choices and processes that affect preservation and interpretation.
b. Learn basic analysis of buildings, spaces, and material culture to gain historical perspectives that are not always part of the documentary record.
c. Learn the issues surrounding the preservation and public presentation of historic sites in a global context, answering questions such as, "How do historic sites tell stories about the past?"
d. Contemplate how the interpretation of Scottish history at historic sites/museums reflects the cultural values and political agendas of the Scottish people and government.
e. Examine major threats to the conservation and preservation of historic sites and artifacts in today's geopolitical society, including the threats of climate change, excesses of tourism, gentrification, and economic inequality.

Students learn much more than course content, however—they learn to experience learning in the context of a foreign country while they broaden their perspectives on cultural values and practices by experiencing life in a neighborhood setting. They understand why learning history in an actual historic city center is more effective than learning it inside a classroom. Students learn about and appreciate a foreign culture and expand their minds, abilities, and confidence to travel to different places and connect with people from different backgrounds. This indirect learning is just as valuable and likely much more memorable than the course-specific content.

COURSE HISTORY

MTSU in Scotland Program 2016-2019

I first offered the *MTSU in Scotland* study abroad program in 2016, after an initial experience leading a successful study abroad program in Rome, Italy, in 2014. From the beginning, I wanted to highlight the approach of looking at a city through the layers of its preserved history. The course theme "International Historic Preservation" reflects my professional focus at the MTSU Center for Historic Preservation (CHP) and presents graduate students in the Public History program with the rare chance to earn credits for their M.A. or Ph.D. program through a study abroad course in their field.

In order to present students with a first-hand experience of fieldwork abroad, I emulated the CHP's partnership approach to projects. In 2016, I made contact with representatives from both Rubicon Heritage, an Irish-based archaeological firm working on a project in Edinburgh, and Edinburgh World Heritage, the independent charity that administers the UNESCO World Heritage Site encompassing the Old and New Towns. Through these contacts, the students were able to participate in both a cemetery beautification workshop with the historic graveyards project coordinator for Edinburgh World Heritage, and a two-day archaeological dig with experts from Rubicon Heritage and also with the city archaeologist of the City of Edinburgh Council. By nurturing these contacts over the years, my students were able to participate in similar workshops in both 2019 and 2022.

These partnerships yield valuable opportunities for students to participate in hands-on service workshops and learn directly from preservation professionals. For example, working with Rubicon Heritage staff, students in the 2016 program began initial excavation and documentation at a 17th-century castle site called Red Hall. Students in 2022 joined the Edinburgh Archaeology Field Service (under the auspices of the City Council) in the excavation of outbuildings at Cammo Estate. In each case, students observed first-hand how material culture evidence is discovered, documented, and interpreted as part of the history of Edinburgh and its vicinity over the centuries, as well as how current organizations manage these sites. Their excitement from "digging up old rocks," as they put it, points to the importance of personal connection when it comes to learning and practicing history and in the connection between history and "real-world issues," such as how a site will impact a public's sense of place (National Council for Public History, n.d.).

Because of my own background in cemetery preservation, I gravitate toward projects involving historic cemeteries. In Edinburgh, I have forged an ongoing partnership with the

Edinburgh Graveyards Project, which is a partially grant-funded initiative within the Edinburgh World Heritage organization. Through this partnership, students have contributed to hands-on projects for the beautification, interpretation, and documentation of some of the historic graveyards within the World Heritage Site designation. For example, in 2019, students spent a whole day cleaning up the "Orphan Section" of Old Calton Burial Ground, which is a small corner of the historic graveyard that was separated from the more prominent main part (where philosopher David Hume and others are buried) by a 19th-century road (see Fig. 9.1). Because this small section is across the street from the main tourist path and can only be accessed by a back alley, it has largely been neglected by the general public and used for "antisocial" purposes (such as littering, drug use, etc.) (Buckham, 2013). When I showed the 2022 group of students the Orphan Section, I was pleased to find that much of the cleaning and beautification efforts the 2019 group had worked on had indeed paid off and that the section was pleasantly inviting and marked by clear signage from the street. The students in 2022 remarked that were proud of what the students in 2019 had done; this brief visit to the Orphan Section helped them see how contributing to a sense of place—even if is not your own hometown—makes you feel like a stakeholder in a community.

Figure 9.1: Students from the 2019 MTSU in Scotland program work to beautify the "Orphan Section" of Old Calton Burial Ground. Photo provided by Stacey Graham and printed with consent of volunteers.

MTSU in Scotland Program 2022 (post-COVID-19)

The 2022 group had the opportunity to beta-test an observational survey for Greyfriars Kirkyard, which is famous largely for the tombs of Greyfriars Bobby, inspiring several character names from the *Harry Potter* series, and for its supposedly haunted nature. Over the course of an hour-long observational period, the students took detailed notes on a prepared rubric concerning visitor activities in the kirkyard. They then discussed their findings with the Graveyards Project Manager and the Graveyard Engagement Officer of Edinburgh World Heritage. Their feedback was used in the creation of a visitor self-survey form and other resources available at the "Making Lasting Impressions" page on the Edinburgh World Heritage website (Edinburgh World Heritage, 2023). Students also contributed to another ongoing project at Greyfriars, the preparation of five selected mural-style tombstones for high-quality photographic scanning. For the greatest amount of stonework detail to be properly scanned, all loose bits of debris must be removed gently so as not to damage the delicate sculpture. Students spent a day using soft brushes and other supplies to clean off these intricate tombstones, which date to the 17th century and are significant for their artwork and association with prominent Edinburgh families. Though it meant getting coated in graveyard dust, students greatly valued the chance to be part of actual preservation efforts in Edinburgh, to learn from experts, and to spend a day actively improving one of the most famous and historic graveyards in Scotland. Their efforts were acknowledged in the latest issue of the Greyfriars Kirkyard Community Project's newsletter (Edinburgh World Heritage, 2022), which gave them a great sense of pride and belonging.

The evolving nature of partnership projects ensures that each study abroad group I bring to Scotland will have a variety of experiences, different from the previous groups yet still within the thematic and experiential scope of the program. The slight differences in locations visited from program to program—most notably on the "Highlands and Islands" excursion—are mainly a matter of logistics within a fluctuating heritage tourism market but have the added benefit of broadening my own familiarity, as the faculty leader, of preservation concerns at various sites to better inform students of examples across Scotland. We went to the famous monastery of St. Columba of Iona in 2016; the town of Kirkwall and the neolithic sites of Skara Brae and The Ring of Brodgar on the Orkney Islands in 2019; and various beautiful natural and cultural landscapes on the Isle of Skye in 2022.

COURSE LOGISTICS

In addition to their academic and hands-on learning, students earn three credit hours through approximately 80 hours of instruction (including walking tours, site visits, and class discussions) during the three-week period. There are no official course prerequisites for this program, mainly because it tends to attract undergraduate History majors and minors who have already taken introductory courses and graduate students already enrolled in Public History or Master of Liberal Arts programs.

PRE-PROGRAM ACTIVITIES

To prepare students for both the content of the course and the realities of living abroad, the first two of the three-hour class periods are held on campus one and two weeks before departure. The first class focuses on the major theme of the course, international historic preservation, by providing a brief overview of Scottish history and politics (including independence referenda and Brexit), the fields of historic preservation and material culture, and the most important preservation organizations in Scotland. The second class covers safety and practical considerations for foreign travel, emphasizing expectations for student behavior as MTSU representatives.

CLASS ACTIVITIES & INTERCULTURAL COMPETENCIES

After our arrival in Edinburgh, I orient the students to their new surroundings in both geographic and historical senses. We start off with walking tours of the Old and New Town sections of Edinburgh, including Calton Hill, Princes Street Gardens, and the Royal Mile. We visit major national museums in the city, such as the National Museum of Scotland, the Scottish National Library, and the National Gallery of Scotland. We also visit preserved sites such as Edinburgh Castle, Holyrood Palace, and Rosslyn Chapel. The 2016 program included a side trip to Glasgow, while the 2022 program also went to the Hunterian Museum, Glasgow Cathedral, and the Necropolis. A "Highlands and Islands" excursion includes a few days in Inverness to experience nearby Urquhart Castle on Loch Ness and the Culloden Battlefield, as well as a day trip to a nearby island of historic interest. The last major component of the program is the hands-on, service-learning workshops we participate in through partnerships with the Edinburgh Graveyards Project and the City of Edinburgh Council (see Appendix 9.2 for the day-to-day schedule). As is the case with place-based learning, students analyze each of these places as primary sources through the stories and material culture that are presented to the public. This builds students' content knowledge about the role these places played in Scottish history and culture, as well as student understanding of how these places are significant to people in the present. For instance, Rosslyn Chapel preserves beautifully intricate stone carvings from the 15th century and interprets the stories of the wealthy family that commissioned the building and the changing use of the chapel over time. When students are there in person, they can also see how other people connect to it not only through its artistic merit, but through its local history, religious value, and its popular (though unsubstantiated) connection to the Knights Templar. Historic preservation is not only about one moment in time but also about how subsequent generations find new, present meaning in the places that connect them to the past.

Through the hands-on workshops, students feel like they are not just taking on new perspective, in terms of learning and experiences, but also giving back to the communities from whom they are learning so much. The workshops represent experiential learning by providing students with the chance to listen to members of the local community and hear what they want to experience at their local historic sites and museums. Students experience first-hand why these places still matter; without an answer to this question, historic preservation is meaningless. I would argue that this enhanced sense of place is an "intercultural competency" that is gained during this program, even if it is discipline-specific at the same time. In contrast to some research on STSAs (Niehaus et al., 2019), I have found that there is not always a clear division between disciplinary and intercultural learning. For example, when this course asks students to contemplate how current Scottish culture and politics affect the stories that are told about the Scottish past at historic sites and museums, it is asking them to be aware of their own cultural attitudes as well as those of the host country at the same time. This is to be expected, as the field of historic preservation asks professionals to analyze why we talk about the past in different ways over time, which forces us to be aware of our changing and enduring values and how they connect or clash with the values of others (Deardorff, 2006).

Beyond the discipline-specific skills that students learn as part of the course, they pick up important "soft skills" through various "meta-curricular" features built-in into the program (Harvey, 2017). This includes, first and foremost, simply living in apartments (locally called "flats") in an Edinburgh neighborhood for three weeks. This allows students to gain skills such as a geographical and spatial awareness of the environment, close observation skills when watching locals for cues as to what to do/where to go, civic engagement skills when using public infrastructure, and increased awareness of themselves as part of a global network of travelers. While these skills aren't articulated within specific, assessed assignments, students nevertheless are given the space, time, and encouragement in which to explore and develop these skills and often derive the most meaning and pride from these experiences, as is clear from their reflection papers. Many of the intercultural competencies that students experience are interwoven into the course content itself so that students are constantly paying attention to the human geography surrounding them and absorbing social norms and practices even while I am constantly presenting them with historical context.

Activities

Walking Tour of the New Town

New Town is the 18th-century planned Georgian extension to the city meant to represent Enlightenment ideals in contrast to the medieval Old Town. The walking tour tasks students with locating prominent monuments, streetscapes, architectural features, etc., based on the walking tour, "Athens of the North," available from the Edinburgh World Heritage website (Edinburgh World Heritage, 2022). This activity emphasized the intercultural competencies listed in Table 9.1.

Table 9.1: Intercultural Competencies in the Walking Tour of the New Town Activity

Knowledge	Skills	Attitudes
• Introduction to Neoclassical architecture • Content learning for Edinburgh history in the 18th and 19th centuries	• Observation of the built environment • Orientation in urban space • Using a physical map • Following directions • Working in pairs and small groups to navigate through space	• Curiosity in the observation of local practices • Stamina in experiencing so much activity on foot across a cityscape

Visit to Culloden Battlefield

Culloden Battlefield is the site of the final defeat of the Jacobites and "Bonnie Prince Charlie" in 1746. Many of the students are already familiar with the story of the battle from the book series/TV show *Outlander*, in which the battle is largely portrayed from the Scottish point of view. Because of this, and because the students are fairly familiar with Scottish culture by the time we visit the site, they usually expect to hear the story from the Jacobite perspective, which renders it a tale of lost hopes and tragic consequences for the Scottish people. While this was once the narrative that the site and its museum presented, the experience that is currently provided explores both the Scottish and the English perspectives of the battle, its lead-up, and its aftermath, using primary sources, which highlight the words of the people who experienced the battle firsthand. Students are always surprised by what they perceive as fairness in the way the story is presented in the museum. The students then have this more balanced narrative in mind as they go on to walk the battlefield grounds and view the famous stone monuments that memorialize the Scottish highlanders by clan and where the English soldiers were supposedly buried. The students make note of this perceived fairness in their site assessment forms that they complete shortly after their visit. The intercultural competencies gained by the students through this activity are listed in Table 9.2.

Table 9.2: Intercultural Competencies in the Visit to the Culloden Battlefield Activity

Knowledge	Skills	Attitudes
• Content on the Jacobite rebellion of mid-18th-century Scotland • Understanding of the event from the perspectives of various figures on both sides of the conflict	• Interpretation of the narrative of the event based on the primary sources and artifacts provided in the museum and on the battlefield • Analysis of the legacy of the battle in Scottish popular memory through battlefield memorialization and other outlets	• Open-mindedness to various viewpoints on a controversial event that still resonates in the present • Sensitivity to ongoing tensions between Scotland and England in the wake of Brexit, COVD-19, and renewed calls for a referendum on Scottish independence

Tasks

Getting around Town

I know from my own experiences as a world traveler that while visiting important sites or participating in fun activities may be the ostensible point of international travel, what gives me the greatest sense of accomplishment is figuring out mundane tasks such as navigating public transportation routes or completing a grocery store run. While these tasks are never articulated as requirements in the course syllabus, they are nonetheless expected, encouraged, and, in most cases, inevitable. I try to provide the framework in which students can best achieve success at these tasks, while also leaving them to their own devices to solve such challenges. On the very first day in Edinburgh, I take the group to the TravelHub outside Waverley Station to get their Ridacards, which are travel passes that will cover their bus fare for the duration of the program. Then I have the students take a bus to find their apartments on their own, which helps them start to develop awareness, agency, and confidence as people who can move about a foreign city unaccompanied by a faculty leader. The intercultural competencies integrated into this task are summarized in Table 9.3.

Table 9.3: Intercultural Competencies in the Getting around Town Task

Knowledge	Skills	Attitudes
• Building self-awareness as one moves through foreign environments where one is at a cultural disadvantage • Knowledge of how the city is laid out and the locations of important city sectors and neighborhoods	• Problem-solving by figuring out bus routes, timetables, and payment methods • Communication with locals who have a different dialect and often a different worldview	• Sensitivity to social etiquette in public spaces • Stepping outside one's comfort zone as an outsider in a local environment • Patience with public transportation delays • Independence as one accomplishes tasks one has never had to encounter in the U.S.

Scavenger Hunt

I try to help set students up for tasks with a brief scavenger hunt on the first day of the program, which challenges them with locating neighborhood staples like grocery stores, post offices, pubs, and banks/ATMs. That way, students notice the service locations they will most likely need to utilize, and they can add those to their mental maps of the city. The intercultural competencies observed in this task are listed in Table 9.4.

Table 9.4: Intercultural Competencies in the Scavenger Hunt Task

Knowledge	Skills	Attitudes
• Learning what the major chains and local branches are for grocery stores, banks, restaurants, cafes, pharmacies, etc., in Edinburgh	• Calculating currency conversion, comparing rates, and figuring out customs forms at the post office • Planning ahead for daily, small-scale grocery shopping (don't forget to bring your plastic bag!)	• Demonstrating humility and open-mindedness when talking with locals and other tourists • Being flexible when faced with options (at stores, restaurants, etc.) that are unfamiliar, inadequate, or unexpected

POST-PROGRAM AND FUTURE CLASS ACTIVITIES

Approximately one week after returning to the U.S., students meet on campus (2016, 2019) or virtually (2022) for one last three-hour class period in which they share their final presentations and reflect on their experiences. While one week may not be considered enough time for adequate reflection, I find that students are beginning to speak like seasoned world travelers, with confidence and perspective gained during the program.

The experience of being at these places in person and dealing with new and unfamiliar cultures can be overwhelming to students, diminishing their understanding of the historical content at the expense of the in-the-moment experiences. Therefore, I would like future class activities to create time for an expanded discussion on course content before we arrive in Scotland. This could be done by adding one additional three-hour pre-departure, in-person class, as well as one or two discussion posts on the learning management system course site.

I am pleased, however, to have found what I believe to be a good balance between scheduled activities and student free time while in Scotland. I am considering giving the students the freedom to schedule their own chosen site visits (for which they will need to fill out a Site Assessment Form), which will encourage a closer analysis of available sites, connecting places to their own interests and curiosity, and taking the initiative of booking tickets, mapping locations, and handling transportation without the faculty leader. I also want to encourage them to step outside their comfort zones more by talking to local people. This will help students better understand the course content of how Scottish people view their history through sites and museums, while also opening their minds to other perspectives.

EVALUATION AND ASSIGNMENTS

The grade breakdown for the course is outlined in Table 9.5:

Table 9.5: Grade Breakdown

Assignments	Percentage of final grade	Type of assessment
Daily assignments	15%	Formative assessment
Final projects	30%	Summative assessment
Reflection papers	15%	Summative assessment
Participation	40%	Formative and summative assessment

I make participation the largest component of the grade because it is the most important. Participation covers conventional course behaviors such as attendance and communication with the faculty leader, but it also covers group dynamics (with each student responsible for contributing positively to the safety and learning experiences of the group) and student responsibility (as representatives of MTSU and the U.S. in general). Therefore, 40% of each student's grade is based on intercultural competency, covering a wide range of expected behaviors and responsibilities. After all, showing up on time to class in this context means navigating your way on foot or by bus to a designated meeting place in the city that you likely never have been to before and calculating how much time it will take to get there.

Site Assessment Form

One of the formative assessments for students is the Site Assessment Form (see Appendix 9.3)—one form for each site we visit, whether it is a museum, castle, cemetery, city block, a pile of ruins that once was a medieval abbey, etc. This form asks the same four questions as a fundamental introduction to site interaction: Who owns and/or operates this site? What kinds of material culture are displayed? What story/stories are told by the site, and in what ways? Who is the audience for this story/these stories? The hope is that students will be able to view any historical narrative presented in any kind of setting as a construction that reflects the vision of a certain set of values and goals in time. This assignment allowed the students to gain the intercultural competencies listed in Table 9.6.

Table 9.6: Intercultural Competencies in the Site Assessment Form Assignment

Knowledge	Skills	Attitudes
• Content knowledge related to specific museums and historic sites on the itinerary	• Critical analysis method applicable to historic sites/museums around the world • Observation, communication, and writing skills	• Respect for other cultures and their history through analysis of their development and presentation

Final Assignments

During our final class period after our return to the U.S., students turn in their final two assignments. The first is a presentation shared with the whole class on a chosen historic site/museum, which assesses the discipline-specific skills they gained through experiential- and theme-based learning. The second is a reflection paper, in which students are asked to evaluate both the academic content they learned as well as their experiences as students abroad, which is more individualized in tone. This paper is a better gauge of students' intercultural competencies and gives me a sense of what they felt were the most important things they learned during the program. While students generally enjoy and learn from the historic site visits (especially the excursions, which are more memorable by nature/design), they almost always point to activities, travels, or even simple wanderings they did by themselves in unassigned free time. I see this as a vindication of the decision to challenge students to step outside their comfort zones and make the most of their opportunities (Harvey, 2017). This assignment helped the students develop the intercultural competencies listed in Table 9.7.

Table 9.7: Intercultural Competencies in the Final Assignment

Knowledge	Skills	Attitudes
• Cultural self-awareness, as one compares one's experiences and expectations abroad to those back in the U.S. • Content knowledge: Overall understanding of basic concepts of historic preservation	• Reflection on one's experiences upon program completion	• Openness to local culture, as evidenced through the frequenting of a favorite neighborhood pub • Taking the initiative for deciding one's own activities during free time (instead of relying on a faculty leader)

STUDENT FEEDBACK

Student feedback comes in different forms. Site Assessment Forms show me how students are developing their analytical and observational skills from week to week. For example, these forms revealed how some of the students were honing their observational skills by considering issues such as accessibility when it comes to museums and sites. Final presentations give me an overall indication of their understanding of the course topic. The student reflection papers are the most valuable for articulating what students felt they learned during the program. Because student course evaluations are focused entirely on the academic content of the course, I find that reflection papers are the best ways to evaluate students' intercultural competencies. Below are two direct quotes received from the student reflection papers. Following each quote, the program year and the intercultural competencies gained by the students are listed.

> "Living, studying, and working in a major international capital city broke through a previously unrealized trepidation within me regarding travel outside this small region of my country; therefore, it made the entirety of the world more accessible and less intimidating. I now feel as if I can, not only travel the world, but turn another of my dreams into a realistic goal: obtaining an internship or job outside the United States within the next several years." (*Student 1, 2022; discovery, risk-taking, stepping outside the comfort zone*)

> "I noticed little in terms of public parking spaces [in Edinburgh], instead seeing numerous bus stops and sidewalks meant for daily usage. It does make me curious about further exploring how this big difference between the U.S. and Europe impacts the preservation of cities, as increased pollution and need for parking space undoubtedly has a strong [effect] on numerous parts of the U.S." (*Student 2, 2022; cultural self-awareness, observational skills, evaluation skills*)

In addition, I implemented a post-course survey in 2022 (see Appendix 9.4) that asked the students to compare their expectations of the program before departure to their actual experiences upon return. The majority of students agreed that their experiences exceeded their expectations, citing their confidence as independent travelers and openness to other cultures as the primary gains from the program (apart from academic learning).

CAVEATS AND REFLECTIONS

Conducting the course at the tail end of the COVID-19 pandemic certainly created additional logistical challenges, as many historic sites now insist on pre-booking tickets and entry times to better control crowd numbers. This meant a greater exercise of organizational skills for students when making plans for free time. They also had a fruitful area of cross-cultural comparison by experiencing the COVID-19 response in Scotland, which at the time, had a 78% vaccination rate compared to a 52% rate in Tennessee.

Overall, the main strength of the course is that it reframes the way students approach historic sites in general. Students come to see places as successive constructions by groups of people over time to help them make sense of their place in the world. This new perspective is both discipline-specific, in that it asks questions about practices in historic preservation, and indicative of intercultural competency, in that it compels students to see how people in other countries conceptualize and preserve their past through places and material culture. The main challenge is time—three weeks is not always enough for students to develop a deeper understanding of why sites tell the stories that they do about the past. I do feel, however, that the seeds of understanding are at least planted during this course and continue to percolate through students' growing awareness for months and even years later. I was impressed how one student in my very first study abroad program in 2014 was so struck by the layering of cultural landscapes emphasized in that course that they brought that approach into other graduate work. Furthermore, the same student participated in my 2019 program as a Ph.D. student and applied the lessons learned in Scotland to a dissertation on agricultural history.

The course is not the only study abroad program offered by the History Department at MTSU, but it is the only one associated with the Center for Historic Preservation. The program, therefore, provides an opportunity for both undergraduate and graduate students in the nationally renowned Public History program to examine issues of historic preservation and public history abroad. It also serves to bolster student resumes when applying for the Public History graduate program as well as for jobs in the field, due to the opportunities it provides students to participate in historic preservation projects in World Heritage Site cities.

The inclusion of intercultural competencies is one of the greatest benefits that students experience in a study abroad program in part because they are unanticipated and therefore experienced authentically by each student. The experience of living in a foreign country provides the overall context into which any specific course information will be processed by individual students. The atmosphere of a bustling, cosmopolitan city such as Edinburgh, with a continuous history stretching back further than the history of the United States itself, influences students' actions and interactions for a period of three weeks. After only a few days, students are usually familiar enough with where they are going that other foreign tourists often ask the students for directions, mistaking them for permanent residents. Adapting to their surroundings as short-term residents requires students to exercise their skills of observation, attention, and openness, which lends itself to critical thinking about the subject matter during site visits and class discussions. Engaging with their environments builds skills at the academic and personal levels in a way that no classroom instruction can duplicate. This sense of place can only be earned by students literally putting their boots on the ground and learning a city by navigating spaces and the people in them.

REFERENCES

Buckham, S. (2013). *The Edinburgh Graveyards Project: A scoping study to identify strategic priorities for the future care and enjoyment of five historic burial grounds in the heart of the Edinburgh World Heritage Site.* Edinburgh World Heritage. https://www.wmf.org/sites/default/files/article/pdfs/Edinburgh%20Graveyards%20Project.pdf

Deardorff, D. K. (2006). Identification and assessment of intercultural competence as a student outcome of internationalization. *Journal of Studies in International Education, 10*(3), 241–266. http://doi.org/10.1177/1028315306287002

Deardorff, D. K. (2012). Framework: Intercultural competence model. In K. Berardo & D. K. Deardorff (Eds.), *Building cultural competence: Innovative activities and models* (pp. 45-52). Stylus Publishing.

Edinburgh World Heritage. (2023). *Greyfriars Kirkyard community learning and interpretation project 2020-2022: Making lasting impressions.* https://ewh.org.uk/explore/projects/greyfriars-kirkyard/

Edinburgh World Heritage. (2022). *Making lasting impressions: The Greyfriars Kirkyard community project.* https://mailchi.mp/4e4fe1a33192/q9i95owqab?fbclid=IwAR06csIo-OPWouW39RLRFWH91Lth1rJ8Xrd4hqdEeqzbL96A8DMQGAV-zxE

Harvey, T.A. (2017). Design and pedagogy for transformative intercultural learning. In B. Kappler Mikk & I. Steglitz (Eds.), *Learning across cultures: Locally and globally* (pp. 109-138). NAFSA: Association of International Educators/Stylus.

MTSU Center for Historic Preservation. (2015). *Annual report: 2014-2015.* https://irp.cdn-website.com/2c253136/files/uploaded/CHP_2015_Annual_Report.pdf

National Council on Public History. (n.d.). *About the field.* https://ncph.org/what-is-public-history/about-the-field/

Niehaus, E., Woodman, T. C., Bryan, A., Light, A., & Hill, E. (2019). Student learning objectives: What instructors emphasize in short-term study abroad. *Frontiers: The Interdisciplinary Journal of Study Abroad, 31*(2), 121–138. http://doi.org/10.36366/frontiers.v31i2.458

Smith, G. A. & Sobel, D. (2010). *Place- and community-based education in schools.* Routledge.

Weiler, P. B., Gorman, A., & Ruble, D. (2022). Protect and preserve: MTSU center works tirelessly to save history before it's too late. *MTSU News.* https://mtsunews.com/protect-and-preserve/

APPENDICES

Appendix 9.1: Reading List from Syllabus

Bucciantini, A. (2018). Beginnings. In *Exhibiting Scotland: Objects, identity, and the national museum* (pp. 1-18). University of Massachusetts Press. https://doi.org/10.2307/j.ctv3s8tv4.6

Bucciantini, A. (2018). Conclusion. In *Exhibiting Scotland: Objects, identity, and the national museum* (pp. 191-198). University of Massachusetts Press. https://doi.org/10.2307/j.ctv3s8tv4.13

Buckham, S. (2013). *The Edinburgh Graveyards Project: A scoping study to identify strategic priorities for the future care and enjoyment of five historic burial grounds in the heart of the Edinburgh World Heritage Site.* Edinburgh World Heritage. https://www.wmf.org/sites/default/files/article/pdfs/Edinburgh%20Graveyards%20Project.pdf

Carrell, S. (2017, August 9). Skye islanders call for help with overcrowding after tourism surge. *The Guardian.* https://www.theguardian.com/uk-news/2017/aug/09/skye-islanders-call-for-help-with-overcrowding-after-tourism-surge

Garavelli, D. (2021, August 22). Insight: The detrimental impact short-term lets are having on urban and rural Scotland. *The Scotsman.* https://www.scotsman.com/news/opinion/insight-the-detrimental-impact-short-term-lets-are-having-on-urban-and-rural-scotland-dani-garavelli-3354863?fbclid=IwAR2AOwHA6eo-e-mjsKBSj9Clgg5roon1rUYd57121homWb2IeP4fnNd78Ps

Gold, J. R., & Gold, M. M. (2007). "The graves of the gallant Highlanders": Memory, interpretation and narratives of Culloden. *History and Memory, 19*(1), 5-38. https://doi.org/10.2979/his.2007.19.1.5

Hume, D. (1758). Of the dignity or meanness of human nature. *Modern History Sourcebook*. Retrieved September 17, 2022, from https://sourcebooks.fordham.edu/mod/hume-dignity.asp.

International Council on Monuments and Sites (ICOMOS). (1964). *International charter for the conservation and restoration of monuments and sites*. https://www.icomos.org/en/participer/179-articles-en-francais/ressources/charters-and-standards/157-thevenice-charter

Morris, W. (1996). Manifesto of the society for the protection of ancient buildings. In N. Stanley Price, M. Kirby Talley, Jr., & A. Melucco Vaccaro (Eds.), *Historical and philosophical issues in the conservation of cultural heritage* (pp. 319-323). Getty Conservation Institute.

Ruskin, J. (1996). The lamp of memory. In N. Stanley Price, M. Kirby Talley, Jr., & A. Melucco Vaccaro (Eds.), *Historical and philosophical issues in the conservation of cultural heritage* (pp. 42-43, 322-323). Getty Conservation Institute.

Trevor-Roper, H. (1983). The invention of tradition: The Highland tradition of Scotland. In E. Hobsbawm & T. Ranger (Eds.), *The invention of tradition* (pp. 15-41). Cambridge University Press.

United Nations Educational, Scientific and Cultural Organisation (UNESCO). (1972). *Convention concerning the protection of world cultural and natural heritage*. http://whc.unesco.org/archive/convention-en.pdf

Viollet-le-Duc, E.-E. (1996). Restoration. In N. Stanley Price, M. Kirby Talley, Jr., & A. Melucco Vaccaro (Eds.), *Historical and philosophical issues in the conservation of cultural heritage* (pp. 314-318). Getty Conservation Institute.

Additional graduate student readings (HIST 6940):

Hague, C., & Jenkins, P. (2005). The changing image and identity of the city in the 21st century: "Athens of the North" or "North of Athens." In B. Edwards and P. Jenkins (Eds.), *Edinburgh: The making of a capital city* (pp. 217-230). Edinburgh University Press. https://www.jstor.org/stable/10.3366/j.ctvxcr958.23

Nora, P. (1989). Between memory and history: Les lieux de mémoire. *Representations, 26*, 7-24. https://doi.org/10.2307/2928520

Smith, H., & Luque-Azcona, E. J. (2012). The historical development of built heritage awareness and conservation policies: A comparison of two World Heritage Sites: Edinburgh and Salvador do Bahia. *GeoJournal, 77*(3), 399–415. https://doi.org/10.1007/s10708-010-9391-5

Smith, L. (2006). *Uses of heritage*. Routledge.

Appendix 9.2: Day-to-Day Schedule (Scotland Itinerary)

Day	Scheduled Activities	Duration
Day 1	Arrival; orientation and introductory walking tour	2 hours
Day 2	Royal Mile walking tour, part 1: Edinburgh Castle to Giles Cathedral	4 hours
Day 3	New Town walking tour: Calton Hill, St. Andrew Square, George Street	4 hours
Day 4	The Mound: National Museum of Scotland, Princes Street Gardens, National Gallery of Scotland	5 hours
Day 5	Graveyard preservation workshop (Day 1 of 2)	5 hours
Day 6	Day trip to Glasgow: Glasgow Cathedral, The Hunterian, Buchanan Street	10 hours
Day 7	Graveyard preservation workshop (Day 2 of 2)	5 hours
Day 8	FREE DAY	
Day 9	Royal Mile walking tour, part 2: Canongate, Museum of Edinburgh, Scottish Parliament	3 hours
Day 10	Holyroodhouse Palace, Holyrood Park: St. Anthony's Chapel and Arthur's Seat	4 hours
Day 11	Excursion to Inverness; walking tour of historic sites in city center	3 hours
Day 12	Bus trips to Urquhart Castle/Loch Ness and Culloden; walk to Clava Cairns	6 hours
Day 13	Ultimate Isle of Skye Day Tour (charter bus)	12 hours
Day 14	FREE DAY in Inverness	
Day 15	Train to Edinburgh; class discussion and reflections	2 hours
Day 16	Historic archaeology workshop (Day 1 of 2)	5 hours
Day 17	Historic archaeology workshop (Day 2 of 2)	5 hours
Day 18	Surgeon's Hall Museums, Rosslyn Chapel	4 hours
Day 19	FREE DAY	
Day 20	Scavenger hunt, final discussion, independent study	3 hours
Day 21	Depart Edinburgh	

Appendix 9.3: Site Assessment Form (Assignment)

MTSU in Scotland Site Assessment Form

HIST 3075/6940: International Historic Preservation

Student Name:
Name of site:
Who owns/operates this site?
What kinds of material culture are displayed?
What story/stories are told by the site, and in what ways?
Who is the audience for this story/these stories?
Additional comments and reactions:

Appendix 9.4: Post-Program Survey

MTSU in Scotland Summer 2022
HIST 3075/6940 (section 002): International Historic Preservation

Post-Program Survey

1. What was the most important thing, concerning the academic content of the course, that you learned from your trip?
2. What was the most important thing, concerning any other aspect of the course, that you learned?
3. What were your biggest challenges while abroad?
4. How was Scotland similar to your expectations? How was it different?
5. How confident do you feel about traveling to other places in the world now?
6. Explain your understanding of what "historic preservation" is.
7. Explain your understanding of what "intercultural competencies" are.

Chapter 10

From One Music City to Another: The History of Western Art Music in Vienna

Joseph E. Morgan

Note: Section II includes Chapters 4-14. These chapters use a standardized template to discuss the details of their respective study abroad programs and reference Deardorff's (2012) framework for intercultural competencies. The use of this template and the intercultural competencies framework are described in the Section II introduction. All courses in this section (except for Chapter 6) were taught through Middle Tennessee State University (MTSU), a mid-sized state school located in Murfreesboro, Tennessee (USA).

This chapter will cover *The History of Western Art Music in Vienna* (MUHL 3020), a short-term study abroad course. The unique goal of this course is to design activities and assignments that bring context to the musical pieces. The context is built into the program by selecting activities that encourage experiential, collaborative, and reflective approaches that lead to holistic learning for the students. This course is the third required music history course for music majors at MTSU. While traditionally offered as an on-campus course, this option was created as a three-to-four-week study abroad program that travels to Vienna during the month of June. This course was created in 2018 and has been offered three times with an average student enrollment of 12.

THEORETICAL FOUNDATIONS

It is worth noting that while all of the program activities were developed organically through the alignment of course objectives and content with what is available in Vienna, the ideals of cutting-edge pedagogy are met here as well. Indeed, as it has evolved, the program has synthesized the diverse ideals of *experiential, reflective, integrative, and collaborative* approaches to instruction.

According to its website, the Association of Experiential Education (2013) defines *experiential* learning as a "...philosophy that informs many methodologies in which educators purposefully engage with learners in direct experience and focused reflection in order to increase knowledge, develop skills, clarify values, and develop people's capacity to contribute to their communities" (Gass, 2013). This approach is often enhanced during the course through *reflective* learning work, which Boyd and Fales define as "...the process of internally examining and exploring an issue of concern, triggered by an experience, which creates and clarifies meaning in terms of self, and which results in a changed conceptual perspective" (Boyd & Fales, 1983, p. 100). The various activities in the course often align as part of an *integrative* learning approach, understood to be "...the ability to make, recognize and evaluate connections among disparate concepts, fields, or contexts..." (Huber et al., 2007, p. 46). In order to enhance the value of the experiences and connections, a number of the activities incorporate *collaborative* learning approaches which describe "...educational approaches involving joint intellectual effort by students, or student and teachers together. Usually, students are working in groups of two or more, mutually searching for understanding, solutions or meanings or creating a product" (MacGregor, 1992, p. 1). Some of the better courses (on campus or off campus) that I have taught involve one, two, or sometimes three of these ideals at one point or another. This study abroad program incorporates all four in an organic and meaningful way.

However, the aspect that makes the course so important to the lives of these students is the transformational learning experiences. According to Strange and Gibson (2017) these experiences can "...move students from perspective[s] that have allowed ethnocentrism and dualistic epistemologies and allow the creation of a new frame of reference that promotes cultural pluralism." Further, as Strange and Gibson (2017) also note, the direct connection between and combination between "strong academic content" and "geographic dimensions" (the history of music and Vienna) can create for the student new meaning structures that are "...more inclusive, differentiating, permeable, critically reflective and integrative of experience" (Strange & Gibson, 2017, p. 87).

COURSE DESCRIPTION

MUHL 3020 surveys Western art music of the 18th-21st centuries, including Classical, Romantic, Modern, and Postmodern periods, covering the classical repertoire of composers like Ludwig van Beethoven, Wolfgang Amadeus Mozart, Franz Josef Haydn, and others. Whether conducted abroad or on our campus, MUHL 3020 is a typical course in the discipline; it is offered at most classical music programs in the United States, and we employ the standard textbook that most programs offer. We use Burkholder et al.'s (2018) *A History of Western Music* coupled with Volumes 2-3 of the *Norton Anthology of Western Music* (Burkholder et al., 2019a, 2019b).

Course Learning Outcomes

At the end of the course, the students will be able to:
   a. Learn critical thinking and aural analysis skills.
   b. Learn pragmatic information in the content area.
   c. Gain knowledge on the influence of socio-economic and political factors on music.

These approaches (*experiential, reflective, integrative, and collaborative*) complement and enhance the course's learning objectives. By studying these musical masterworks in the places they were composed, students learn critical thinking and aural analysis skills. They also learn pragmatic information such as the names, time periods, and characteristics of major historical periods and styles. Students then set them within a broad, generalized knowledge of repertoire, formal procedures, genres, and compositional procedures, their relevance to other eras and repertories. This is meant to provide context to the works that they have already studied on their own instruments in the years previous to the course. Finally, a primary objective of the course is to introduce the influence of religious, socioeconomic, and political factors on music. MTSU's accrediting agency, the National Association of Schools of Music (NASM), mandates that an essential competency is "the ability to work intellectually with relationships between music and music literature within cultural/historical contexts. [As well as a] Knowledge of a variety of cultures, various historical periods…" (NASM, 2021, p. 107). These outcomes are required for both the study abroad and the domestic version of the class.

COURSE HISTORY

The origin of the MUHL 3020 study abroad version came about rather surprisingly and as a result of positive leadership and connections from both the School of Music and the Department of International Studies. As a researcher, I had the opportunity to present a paper in Florence, Italy, and the head of International Studies at the time connected me with a person in Florence interested in hosting study abroad coursework there. It turned out that the program might be a little too expensive, and I was asked if there might be another place that I might like to teach abroad. At that moment I was preparing on the symphonies of the "first Viennese School" and told him Vienna with a smile knowing that it very well might be one of the most expensive cities in Europe to visit.

Shortly thereafter, the then Director of the School of Music told me how Webster University had established campuses across the globe, from Ghana, to China, to Vienna. He put me in touch with the administration there, including the office of student services, and I soon had a classroom and a housing service in the heart of Europe. I visited in 2017 to ensure that the accommodation and classrooms were appropriate, and I took my first set of students in 2018. Having taken the time to build the program myself, and through the use of contacts at Webster University, we have found a way by which we can offer an affordable option for our students to study in one of Europe's most expensive cities.

COURSE LOGISTICS

The course is typically offered every semester in the classroom, and the summer study abroad is a complement to the classroom experience, with both versions providing three credit hours. The students and I meet in a classroom at Webster University in Vienna, which is housed in the historic Palais Wenkheim, in the 2nd district, close to the city center. The course is primarily for music majors but is open to students who are looking for a study abroad elective and can read music well.

PRE-PROGRAM ACTIVITIES

I have built the course primarily on the theoretical foundations of experiential learning. It is from this area that most life- and perspective-altering moments take place. However, in several ways, I amend this approach with assignments and activities built from ideas around reflective, integrative, and collaborative approaches.

The pre-program activities require the student to develop a certain amount of independence in preparing for the trip. This includes applying for scholarships, whose applications require essays and letters of recommendation, as well as the acquisition of a passport, ticket, vaccines, and much else. These things happen with very little instructional support, as my program is run on a shoestring so that it can be affordable by our typical students, who are often working, middle-income, and first-generation students. Simply put, the amount of individual work that the student, who is often around 20 years of age and perhaps still living with their parents, must accomplish to meet me in a classroom in Vienna on the first day is incredible unto itself.

CLASS ACTIVITIES & INTERCULTURAL COMPETENCIES

The program activities fall into roughly three categories: concerts, museums, and field trips to significant spaces. For concerts, the students are exposed to the world-class cultural performing ensembles in Vienna, including but not restricted to the state-sponsored opera and symphony. For the museums, Vienna was long the seat of the Astro-Hungarian empire and holds outstanding collections of historical and artistic treasures. We visit at least seven museums during the trip. Related to these trips to museums are the trips to significant spaces. Vienna itself is home to a vast number of musically relevant historical spaces including the preserved homes of Ludwig van Beethoven, Johannes Brahms, Franz Schubert, Wolfgang Amadeus Mozart, Arnold Schoenberg, and others. Trips outside Vienna have included Franz Josef Haydn's castle in Esterhazy, Mozart's childhood home in Salzburg, and other cultural encounters therein. Indeed, a primary component of the experiential character of the program is the fact that during the visit, students see how historical and cultural artifacts express and represent cultural values. This experience provides a glimpse of alternative cultural and social solutions, some better and some worse, to simple and complicated problems, whether they be historical monuments, city infrastructure, artistic funding, religious expression/difference, or many others.

For a more specific discussion of the class activities, tasks, and assignments, I have chosen to focus on eight class activities that serve both as a highlight for the program and as a remarkable pedagogical experience. To emphasize this, I have added a table after each assignment section that describes which knowledge, skills, and attitudes are engaged within each particular assignment. However, it should be emphasized here that these identified best practices and pedagogical theories are limiting and reductive. In reality, these and other approaches mentioned earlier (experiential, integrative, and collaborative) all work together in a mutually reinforcing way to create a holistic, transformative experience.

1. The Scavenger Hunt (aka "The Great Race")

The idea for the first assignment, the scavenger hunt, was given to me by a colleague and former Director of the School of Music who apparently conducted study abroad trips to London on a semi-regular basis. It is probably the most pragmatically impactful assignment on the list and is an invaluable guide in collaborative learning. The day after we arrive in Vienna, students are required to "pair up," locate 14 artifacts, and then document them through a selfie that indicates that they were there.

The list includes landmarks featuring significant academic content knowledge that our course will visit during our time in the country. It also includes pragmatically important locations, such as Webster University where our class meets, in addition to some basic, fun, tourist things. The goal of the assignment is to get each student comfortable with public transportation in Vienna (as many have not experienced public transportation before), foster a sense of comfort wandering in a foreign city, and engage skills in problem-solving and creative thinking. Other acquired skills that cannot be overestimated are the use of maps, communication with locals, and problem-solving, all of which require strong attitudes of empathy, risk-taking, and stepping outside of their comfort zone (see Table 10.1 for a list of competencies). The teamwork aspect is great fun, and in some variations, I assign the teams in order to break up any cliques that I see might be developing among participants. Refer to Appendix 10.1 for a complete list of artifacts for this activity.

Table 10.1: Intercultural Competencies for Scavenger Hunt Activity

Knowledge	Skills	Attitudes
- Culture-specific knowledge - Academic content knowledge	- Creative thinking - Problem-solving - Map reading	- Risk-taking - Discovery

2. St. Stephen's Dome Tour

Visiting St. Stephen's Dome is a typical tourist activity in Vienna. The cathedral is a late medieval Romanesque and Gothic structure with an ornate roof and is the central monument at the center of Vienna's busiest district. The church and its parish are the seat of the Archbishop of Vienna, in the capital city of a country that considers itself to be Roman Catholic. While large, Gothic cathedrals are a rather common thing in Europe, as nearly every major metropolitan area is complemented with one, it is rather rare in the United States, and many of the study abroad students have never seen such an ornate structure and edifice on a sacred building. Before entering, we engage with cultural self-awareness and understanding other's worldviews by talking about behavior and how there is an expectation of dress (e.g., covered shoulders), and that the students should adopt an attitude of respect with regard to their presence in this holy place.

In order to integrate the Cathedral with our lecture during the tour, I tie our discussion of the ornate cathedral to the historical differences between Protestant and Roman Catholic sacred music. The lecture content can include the singing of the congregation and Roman Catholic sacred music, which can be considered more ornate—differences that are bound up with the religions themselves—justified through faith alone, or faith and good works. The students garner the skills to observe and analyze the ornate chant, building, and art as the community's expression of faith. With this activity, it is possible for some students to gain an open-minded understanding of religion in different contexts, regions, and countries. This activity completes cultural bridging and hits a number of important competencies including attitudes, bringing students outside of their comfort zone, allowing them to understand others' worldviews, and creating culture-specific knowledge as seen in Table 10.2.

Table 10.2: Intercultural Competencies for St. Stephen's Dome Tour Activity

Knowledge	Skills	Attitudes
• Cultural self-awareness/understanding • Understanding others' worldviews • Academic content knowledge	• Observe • Interpret	• Open-minded • Respect

3. Mozart's Apartment vs. Haydn's House in Eisenstadt

The third activity takes place over two days at the end of the first week of our visit. Wolfgang Amadeus Mozart and Franz Josef Haydn are considered to be the founders of the first Viennese school in musical composition. They were friends and colleagues who influenced and supported each other's work. On our visit to Mozart's apartment, we discuss his struggles and ultimate failure to find gainful employment at a court that could securely subsidize his artistic works. The next day, we visit the Esterházy Palace in rural Eisenstadt, a suburb of Vienna, where Haydn was employed by the Esterházy family. Mozart had the benefit of a central apartment and the culture of Vienna, but Haydn enjoyed the stability of regular work. Through discussion and a reflective approach, the two different biographies provide an excellent lesson in specific historical content knowledge but also an avenue for developing a related skill like music education or music industry. The biographies parallel and provide a deeper understanding of the decision in careers and goals that the students are facing themselves—whether to pursue a career in performance or undertake a career in music education and/or the music industry. The broader lesson tends to be that while the financial reward of a career in performance may provide access to wealth, it lacks the stability of a career in education. The competencies addressed in this activity are listed in Table 10.3.

Table 10.3: Intercultural Competencies for Mozart's Apartment vs. Haydn's House Activity

Knowledge	Skills	Attitudes
• Academic content knowledge • Culture-specific knowledge	• Observation • Relate	• Empathy • Flexibility

4. Standing Room Only at the Opera

As a group, we attended a couple of operas, standing room only, at the *Staatsoper*. While I usually incorporate one seated ticket for around €75 into our budget, the standing-room spaces are around €10 per opera. The students usually see three or four operas standing during the program because they have a better view than the more expensive seated tickets. I provide music-historical context for the operas we see and then we compare the ticket prices and the different approaches to funding between Nashville and Vienna. The fact that Vienna, as one of the smaller European cities, is able to produce world-class opera productions can be connected to the fact that the state subsidizes the productions greatly. Artistic production is understood by the Viennese as a currency itself and worth the cost, while more capitalistic approaches, like those in Nashville, can yield productions equally good to those from Vienna but are prone to inconsistency in quality. In this activity, the academic content knowledge and culturally-specific knowledge lead to an awareness of differences in artistic culture (see Table 10.4 for a complete list of cultural competencies in this activity). These lessons are revisited throughout the program with visits to the symphony, the Summer Night Concert, and affordable museums in Vienna.

Table 10.4: Intercultural Competencies for the Opera Activity

Knowledge	Skills	Attitudes
• Academic content knowledge • Understanding others' worldviews • Culture-specific knowledge	• Problem-solving • Observe	• Respect • Withholding judgment

5. The Cooking Lesson

For this activity, the group works together, gathering tremendous skills in teamwork and leadership under the direction of a chef to cook a traditional Austrian meal, from appetizer to dessert, *schnitzel* to *strudel*. I was surprised at this lesson because I originally scheduled it as a way that the students might get to meet each other. However, particularly with the inclusion of a great chef/personality, the activity becomes much more rewarding. Through cultural self-awareness/understanding, the students discover much about their perceptions of others through food, their resilience in terms of their ability to cook for themselves, patience in the inherent teamwork required of the activity, as well as the specific cultural knowledge of cuisine. Additionally, the chef will end dinner with extended stories of the Vienna Opera. Although there is not much in terms of scholarly musicology in this activity, it will remain in my program because it creates a great deal of intercultural competency and promotes the general growth of all students involved (as listed in Table 10.5).

Table 10.5: Intercultural Competencies for The Cooking Lesson Activity

Knowledge	Skills	Attitudes
• Cultural self-awareness/understanding • Understanding others' worldviews	• Leadership • Problem-solving	• Resilience • Patience

6. The Jewish Museums

At about halfway through the study abroad course, the class lectures pivot from the idealism and industrialization of the 19th century to the Modernism that accompanies the onset of the 20th century. Part and parcel of that discussion is the shift from the utopian ideal of technology to the deep pessimism that accompanied the realization that technology did not improve man's condition but rather enhanced its ability to commit atrocities. This perspective led to the creation of German Expressionism, and there are very few places where this movement and aesthetic development occurred more closely than in Austrian culture.

Within the course, the works and biographies of Jewish composers Arnold Schoenberg and Anton Webern, members of the "Second Viennese School," are studied for their dark aesthetic, negativity, and the way they had to flee Austria when the Nazis came to power. Then as an activity, we visit Heldenplatz, the Hofburg Imperial Palace, and the balcony where Adolf Hitler declared the *Anschluss* (the annexation of Austria to Germany at the beginning of World War II). As we stand in the square, students look up images from Hitler's speech on their own phones and see the quarter-million Nazi sympathizers that came out on that tragic day to show their support.

The next day we visit the Jewish Museums which depict not just the Holocaust, but more than a millennium of atrocities committed against the culture by Austrians in and around Vienna. A critical and more sophisticated understanding and observation of the city soon emerges that emphasizes analysis of cultural awareness, culturally specific knowledge, and academic content knowledge. The discussion leads to Austria's way of dealing with its dark history, and empathy leads to inevitable comparisons with the often dark history of the United States, such as slavery, the Civil War, and the Civil Rights movement. Answers are rarely revealed, but the broader goals of cultural self-awareness, understanding others' worldviews, empathy, and an ability to understand common problems with different solutions are obtained rather easily. A list of competencies for this activity are in Table 10.6.

Table 10.6: Intercultural Competencies for The Jewish Museums Activity

Knowledge	Skills	Attitudes
• Cultural self-awareness/understanding • Academic content knowledge	• Observation • Analysis	• Open-minded • Stepping outside comfort zone • Empathy

7. Heiligenstadt

This activity undertakes a visit to Beethoven's house in Heiligenstadt, then a suburb of Vienna, now part of the broader city. This was the place where he wrote the famous Heiligenstadt testament which deals with his growing social isolation due to his increasing deafness. The night before the visit, I have them read the document, and then during the visit, we see various exhibits which depict the stages of his increasing deafness and his decision to compose and persevere nevertheless. Finally, I have them write a short testament about their own struggles and what makes them persevere. Apart from the academic content knowledge, I believe the lesson teaches a great deal about resiliency, patience, articulation, and self-dependence, and it is perhaps one of my favorite lessons of the trip. Refer to Appendix 10.2 for the writing prompt for this activity, and Table 10.7 for a list of competencies in this activity.

Table 10.7: Intercultural Competencies for Heiligenstadt Activity

Knowledge	Skills	Attitudes
• Academic content knowledge • Cultural self-awareness	• Relatability • Self-dependence	• Resiliency • Patience

8. The Self-Reflection

The final activity is due two weeks after the course ends. It is a self-reflection that asks the students to evaluate the program and its value to their own lives, including cultural observations and what they have learned that might be used to enrich the lives of those around them. Topics covered will reveal the emerging cultural self-awareness/understanding and culturally specific knowledge (see Table 10.8 for a complete list of competencies in this activity). As a simple self-reflection, it positions the program and their privilege to be on it as part of the social contract of their education: a responsibility to contribute to the society that has provided such opportunities.

Table 10.8: Intercultural Competencies for the Self-Reflection Activity

Knowledge	Skills	Attitudes
• Cultural self-awareness/understanding • Cultural specific knowledge	• Articulation • Communication skills	• Empathy • Adaptability

POST-PROGRAM AND FUTURE CLASS ACTIVITIES

For a post-program assignment, I have the students write a reflective paper on what they have learned, what a citizen of Tennessee might learn from Vienna, and what a citizen of Vienna might learn from Tennessee. The assignment is empowering and provides some very thoughtful responses.

While I find this trip to be successful, there is room for it to grow. I foresee taking future classes to the nearby city of Prague and the Nazi concentration camp Mauthausen. However, there is tension with this, because I do not wish to fill every moment of the trip with a preset experience. These students need time to consider what they have seen, do their homework, and explore the city for themselves. Their own explorations can enrich and individualize the program for each student. Other improvements that I would like to undertake include finding more funding for scholarships, as this opportunity should be available to any music major. I would like to also improve opportunities for our students to meet more Viennese students.

EVALUATION AND ASSIGNMENTS

The course requirements for the study abroad version are the same as the classroom version offered at MTSU. The final grade is based on five factors as seen in Table 10.9.

Table 10.9: Evaluation Breakdown

Assessment Type	Percentage of Final Grade
Formative Assessments:	55%
• Participation (attendance)	15%
• Nightly Reading Quizzes	15%
• Brief Writing Assignments	25%
Summative Assessments:	45%
• Midterm	20%
• Final (comprehensive of the whole semester)	25%

Of the formative assessments, the battery of reading quizzes are made from simple multiple-choice questions that help them to direct their reading. These quizzes are set for a limitless number of retakes and typically the students ace them after a number of tries. For the summative assessment, the midterm and final are typically large exams, but their value is not so much that a student can get a D on either and still obtain an A for the final grade. As such I am privileging the formative role of all assignments. Participation is rarely a difficulty in these programs. Most important, however, are the written assignments. These are roughly 500 words long and require not only knowledge but perspective.

CAVEATS AND REFLECTIONS

I feel that this is a very successful course and find that it provides a unique experience for students in Middle Tennessee. One that they might find at distant, larger, and much more expensive schools, if they are lucky. To be able to offer this opportunity to integrate the study of classical music with an intercultural experience in Vienna fulfills the stated purpose of Middle Tennessee State University. This purpose includes, among other things, supporting student learning through unique programs and effective teaching methods, including experiential and integrative learning. From my perspective, weaknesses of the program include student participation and funding constraints. For example, I wish that I could take more students into the program, and I would like to develop scholarship opportunities to assist with this. That said, I think of this study abroad as perhaps the most important contribution I make as a teacher. The opportunity to introduce these students to such history and culture in such a personal way is an ideal that any music teacher would embrace.

REFERENCES

Boyd, E., & Fales, A. W. (1983). Reflective learning: Key to learning from experience. *Journal of Humanistic Psychology, 23*(2), 99–117. https://doi.org/10.1177/0022167883232011

Burkholder, J. P., Grout, D. J., & Palisca, C. V. (2018). *A history of Western music.* W. W. Norton.

Burkholder, J. P., Palisca, C. V., & Grout, D. J. (2019a). *Norton anthology of Western music volume II: Classic to Romantic.* W. W. Norton.

Burkholder, J. P., Palisca, C. V, & Grout, D. J. (2019b). *Norton anthology of Western music volume III: The twentieth century and after.* W. W. Norton.

Gass, M. A. (2013). *Frequently asked questions.* Association for Experiential Education: https://www.aee.org/what-is-experiential-education

Huber, M. T., Hutching, P., Gale, R., Miller, R., & Breen, M. (2007). Leading initiatives for integrative learning. *Liberal Education, 93*(2), 46–51.

MacGregor, B. L. (1992). What is collaborative learning? In A. Goodsell, M. R. Maher, & V. Tinto (Eds.), *Collaborative learning: A sourcebook for higher education.* National Center on Postsecondary Teaching, Learning, and Assessment at Pennsylvania State University.

National Association of Schools of Music. (2021). *Handbook: 2022-2023.* National Association of Schools of Music. Retrieved from https://nasm.arts-accredit.org/accreditation/standards-guidelines/handbook/

Strange, H., & Gibson, H. (2017). An investigation of experiential and transformative learning in study abroad programs. *Frontiers: The Interdisciplinary Journal of Study Abroad, 29*(1), 85–100. https://doi.org/10.36366/frontiers.v29i1.387

APPENDICES

Appendix 10.1: List of Artifacts for Scavenger Hunt Activity (Vienna, Austria)

In this assignment the students are asked to take and submit a "selfie" of themselves standing by, or with:

1. The Hofburg
2. St. Stephen's Cathedral
3. Apfel Streudel (or another sweet)
4. Prater Park
5. Danube Canal
6. Wiener Staatsoper
7. The monument to Empress Maria Theresa at Maria-Theresien-Platz
8. The entryway to Webster University's building
9. Musikhaus Doblinger
10. A nice bratwurst
11. Entrance to the Pasqualati Haus
12. Schubert's House
13. A bust of any composer
14. Someone dressed like Mozart or Haydn

Appendix 10.2: Writing Prompt for Heiligenstadt Activity

Consider that the Heiligenstadt Testament is an apology for Beethoven's behavior, a description of his greatest obstacle, and a reason why he persevered. A career in music is a difficult endeavor to be sure. For this assignment, in under 500 words, I would like you to create your own "Heiligenstadt Testament." Address it as Beethoven did, to whomever is most important in your life. Describe the greatest obstacle you have confronted in your journey as a musician and how you plan to deal with it in the future. Then explain why you persevere, what is it about this profession that draws you and drives you.

Chapter 11

Intercultural Competency Education Via Food

Tony V. Johnston

Note: Section II includes Chapters 4-14. These chapters use a standardized template to discuss the details of their respective study abroad programs and reference Deardorff's (2012) framework for intercultural competencies. The use of this template and the intercultural competencies framework are described in the Section II introduction. All courses in this section (except for Chapter 6) were taught through Middle Tennessee State University (MTSU), a mid-sized state school located in Murfreesboro, Tennessee (USA).

The course entitled *International Agriculture* (AGBS 5800) examines food as an avenue to explore international cultures and was first offered in Mendoza, Argentina. Mendoza is a city in the westernmost part of the country, close to the Andes Mountains. Mendoza province is the source of most of Argentina's fruit and vegetable production, processing, and export, and the city of Mendoza is centrally located within the province. This course puts focus on cuisine culture as a vehicle to learn about the everyday lives of people and provides opportunities for students to reflect and critically think about the deeper differences that exist across cultural boundaries. The course has been taught in Mendoza seven times (2011-2023) and a total of 67 students have participated.

THEORETICAL FOUNDATIONS

Two pedagogical approaches are utilized at different times in this course. Study abroad courses are inherently experiential, as students must learn to adapt to the study abroad environment in addition to learning the content being taught (Kolb, 1984), but exactly how the experiences encountered are integrated into the curriculum can vary. For this course, the integrative pedagogical approach (Yadav, 2022) is utilized during the execution of "class time" since the students are physically present in the fields and factories in which agricultural goods are produced, processed, and shipped. The topics being discussed, such as agricultural production and trade, are literally at hand and underfoot, and almost everything being taught relates to the application of science, math, and economics. This course is designed to be integrative; every activity, including pre-planned meals, "free time," and even transportation time, is utilized as an opportunity for formal and informal student instruction and guidance. This addresses one of the most important issues that impact pedagogical success: confidence in and comfort with the instructor. This is especially critical in the study abroad environment, where the instructor is frequently viewed as a "lifeline to home" in addition to the person teaching the course. Group-based informal contact with students in the class is critical to rapidly establishing credibility and confidence and reducing fear and stress (both expressed and internalized).

To help students connect the dots between activities and desired educational outcomes, students are briefed for each activity via a short lecture detailing what the students will encounter and providing context prior to activity execution. At activity completion, students are prompted for reflection and guided toward desired educational outcomes. Prior to scheduled free time, students are invited to join the instructor in unscheduled, casual activities, such as a meal or a visit to a local site of interest unrelated to the class. Although students do not always take part in unscheduled events, word quickly spreads that these opportunities are interesting, entertaining, and worthy of participation.

After the students return home, a reflective essay assignment (discussed in detail later) is used as a reflective pedagogical exercise (Yadav, 2022). Although the primary academic objectives of the class have been achieved during class time, reflection provides a powerful means of reinforcing the greater lessons of studying abroad, including the commonality of humanity, the beauty of world cultures, and humanity's interdependence. The importance of this exercise cannot be overemphasized.

COURSE DESCRIPTION

This course was specifically designed to be taught abroad. Students are taken to countries outside the U.S. to explore first-hand how agricultural practices differ in other countries and how commodities are delivered from those locations to the U.S. and other export destinations. The course was taught via a combination of discussions, lectures, and visits to agricultural production fields, fruit and vegetable processing facilities, grocery store warehouse operations, and export operations. During these visits, students talked with owners, managers, and supervisors of each business. All activities took place within a two-hour drive radius of the city of Mendoza. Because there was no textbook available that met the needs of this course, a customized course packet, consisting of articles and agronomic information, was created to accompany the course.

Course Learning Outcomes

The primary learning outcomes for this course are:

a. Recognize limitations that nature and geography impose on agriculture on a global scale.
b. Recognize the role that economics plays in the marketing of agricultural products.
c. Recognize logistics as a key factor that influences commodity prices and that transportation within a country or continent can be more difficult than across oceans.
d. Understand that individual farmers decide what to produce based on market forces and national governments work to influence market forces.
e. Understand that currency exchange rates significantly affect the value of agricultural crops in international trade.

f. Recognize that labor costs and technological differences between countries significantly impact the relative cost of production (and therefore, value) of agricultural products.
   g. Recognize that low rates of agricultural mechanization do not always translate into higher costs of production.
   h. Recognize the interdependence between countries required to feed the world.

COURSE HISTORY

The course was developed in the Middle Tennessee State University (MTSU) School of Agriculture as part of the Agribusiness major in the late 1990s. No such course previously existed at MTSU, and the primary purpose was to teach concepts related to international trade in agricultural products. A critical component of this class was the availability of locally based personnel who can identify potential companies and personnel to visit with and make arrangements for transportation. In the case of Mendoza, the same company has been utilized for almost 15 years because of their ability to make all arrangements and respond to both local circumstances and academic objectives. Although this stability aids in the success of the course, there are changing circumstances between planning and execution each year. As a result, an updated and detailed schedule is provided to each student upon arrival.

COURSE LOGISTICS

This is a 3-credit hour upper division course where almost all instruction occurs in a non-traditional manner. It is frequently difficult to find traditional classroom space in the study abroad environment, and, as opposed to teaching in a traditional setting, the entire day can be utilized for instruction while teaching abroad. Meals, most of which are either pre-paid or coordinated by the instructor, are valuable teaching and learning opportunities. Time in transit to and from scheduled meetings can be utilized to prepare students for what they will see and whom they will visit and to emphasize key points of the experience/discussion. Formal lectures, when necessary, may be offered in city parks, when the weather allows, or in the hotel conference room. In this 17-day class, a total of 272 contact hours are available for instruction (16 hours/day), of which only 7 hours are scheduled for traditional classroom time. The course is designed as a senior-level agribusiness major elective course and includes several agribusiness prerequisites, but exceptions can be made for non-agribusiness majors to take the course. Non-agriculture majors are typically deficient in their awareness of agriculture in general, and especially unaware of how food gets from a farm to the store where they purchase it. The philosophy behind making exceptions to enrollment in this course is that non-agricultural majors will, by exposure to the course itself and interaction with agribusiness majors during the conduct of the course, substantially increase their comprehension of the world food supply system.

PRE-PROGRAM ACTIVITIES

The course itinerary must be prepared well in advance of the class, and it should be designed to accomplish the stated learning objectives. This is the single most important value of an in-country logistics provider because that company identifies the people, places, and events available to help you accomplish your goals. For this course, the logistics provider was provided with both the learning objectives and a list of suggested commercial operations (not individual companies), venues, and civilian or governmental positions that would address each objective. The logistics company then identified options for each learning objective. Through email conversations, selections were made and an itinerary was built. In addition, prior to departure, students were briefed on what to expect in Argentina and a long list of other topics including expectations of behavior, what to and not to pack, currency exchange details, and what kind of laundry options were provided (see Appendix 11.1 for a list of pre-departure discussion topics).

CLASS ACTIVITIES & INTERCULTURAL COMPETENCIES

Visits to commercial farming operations were arranged to address course learning outcomes *a, c, d,* and *f*. Since only 2% of U.S. residents live on a ranch or farm (Farm Bureau, 2021), it is highly likely that visits to farming operations are totally new experiences for most students and a key component of the integrative pedagogical approach taken in the class. Visits to commercial processing operations involved in the export of their products (e.g., wineries, fruit and vegetable canning operations) and a supermarket distribution center were arranged to address course learning outcomes *b, c, e, g,* and *h*. Access to commercial food processing facilities in the U.S. has always been relatively restricted for probably obvious reasons, but the recent COVID-19 pandemic and the heightened need to ensure the safety of our national food supply have made access even more difficult for non-employees (Brackett, 2021). Therefore, processing plant and food distribution center visits, practically impossible to accomplish in the U.S., are extremely valuable experiential learning opportunities. Cultural awareness was repeatedly addressed by scheduled/pre-arranged meals, interactions with a panel of expatriate entrepreneurs who had immigrated to Argentina and established companies there, and the innumerable opportunities to accompany students as they learned the city, shopped, sought daily meals, bought their daily gelato, and enjoyed the parks in the city. Highlights of the program itinerary are presented in Appendix 11.2. One of the most important considerations for faculty members conducting courses abroad is to be flexible and always have alternatives in mind for each of your planned activities. Despite careful planning and arrangements made in advance, unexpected events occur and circumstances change, requiring a change of plans.

Class activities for *International Agriculture* are always, to some degree, adjusted to reflect the presence and subject matter of any other courses being offered in parallel. It is critical to note, however, that group activities are always preferred over individual activities. Students studying abroad are inevitably sharing rooms, meals, and transportation with one another, and they may not have known each other before embarking on the class. This provides an ideal opportunity for students to learn how to work with others whom they may or may not know much about, which is a situation we all experience when we take a new job and make other life changes. In this section, some representative activities, tasks, and assignments from the course will be presented while also identifying key integrated intercultural competencies.

Welcome Lunch and Local Tour

The first formal activity of the class is a welcome lunch, which features empanadas (individual meat, cheese, and/or vegetable pies), the local version of pizza, and drinks. Having flown overnight and knowing that the first pre-planned dinner is scheduled for much later in the evening (which is typical for Argentina), this lunch is a necessity. As food is consumed, students are offered an informative and entertaining presentation on Argentine culture and an orientation to the city of Mendoza.

The welcome lunch is followed by an open-air bus tour of the area immediately around the hotel, which includes five major inner-city plazas: Plaza Independencia, Plaza Chile, Plaza España, Plaza San Martin, and Plaza Italia, and General San Martin Park, a major park on the western side of the city. San Martin Park is heavily utilized because of the wooded and open spaces available for recreation in addition to the city zoo, Juan Cornelio Moyano Museum of Anthropological and Natural Sciences, Grego Frank Romero Day outdoor amphitheater, and the Army of the Andes Monument, which celebrates the liberation of Argentina from rule by Spain. At the end of this tour, students are dropped off at Anna Bistro restaurant a few blocks from the hotel for their first Argentine dinner. The after-dinner walk back to the hotel is generally the final prelude to participants enjoying a good night's sleep. This activity provides the students an opportunity to gain the intercultural competencies identified in Table 11.1.

Table 11.1: Intercultural Competencies in the Welcome Lunch and Local Tour Activity

Knowledge	Skills	Attitudes
• Geographic awareness • Cultural awareness	• Navigation skills • Culturally appropriate communication skills • Observing and interpreting new information	• Adaptability • Acceptance/open minded • Stepping outside one's comfort zone

Grocery Shopping and Scavenger Hunt Task

Because the accommodations include a kitchenette, students want to visit a grocery store shortly after arriving to stock up on water and snack foods to keep in their rooms. It took a visit to the grocery store with students to recognize the potential value of formalizing the learning that occurred during the trip. Not all students who visit Argentina can speak or read Spanish, and it quickly became obvious that students were shopping by sight rather than by reading the directional signs or package labels. Pictures on packages were immediately identified as vitally important and information could be gleaned from locational clues (e.g., proximity to similarly sized/shaped products with pictures), or Spanish-speaking students could be utilized to interpret. The students are so focused on their efforts to identify and purchase familiar and potentially edible unfamiliar food items, they didn't see the bigger picture the store offers.

In response to this observation, a simple exercise (see Appendix 11.3) was designed along the lines of a scavenger hunt to direct students to see what they otherwise would not. Both culturally unique and "typical American" food items were selected, and students are challenged to find them. In addition, questions are formulated to direct attention to both subtle and obvious distinctions between U.S. stores and familiar food items and Argentine grocery store items. Students are organized into teams of 2-3 depending on the size of the class, and Spanish-speaking students are distributed amongst the teams. For the first class, the entire group was sent to the store, regardless of whether they had previously visited it. For all subsequent classes, this exercise was used as the first formal learning opportunity upon arrival, knowing that repeated visits to the grocery store would be made and, whether consciously or unconsciously, the lessons learned will be emphasized with each visit. Intercultural competencies gained by the students through this task are tabulated in Table 11.2.

Table 11.2: Intercultural Competencies in the Grocery Shopping and Scavenger Hunt Task

Knowledge	Skills	Attitudes
• Food customs awareness • Awareness of local economics (food prices)	• Teamwork • Observation • Interpretation • Evaluation • Analysis • Communication	• Acceptance • Patience • Flexibility • Discovery • Respect

Field Trips

The next several days of the program focus on visits to distinct agricultural production areas throughout Mendoza province, including the Uco Valley, Maipú, and Luján de Cuyo, to explore the variety of crops produced and processing facilities located nearby. The co-location of processing facilities near production areas is a key principle of agricultural economics and is a major reason food costs around the world are as low as possible. As various areas are visited, pre-paid meals are incorporated into the daily schedule to expose students to the culture and, more specifically, the variations within the culture of Argentina. Each of these meals offers opportunities for the students to experience and discuss the differences they note between U.S. and Argentine customs. Intercultural competencies integrated into this activity are summarized in Table 11.3.

Table 11.3: Intercultural Competencies in Field Trip Activities

Knowledge	Skills	Attitudes
• Specific crop production knowledge • Export market knowledge • Awareness of local agricultural labor practices	• Listening • Observing • Interpreting • Analyzing • Communication	• Empathy • Curiosity • Tolerance • Flexibility • Adaptability

Traditional Day of Activities

One highlight of the class is the day spent at Cerro Arco Park in the foothills of the Andes Mountains. Located just outside the Mendoza city limits, this is the highest point adjacent to the city and many telecommunications towers are installed on the peak. Many residents use the rough road to the peak as a recreational area, and a local restauranteur and mountaineer has established a restaurant, Puerta de la Quebrada, at the base of the hill. This restaurant features extensive outdoor seating, a traditional mud oven fired by local wood in which most of the food is cooked, and cooking classes for individuals and groups who want to learn about traditional Argentine dishes. The *asado*, which is both the traditional barbeque of Argentina and the traditions around its preparation, is more than just a dish. It is truly a cultural icon and is significantly woven into Argentine culture.

On this day, students may choose to hike to the peak (an approximate 2.5-hour round trip) or stay at Puerta de la Quebrada for a cooking class before the meal itself. Those who participate in the cooking class are taught as they prepare the empanadas that start the meal and the deep-fried quince-filled dessert pastries that end the meal. A second highlight of the day is when the owner of Puerta de la Quebrada is asked to talk about either his multiple climbs of Aconcagua, the highest peak in South America, or his research into the ancient residents of the local region of the Andes. Both groups enjoy a completely traditional day of activities based on their preferences and enjoy the most traditional of Argentine meals. The intercultural competencies observed in this activity are identified in Table 11.4.

Table 11.4: Intercultural Competencies in the Traditional Day Activities

Knowledge	Skills	Attitudes
- Historical awareness - Cultural knowledge - Geographic knowledge - Comprehension of local growing conditions	- Creativity - Teamwork - Listening - Observing - Relating - Communication	- Acceptance - Empathy - Open mindedness - Respect - Stepping outside one's comfort zone

Research Station Visit

Because agriculture is such an important part of Argentina's economy, federally sponsored research stations have been established around the country to advance the science of agriculture and the practical application thereof. The facility for the Mendoza province is located a short 15-minute drive from the center of Mendoza, making it ideal for the exploration of the more technical aspects of agriculture. At this research station, nuts, grapes, tree fruits, ornamental plants, and field crops such as garlic, corn, and beans are under constant experimentation and analysis. This facility is visited for a portion of one day. Several of the research scientists working there share their research areas and provide an overview of the importance of that research to agricultural production with the students in the class. This visit is key to emphasizing the scientific value of the class and the trip itself. This activity allowed the students to focus on the intercultural competencies identified in Table 11.5.

Table 11.5: Intercultural Competencies in the Research Station Visit Activity

Knowledge	Skills	Attitudes
• Local agricultural practice knowledge • Agricultural research priority (for Argentina) knowledge • Awareness of Argentina's agricultural worldview	• Listening • Observing • Analyzing • Technology • Communication	• Resilience • Respect • Adaptability • Discovery • Empathy

Recreation Activities

Students (and faculty alike) need downtime during study abroad programs, so two recreational days are incorporated into the class. One day is left to the student to decide what they would like to do, and they are provided a list of "vetted" options in the immediate area to choose from. The most popular of these options is an outdoor activity company named Argentina Rafting. Founded by a U.S. citizen and her Argentine husband, Argentina Rafting offers zip line, white water rafting, mountain biking, rock climbing, sky diving, hiking, paragliding, horseback riding, stand-up paddling, and kayaking adventures. From a practical point of view, the best features of this option are that the company operates an office that is a 15-minute walk from the hotel, at which students may choose and pay for their chosen activities and arrange for round-trip transportation from the hotel to the facility, which is located about an hour outside the city limits.

The second recreational day of the trip is scheduled to be spent at the Cacheuta Hot Springs Thermal Water Park. The naturally heated mineral waters in the pools, beautiful vistas, and ample accommodations for lounging at the facility provide a relaxing respite for all participants. The day at the park includes a buffet lunch which features countless traditional Argentine dishes and chefs on hand to prepare dishes that are not ready-made. The only way to describe this experience is that everyone in the group is pampered. Through these recreational activities, the students could gain intercultural competencies as listed in Table 11.6.

Table 11.6: Intercultural Competencies in Recreation Activities

Knowledge	Skills	Attitudes
• Cultural self-awareness • Understanding other' worldviews	• Listening • Observing • Interpreting • Communication	• Risk taking • Tolerance • Flexibility • Adaptability

Research Paper Presentations

One of the last scheduled events of the course is the presentation of the students' research to the class. The students are allowed to select their topic from a list provided in the syllabus, all of which are fruits, vegetables, nuts, and spices not produced in the U.S. Regardless of the level of agricultural familiarity amongst the students enrolled in the study abroad course, awareness of and familiarity with crops produced abroad is inherently low. This exercise provides students another opportunity to hone their public speaking skills and share their research on unfamiliar crops that are exported to the U.S. (and other countries). Academically, it also reinforces the central idea of the class: humans around the world are dependent on each other to provide the foods and organic materials we want to consume. This assignment helps the students develop the intercultural competencies listed in Table 11.7.

Table 11.7: Intercultural Competencies in the Research Paper Assignments

Knowledge	Skills	Attitudes
• Understanding others' worldviews • Country-specific knowledge • Academic content knowledge	• Communication • Creative thinking • Interpretation • Analysis • Articulation	• Discovery • Respect • Patience • Withholding judgment

POST-PROGRAM AND FUTURE CLASS ACTIVITIES

Post-program assessment and reflection are perhaps the most important aspects of studying abroad. Upon both the arrival in another country and the return home, students undergo a type of culture shock. Outbound culture shock occurs as the student notices all the differences between the new environment and the place they call "home." In contrast, inbound culture shock takes time to develop, as the traveling student internalizes everything experienced while abroad and readjusts to living at home.

The final assignment of this course is a post-return reflection paper adopting the reflective pedagogical approach (Yadav, 2022). The unusual, and strict, stipulation for this assignment is that students may not begin writing the paper until at least 30 days after their return. Time must be allowed for the euphoria of a successful trip and return home to diminish, after which the students can focus on their changes of perspective, newfound awareness of the prevailing culture at home, and their experiences abroad. To accommodate this post-trip assignment due date, the program must be scheduled early in any given semester.

Each offering of this course is potentially executed in a different country, making it critical that the itinerary always be flexible. Fortunately, agriculture is practiced around the world, and there are always opportunities for teaching it. The most important aspects of successfully teaching the course are to have a large set of teaching options and to constantly add to those options; for example, formal and informal lectures, prepared exercises, guest speakers, visits to production centers and processing facilities, panel discussions by local entrepreneurs, and interaction with local academic and research faculty, staff, and students.

Commercial leisure activities are not always readily available in all locations, so it is also critical that free leisure activities such as walking, hiking, and good, old-fashioned sightseeing are always available. Safety is always a concern, so it is not necessarily advisable to encourage or allow students to "wander aimlessly" for recreation. Organized, and, if at all possible, pre-vetted leisure activities are strongly recommended.

Agricultural class activities are also frequently limited by the season of the year. Offering a course during the planting or harvesting seasons provides the opportunity for students to participate in those activities as part of a class. Classes offered at other times of the year turn the focus of the course to a reliance on the availability of guest lectures, panel discussions, and interaction with experts in research environments.

EVALUATION AND ASSIGNMENTS

This course is graded using the rubric in Table 11.8.

Table 11.8: Course Rubric

Assessment Type	Criteria	Percentage of Grade
Formative	Pre-departure meeting attendance and preparation	5%
Formative	Participation and engagement in workday activities	20%
Formative/Summative	Daily reflections while in the host country	15%
Summative	Research paper (written submission)	25%
Formative	Presentation of research paper to the class	25%
Summative	Final integrated reflective essay	10%
Total		100%

Student evaluation is a subset of the larger objective of establishing behavioral expectations for the study abroad course. Both students and faculty members are in a nontraditional educational environment while abroad and the options available for addressing inappropriate behavior are limited. Therefore, expectations must be clearly elaborated upon. While abroad, formative assessment activities predominate as a necessity. However, students must be aware of and not ignore the summative assessment assignments that will be submitted well after their return home.

Many students who study abroad have not previously left their home country, making the experience stressful in unexpected ways. However, that stress is most likely the driving force to learning in the study abroad environment. Students must be or become better self-directed learners while abroad, and the pre-departure briefing, participation in activities while abroad, and daily reflections offer excellent opportunities for the instructor to monitor and assess learning progress in real-time. Summative assessment is actually the easier format of the two to measure because the documents submitted can be graded well after returning home.

STUDENT FEEDBACK

Although no formal student surveys have been conducted for this course, student feedback abounds. MTSU offers a formal opportunity for students to assess each class and instructor, which is somewhat informative, but the more significant feedback is generally provided by comments made to the instructor and most importantly, to student peers. The ideal situation for study abroad courses is consistently offering a course and relying on participating students to create a "buzz" amongst their peers to ensure future enrollment. It must be noted that generating demand based on previous students' experience in upper-division study abroad courses is more difficult than lower-division courses because upper-division students are more likely to be close to graduation and as such, do not interact as much with the potential market for future offerings of the course.

The most common response (both verbal and written in the reflective essays) is a desire to return to the country visited as well as a description of the values the students have internalized after the experience abroad. Most find the study abroad experience to be "life-changing" and report a newfound desire to explore other countries not yet experienced. Even students who were injured, became ill, or received devastating news from home while abroad have related their experiences as "life-changing." The most academically rewarding students are those who relate that going abroad and seeing fruits and vegetables being grown, processed, and packaged with labels written in English for familiar brands opened their eyes to the interdependence of the world's population. Being abroad revealed they thought the U.S. is completely self-sufficient; this class allowed them to look, with different eyes, at their own culture. The abstract concept of cultural competency took on new meaning by simply being abroad.

A favorite outcome for participating students is the opportunity to tell potential employers they have studied abroad as part of their degree program. For example, one student who took the course included his study abroad experience in his resume. In his first job interview, the bulk of the time was spent discussing mutual experiences in Argentina, and the student was hired.

CAVEATS AND REFLECTIONS

This course was created in response to a growing recognition of the international nature of agriculture, and in particular, agribusiness, the business of agriculture. Multinational corporations are very common today, as they were in the 1990s when the course began. In fact, many of the first multinational corporations were and are still involved in the business of agriculture. In the late 1990s, there were no academic courses at our university that specifically focused on the multi-billion-dollar industry that is agriculture on an international scale. It took time to, first, acknowledge the need for such a course, and, second, recognize the potential value of teaching such a course in an abroad setting. Even educators must evolve, and all evolution takes time.

The projected (and realized) strength of this course is the experience students gain by being abroad. Intercultural competency is a valuable life skill that can only be learned by meeting and interacting with people from other cultures. As the most basic of human needs, food is an ideal tool for teaching intercultural competency since none of us needs food more than anyone else. Focusing on food also powerfully illuminates humanity's worldwide interdependence and the need for trade.

Having experienced another culture for a short period of time also places these students in a very small but significantly elevated category of job seekers, and employers recognize their value. Employers know it is not necessary to know about every culture in the world, it is just important to be aware that differences in culture exist and be willing to learn about and identify those differences. Students who study abroad have already internalized these lessons and make highly valuable employees in our modern, highly interconnected world.

Challenges to teaching abroad abound, but the most significant challenge in teaching this specific course is finding the right contacts in the chosen country. Teaching the course in Argentina is very simple because the hard work has been done. Relationships have been made, contacts have been established, superior logistics providers have been identified and used repeatedly, and familiarity breeds comfort. The hard work of identifying a logistics provider, planning around national holidays and transportation bottlenecks, and coordinating with potential and intended speakers must be done from scratch, and it is a time-consuming task. In my opinion, study abroad is unnecessary if the objective is to create run-of-the-mill graduates, but if the objective is to help students stand out amongst their peers, the time and effort required are well worth the investment.

Very few subjects or problems can be addressed by simple or single-dimensional answers, and the *International Agriculture* course, being focused on the worldwide system we depend on to feed ourselves, is no exception. A new course delivery model was developed to expand the learning potential for students of both *International Agriculture* and related courses: teach two courses simultaneously while abroad. Non-agriculture instructors were invited to teach their courses at the same time as *International Agriculture* while abroad, and all students would be exposed to the content of both classes. The first course offered in conjunction with *International Agriculture* in Argentina was an upper-division marketing class. Since all products are marketed and so many Americans are unaware of where their food comes from, the combination of these courses was seen as a natural fit. Students in both courses learned extensively from each other as they discussed and explained course content formally and casually.

The second course offered in conjunction with *International Agriculture* was an aerospace course focused on remote sensing using remotely piloted vehicles, known today as, "drones." When these courses were offered together, agriculture and aerospace students worked together to collect data from agricultural fields, analyze the data, and report on how this data could be used to improve crop health, yields, and values. Students were assigned to teams composed of members of both courses, who then worked together to present their data to the instructors of the courses.

As counterintuitive as it might seem, teaching this course in conjunction with a second related course is also an outcome multiplier. The planning and execution of the course are somewhat more complicated when two (or more) faculty member(s) and their students are involved, but the synergistic effects of co-teaching are significant. If the faculty members involved take the time to carefully plan their courses and coordinate on venues visited, lectures provided, and expected outcomes, the teaching of the courses is much easier. Having a second faculty member present while abroad also helps ensure continuity of operations if a student, or even a faculty member, falls ill or otherwise requires independent assistance.

Faculty who wish to teach abroad take on an enormous amount of responsibility beyond the basics of teaching their courses, and many of those extra responsibilities can be shared if two or more classes are taught simultaneously. By teaching multiple courses simultaneously and collaboratively, instructors can highlight the ways course content is interconnected and help students understand that like intercultural competency, course content should not be understood to exist in isolation. Course content and intercultural competency, therefore, can and should be taught simultaneously.

REFERENCES

Brackett, E. (2021). Tightening physical security at food processing plants. *Processing*. Retrieved Feb 8, 2023, from https://www.processingmagazine.com/maintenance-safety/article/21222723/tightening-physical-security-at-food-processing-plants

Deardorff, D. K. (2012). Framework: Intercultural competence model. In K. Berardo & D. K. Deardorff (Eds.), *Building cultural competence: Innovative activities and models* (pp. 45-52). Stylus Publishing.

Farm Bureau (2021). *Fast facts about agriculture & food*. Retrieved Feb 8, 2023, from https://www.fb.org/newsroom/fast-facts#:~:text=Farm%20and%20ranch%20families%20comprise,2%25%20of%20the%20U.S.%20population

Kolb, D. A. (1984). *Experiential learning: Experience as the source of learning and development*. Prentice Hall.

Yadav, K. (2022). *Pedagogy as a tool of effective teaching and learning*. Evelyn Learning. Retrieved Feb 8, 2023, from https://www.evelynlearning.com/pedagogy-as-a-tool-of-effective-teaching-and-learning/

APPENDICES

Appendix 11.1: Pre-Departure Discussion Topics

Finances
- Currency exchange
- How much cash to bring
- Travel purses

Health and Safety
- Immunizations
- Medications/medical disclosure
- Carrying of valuables around town
- Safety in the room

Food, Clothing and Housing
- Proper dress
- Medium sized suitcase/limited clothing
- Alcohol consumption
- Food in country
- Housing arrangements
- Nested suitcases
- Light jacket

Travel and Weather
- Travel buddies
- Driving/Cabs
- Where to meet at the Nashville airport
- Weather
- Itinerary/changes
- Water purchases

Things to Bring
- Power converters
- Laptops
- Course syllabus
- Cell phones
- Viber (app)
- External HD/Zip drive
- Preparatory language training
- Expected behavior

Appendix 11.2: Daily Program Itinerary

Day	Morning	Afternoon	Evening
Day 1		Arrival, welcome lunch (light)	Open air bus tour of the city and pre-arranged dinner
Day 2	Tours of Agricultural Research Station, Commercial Olive Oil Production Company, and Winery	Pre-arranged lunch and tour of vineyards	Daily reflection, lecture
Day 3	Cooking class, hike with local citizens, and lunch	Cooking class, hike with local citizens, and lunch	Guest lecture on Argentina Wine Industry
Day 4	Pre-planned recreation day with lunch	Pre-planned recreation day with lunch	Guest lecture on Argentina Wine Industry
Day 5	Grocery Store Activity and Reflection	Grocery Store Activity and Reflection	Formal Dinner
Day 6	Guided tour of city and lunch	Guided tour of city and lunch	Course related movie viewing (non-commercial) and reflection
Day 7	Tour of horse farm and lunch	Tour of horse farm and lunch	Expat entrepreneur panel discussion
Day 8	Tour of commercial nursery and large-scale winery; lunch	Tour of commercial nursery and large-scale winery; lunch	Daily reflection, lecture
Day 9	Tour of chicken and fruit/vegetable processing plants; lunch	Tour of chicken and fruit/vegetable processing plants; lunch	Daily reflection, lecture
Day 10	Spa day/lunch	Spa day/lunch	Daily reflection, lecture
Day 11	Free day (laundry, shopping, etc.)	Free day	Free day
Day 12	Tour of commercial nursery and large-scale winery; lunch	Tour of commercial nursery and large-scale winery; lunch	Daily reflection, lecture
Day 13	Tour of small-scale farm operation, larger scale winery and lunch	Tour of small-scale farm operation, larger scale winery and lunch	Daily reflection, lecture
Day 14	Tour of supermarket distribution center, conference with management	Tour of supermarket distribution center, conference with management	Daily reflection/lecture

Day	Morning	Afternoon	Evening
Day 15	Visit local retail venture owned by Argentinians, meet with owners	Visit local retail venture owned by Argentinians, meet with owners	Dinner on own
Day 16	Research Presentations/Discussion	Research Presentations/Discussion	Daily reflection, lecture Prep for departure
Day 17	Departure		

Appendix 11.3: Supermarket Exploration Exercise

CarreFour Supermarket Exploration Exercise
The class has been divided into groups and each group has been assigned one or more of the food groups listed below to explore and analyze in the CarreFour Supermarket near our hotel in Mendoza. You will report on your observations to the entire group when we return from the market. Everyone in the group must participate in the presentation of your report (remember, everyone is being graded).

Your report will provide a basis on which to make inferences about Argentine culture and international agriculture. Specifically, you should focus on what products are offered in the store as well as how much of any given product is there. We are most interested in how this store is different from the typical grocery megastore in the U.S. and where the products being sold here are sourced from.

Your report must include the following points at a minimum:
1) Description of the types of products available, focusing on products similar and different from those sold in the U.S.
2) Relative price (in U.S. dollars and dollars/lb., as applicable) for the products available.
3) Placement of the products in the store and on the shelves.
4) Variety range and number of competitive products available.
5) Implications of the product placement, number of options available and prices.
6) Sources of products sold (Argentina or somewhere else in the world).
7) Total floor space devoted to your assigned products (compare to typical floor space devoted to these products in the U.S.).

Each group will be assigned to explore one of these sets of products:
- Meats (including cold cuts) and Cheeses
- Produce, Spices, and Non-alcoholic drinks
- Breakfast Cereals, Canned Goods, and Dry Goods
- Breads, Crackers, and Cookies
- Dairy Products, Eggs, and Frozen Foods

Each product group includes a variety of different products. Be sure to investigate all of them. Finally, we will use the posted exchange rate for pesos to dollars in the bank on the opposite corner from the store. Don't forget to write it down to allow you to make your comparative calculations.

Chapter 12

International Management: Exploring Educational and Cultural Immersion in the Chinese Environment

Sesan Kim Sokoya

Note: Section II includes Chapters 4-14. These chapters use a standardized template to discuss the details of their respective study abroad programs and reference Deardorff's (2012) framework for intercultural competencies. The use of this template and the intercultural competencies framework are described in the Section II introduction. All courses in this section (except for Chapter 6) were taught through Middle Tennessee State University (MTSU), a mid-sized state school located in Murfreesboro, Tennessee (USA).

The course entitled *International Management: Globalization in China* (MGMT 6770) is a short-term study abroad course that exposes students to the challenges and opportunities that multinational companies face as they operate across national boundaries. The unique aspect of this course is its emphasis on the Chinese management environment as it relates to political, economic, and cultural factors. The course is delivered as an in-person course, with class lectures taking place at Hangzhou University in China, visits to business offices and manufacturing facilities, and cultural excursions in the Chinese cities of Shanghai, Hangzhou, and Beijing. The program has been conducted four times, from 2016 to 2019. The program takes place during the May term each year. The number of students averages about nine each year.

THEORETICAL FOUNDATIONS

The pedagogical approach to the program leans heavily on an experiential approach (Harvey, 2017). The curriculum and co-curricular activities in the program reflect the various stages in Kolb's Experiential Learning Cycle (Kolb, 1984), with an emphasis on concrete experience and reflective observation. However, there is also the recognition that self-awareness and the ability to evaluate in an objective manner enhance learner experience (Weimer, 2013). We spend time exploring the differences in some of the environmental factors that affect the practice of business. We specifically focus on the political, economic, legal, and cultural factors that impact business across national boundaries. There is the belief that this foundation will enhance learning and understanding as the learners engage in different environmental contexts.

COURSE DESCRIPTION

The course's objective is to familiarize the students with the global environmental forces surrounding international business operations of Multinational Companies (MNCs). The comparative management issues facing MNCs are addressed in the course with an emphasis on the Chinese environment. The course and associated extra and co-curricular activities are designed to sensitize students to differences in the environments in which MNCs operate.

The study abroad course is designed in such a way that in addition to the academic content, students are given multiple opportunities to experience a different business and cultural environment. Lecture materials are designed to give students exposure to different theories of international management and trade and cross-cultural management. The study abroad trip to China allows students to experience some of these nuances of cross-cultural management and to be exposed to perspectives on relevant topics from outside of the United States. For example, during our study abroad program, some of the lectures are provided by Chinese professors, and our U.S. students are also in class with Chinese students. Listening to and discussing with Chinese professors and colleagues prove to be invaluable educational and cultural experiences. No textbook is assigned for the course. However, there is a reading list with articles from *The Harvard Business Review*, for example, that I modify from year to year. A sample reading list of assigned articles is included in Appendix 12.1.

Course Learning Outcomes

After taking the course, students should have a good understanding of the following:

a. International trade theories and motivations of MNCs.
b. The environmental factors that influence the motivations and strategies of MNCs.
c. Impact of environmental factors in the application of management theories across national boundaries.
d. The environmental factors and how they shape globalization in China.
e. An awareness of the required cultural competency for managers operating across national boundaries.

COURSE HISTORY

The course was developed as a logical extension of the *International Management* course that I normally teach on campus. The course was designed to expose students to the environmental factors that impact how companies are managed across national boundaries. In addition to political and economic factors, the course tends to emphasize the importance of cultural understanding and adaptability as managers perform their duties across national borders (Chang, 2010). An earlier version of this course also taught by me was done as a study abroad course, with trips to Finland, Sweden, and Estonia. These countries represent different economic and political systems compared to China, which is more of a communist state and an emerging economy. As one can imagine, the history of these countries has an impact on their present-day economic system.

With the increasing role of China in globalization and its position as a trading partner for the U.S., the motivation was to further explore the environmental factors that impact Chinese MNCs and other MNCs that operate and compete in the Chinese environment. After an initial exploratory visit and with the help of a faculty colleague, the decision was made to teach a study abroad course in *International Management* with special emphasis on the Chinese environment. The study abroad program in China was designed to expose our students to these environmental factors as they specifically relate to China and give the students the opportunity to learn how to understand and navigate in a place where the environment is significantly different.

COURSE LOGISTICS

The course *International Management: Globalization in China* is a 3-credit hour graduate-level elective course open to students in the College of Business. Historically, most of the students in the program have been MBA students, but we also had students pursuing graduate degrees in finance, accounting, and management participate in the program. Upper-level undergraduate students (seniors) with relevant experience have been allowed to participate in the program. Because there are both undergraduate and graduate students, there are some differences in the expectation of the term paper. However, the exams are the same for all students. Given the very few undergraduate students that participate in the China trip, the expectations and evaluations are broadly geared towards graduate-level work. There are no course prerequisites for the program. In-class instruction hours for the program are about 35 hours. The study abroad program is for a duration of three weeks, with two weeks outside the country and one week in the U.S.

PRE-PROGRAM ACTIVITIES

In addition to the pre-departure orientation conducted by the Office of Education Abroad, we meet with the students daily for three hours each evening from Monday to Thursday in the week prior to departure. During those meetings, we discuss some of the logistics of the trip to China and the expectations of the participants. Students are given general information about China, including a brief cultural and geographical history. This is done by a faculty colleague who is a Chinese national and native speaker. Pre-departure activities also include some lectures on globalization, the importance of emerging nations, and some of the trends in international trade and globalization. Finally, given the students' diverse backgrounds, we create opportunities for them to get to know each other since they will be living in proximity for a couple of weeks.

CLASS ACTIVITIES & INTERCULTURAL COMPETENCIES

Upon arrival in China, activities include class lectures and discussions, excursions, visits to business office and manufacturing facilities, and group activities with Chinese students. Class lectures and discussions are primarily facilitated by me, as the instructor of record. In addition to the students from MTSU, we also have in the class Chinese students studying business programs at our host institution in China. The students have English language proficiency, so discussions are always in English. Some of the class lectures and discussions are facilitated by Chinese colleagues, and this gives our students an opportunity to get a different perspective on issues and topics being discussed. Class activities include a written examination which is graded and used as part of the final grade. Students are also required to write a term paper for the course. During class discussions, we sometimes have students work in groups, with each group being a good mix of Chinese and American students. This allows them to consider multiple perspectives on the issues we are discussing and learn how to work well with others. The study abroad program in China is designed in such a way that students can experience some of the theories that we discuss during our class meetings. For example, when we visit a government-sponsored and funded business incubator, the students get to experience what public-private partnership looks like in the Chinese context. I would also suggest that attending a lecture given by a Chinese professor adds some experiential flavor to the learning experience.

On each trip, we plan a few excursions and business office and manufacturing facilities visits. The goal of these visits is to give our students an opportunity to see how businesses operate outside of the U.S., to learn about the influence of environmental factors, and how MNCs adapt in another country. Visits include a Chinese-owned and operated company, a foreign MNC operating in China, Chinese start-up organizations, and an organization that represents a public-private partnership in China. Here we make use of contacts initiated by my Chinese colleague at MTSU with his connections to the Confucius Institute and faculty colleagues at Hangzhou University. We also make sure that different industries such as financial services and manufacturing are represented in our visits. In addition to these types of visits, we also visit places of cultural significance in China. On each trip, we provide opportunities for our students to work in groups with Chinese students on non-class related projects, which may include craft-making activities and cooking lessons. These types of interactions allow our students to learn how to work with other people and understand cross-cultural group dynamics in a non-threatening environment. See Appendix 12.2 for a travel itinerary.

Students in the program are expected to participate in different class activities during the program. Some of these class activities are conducted before the actual trip, but most of the class activities occur during the trip. Students are expected to attend class lectures and discussions daily. The class meetings average about 4-6 hours a day. A typical day consists of class lectures from 9:00 am to 12:00 pm, a lunch break, and then class again from 1:00 pm to 4:30 pm. Some of the lectures and discussions are in a typical classroom setting, and some take place in the conference rooms of the companies or organizations we are visiting. Most of the classroom lectures are given by me as the instructor of record, although some are given by Chinese colleagues that teach in the host institution, and by industry executives that may be conducting the tours to the facilities we are visiting.

As one can imagine, the schedule for each day and week will tend to change depending on how successful we are in coordinating the schedule for visiting organizations and the availability of the guest lecturers. Detailed below are examples of class activities, tasks, and assignments for a few days in a typical week.

Lectures

Class Lectures on the Environment of International Management

In this module, we explore the environmental factors that impact the operations of multinational companies and how and why they operate across national borders. We pay particular attention to economic, legal, cultural, and environmental factors. Class lectures and academic journals that relate to this topic are discussed. Examples of MNCs operating in multiple environments are also given to illustrate the need for companies to be nimble as they move across national boundaries and encounter these different environmental factors. During class discussions, U.S. students are grouped with Chinese students to further discuss some of the issues highlighted during the lecture. The mixed group class discussions are a great opportunity for our U.S. students not only to learn about the Chinese environment but also to get a better understanding of why some U.S. companies operate the way they do. As a result, both US students and their Chinese colleagues have a better appreciation for each other's culture.

On the first day or two of our trip, we arrange for our U.S. students to go out and eat dinner in a typical local restaurant with the Chinese students. By this time, the level of curiosity about some of the nuances of Chinese culture is high, and some of the preconceived ideas about Chinese culture are already being challenged. The class discussion also gives our students an insight into the Chinese students' perception of U.S. culture. The level of learning and understanding over the two weeks in China is noticeable, as evidenced in some of the reflection papers that students submit at the end of the trip. Being able to understand that neither Chinese nor U.S. culture is monolithic is eye-opening and the cultural competency of the students improves. The class lectures help the students better understand that the culture in China has some regional variations just like in the U.S. For example, they are able to recognize that a large percentage of China is still very rural, and Beijing and Shanghai do not represent the country.

Guest Lectures

These are typical classroom lectures on selected topics, but they are delivered by Chinese colleagues. These lectures tend to focus on the general Chinese perspective on globalization and the perceived impact of globalization on the Chinese population. These lectures coming from Chinese professors are an opportunity for our students to have alternative perspectives on a very timely topic of critical importance to national competitiveness (Pan, 2011). These lectures help give a unique insight into how some of the international trade theories that we discuss play out in practice. There is also evidence from reflection papers that a portion of students have experienced a significant shift in previously held opinions on some issues. Another additional learning opportunity with guest lectures is that our U.S. students are exposed to the "classroom culture" with a Chinese professor. These classes and guest lecture activities provided the students with the intercultural competencies identified in Table 12.1.

Table 12.1: Intercultural Competencies in Lecture Activities

Knowledge	Skills	Attitudes
• Understanding of the role of the Communist Party in business in China • Understanding that some of the priorities of governments and businesses may not be the same as in the U.S.	• Developing the ability to ask the appropriate question.	• Openness to other forms of business operations. • More inquisitiveness on the part of students.

Site Visits

Visits to Government-Sponsored Incubator Units

The program is intentionally designed to let students experience many of the theories we cover in the course lectures. We have a few visits/excursions scheduled to be able to achieve this objective. The visit to the government-sponsored incubator venue is one that demonstrates the importance of public-private partnerships in China to improve the national competitiveness of the country.

During these visits, students learn how government funds are used in workforce development in China for the private sector (Ke et al., 2010). These visits are of great significance because the operation defies the assumptions of how a communist economy works. This is a good lesson for our students in the nuances of the intersection between private and public sector enterprises in China. This is an experience that our students would not have had without such a trip. These visits demonstrate some of the steps taken by the Chinese government to maintain its national competitiveness.

Visit to a Foreign MNC Operating in China

We also visit the manufacturing operations of a German company that manufactures automobiles for the Chinese market. This visit allows us to observe how those operations in China are different from operations in the home country of the company or subsidiaries in other parts of the world. Students can learn how the leadership and motivation techniques used in this plant are influenced by Chinese culture and government regulations. During this visit, students are required to identify differences they observe in China and how some could be explained by Chinese culture and others by the culture of the MNC's parent country. Being able to observe the differences in practice enhances the students' cross-cultural competency skills, and hopefully makes them more understanding employees or managers when they collaborate with people from other cultures.

Visit to a Large Chinese MNC

On one of the tours we take, we visit the largest Chinese retail outfit with a global footprint. While some of the students have heard of Alibaba Trading Company, they were not aware of how big and well-ingrained the company is in China. The tour of multiple operations of Alibaba and its headquarters is an opportunity for students to learn how technology is used to serve the interest of consumers, the company, and the central political administration of the country. Students can observe how a large private company operates in a communist economy and consider how their stereotypes are challenged. This is a great example of a public-private partnership, which is an increasingly popular dimension of international trade.

Visit to the Financial District in Shanghai

During our stay in Shanghai, we visit Shanghai's Financial District (Lujiazui) located on the east side of the Huangpu River, directly across from the Bund in Shanghai, China. The tour and lectures in the Financial District give our students some awareness of the role that China plays in globalization and the movement of capital to facilitate trade in that region of the world. The presence of major financial institutions from outside of China with offices in the district and the number of expatriates that work in the district allow our students to learn more about managing human resources across national borders. Through these various excursions and site visits, students were able to gain the intercultural competencies listed in Table 12.2.

Table 12.2: Intercultural Competencies in Site Visits Activities

Knowledge	Skills	Attitudes
<ul><li>Understanding some unique business cultures in China</li><li>Supply chain activities of companies</li><li>Better understanding of business relationships</li><li>Learning about culture</li></ul>	<ul><li>Ability to navigate the transportation system</li><li>Communicating better with Chinese business professionals</li></ul>	<ul><li>Increased level of confidence</li><li>Openness to new ideas</li><li>Willingness to try new ways of doing things</li></ul>

Extra and Co-Curricular Activities

Lecture and Visits to Historical and Culturally Significant Sites in China

Some of the major extracurricular activities we engage in while in China are visits to historically significant cultural sites. With such visits and accompanying lectures, our students learn about the history of China and the impact of that history on modern-day China. These visits and lectures give students a better understanding of the impact of legal and cultural factors on business operations in China.

Co-Curricular Activities

With the privilege of having local Chinese students in our classes while in China, we engage in a few curricular activities that are designed to give better insight into aspects of Chinese culture and facilitate opportunities for long-lasting friendships. Some of these activities include soccer games, craft lessons, dumpling-making (cooking) lessons, and shopping in local markets. With guidance, students are allowed to navigate the day-to-day living of Chinese citizens by taking local transportation and conducting exchanges in the local market. These intercultural contacts tend to lead to positive effects and help to eliminate some stereotypes (Visbal, 2009). Based on feedback from both American and Chinese students, it is safe to say that these extracurricular activities are perceived as fun, and they enhance the intercultural competency of both groups of students. We can notice how much more comfortable the American students are in interacting with their Chinese colleagues by the end of the trip. Before returning to the U.S., some of them are able to venture out on their own, and to an extent, successfully navigate life in China as temporary visitors. These extra and co-curricular activities enabled the students to develop invaluable intercultural competencies as tabulated in Table 12.3.

Table 12.3: Intercultural Competencies in Co-Curricular Activities

Knowledge	Skills	Attitudes
• Better understanding of Chinese history and possible impact on business practices	• Navigation • Communication	• Better appreciation of home culture • Better understanding and appreciation of other cultures • Awareness of unintended prejudice • More world mindedness

POST-PROGRAM AND FUTURE CLASS ACTIVITIES

Upon return from the study abroad experience, students are also required to submit a reflection paper. The students are required to reflect on at least the following: a new revelation about Chinese culture; new business concepts learned as a result of the trip; ideas they would pass on to those who may want to do business in China; new things learned about themselves; significant changes in their thought process as a result of the trip (such as doing away with stereotypes); and any lasting perspective about globalization in general.

For future programs, I plan to be more deliberate in evaluating the intercultural competencies of the participating students. It would be worthwhile to evaluate the level of cultural sensitivity that students have before and after participating in the study abroad program. Administering a global aptitude test or a world-mindedness test before and after the program will be introduced in the future. I also plan to take greater advantage of the available technology to immerse the students in the culture of the host country. For example, we could organize pre-departure Zoom meetings with the Chinese students who would join us in our study abroad class sessions. This may help in reducing the length of time it takes to be comfortable with socializing when we get to China by pairing up the students via Zoom and give them an assignment.

EVALUATION AND ASSIGNMENTS

Students were evaluated based on their performance in three areas. There were two essay examinations, participation in discussion activities in class and during co-curricular activities, and a term paper, which included a section on the reflection of the study abroad experience.

- Examinations - 100 points
- Class participation - 50 points
- Term Paper/Reflection on Trip - 150 points

The grading criteria did not explicitly include intercultural competencies; however, there was evidence in the student term papers that students demonstrated an appreciation of intercultural competency because of exposure to the Chinese environment. Class participation in discussion groups and visits to the company/excursion sites are more formative types of assessment, while the reflection paper and written exams are more summative.

STUDENT FEEDBACK

The students' feedback has always been incredibly positive. Many of the program students are newer to foreign travel, and many of them had not been exposed to diverse cultures outside of the United States. A few of them have had limited travel to Canada and resort destinations in Mexico and the Caribbean. With that type of background, they are a group that is prime to experience a totally different culture and develop intercultural competencies. As stated earlier, we do not use any formal survey to measure the level of pre- and post-trip level of cultural awareness, but there is enough qualitative and anecdotal evidence of students that go on the program having more global and cultural awareness after the trips' discussions.

Some days tend to be long in the classroom, but that is unavoidable given the necessary content of the course and the scheduling of business offices and manufacturing plant visits and excursions in the limited time we have in China. The students enjoy interacting with the Chinese students that participated with us in the program, and some of them have become lifelong friends. A few of the students find it burdensome to navigate the public transportation system in a big city, but many of them think of it as a challenge and an opportunity to learn. Initially, some of the students had a hard time adjusting to the local diet but did not consider it a major problem with the increasing number of alternative food choices in many places in China. The length of time in China seems to be perfect given the work schedule and other obligations of many of our students at home. Students reported that there was a good balance between the curriculum and the co-curricular activities throughout the program.

CAVEATS AND REFLECTIONS

After four iterations of the study abroad course in China, we have had the opportunity to refine the program and include many elements that make for a good cultural and educational experience for our students. For example, in the first year of the program, we did not have Chinese students participate in our class lectures and discussions. Inviting Chinese students and guest lecturers has enhanced the educational experience and allowed our students more insight into Chinese culture, so this will continue to be part of the program.

The last trip was in 2019. As for the future of the program, COVID-19 will continue to make study abroad in China difficult. The mobility restrictions by the Chinese government do not help, and truth be known, many Americans are still very reluctant about traveling to China (U.S. Department of State, 2023). However, after five of these trips to China and teaching this course both in China and at home, there is no doubt that the program has been of benefit to our students, the College of Business, and the university. It has given students the kind of exposure that one would expect from a program that offers a business major. Globalization is here to stay and understanding the nuances of the subject matter and from the perspectives of other stakeholders is very important. Being able to learn, visit, and observe in a small way how one of the biggest economies operates is of great advantage. The experience broadens the perspective of our students. Our interaction with local Chinese students is also of great benefit to those students since we have a forum for increasing mutual understanding between the two groups. In addition to increasing my knowledge base, my experiences in China (and other countries for study abroad) have made me a better instructor. I think the same is true for our students. Some students have expressed that being students overseas and interacting with Chinese professors and students has given them the opportunity to be better students and employees when they return to the U.S. Finally, based on student feedback, the experience has also helped them in having more appreciation for their home country.

It would be desirable if more students were able to experience the opportunity to study abroad. In addition to the challenges of funding the trip, the mindset in terms of the importance of study abroad is not prevalent among the American population and students within our College of Business. Our college has been very generous in providing scholarships to students going to study abroad (for example, each student who is a College of Business major gets an additional $1,000 for a study abroad program) and encourages faculty members to develop study abroad programs. This program would have been more challenging if not for the help of a colleague on campus who was able to help with the logistical details in China. Having local partners in Chinese universities is a major plus for our program.

The program is at the very core of the mission of our College of Business. It is an integral part of preparing our students for an increasingly globalized business world, which is characterized by interdependencies among countries and multinational corporations. This is one of the reasons that the College has been generous in funding students for study abroad programs.

REFERENCES

Chang, S. J. (2010). When East and West meet: An essay on the importance of cultural understanding in global business practice and education. *Journal of International Business and Cultural Studies, 2*, 1–13. https://ir.library.illinoisstate.edu/fpfil/1/

Deardorff, D. K. (2012). Framework: Intercultural competence model. In K. Berardo & D. K. Deardorff (Eds.), *Building cultural competence: Innovative activities and models* (pp. 45-52). Stylus Publishing.

Harvey, T. A. (2017). Design and pedagogy for transformative intercultural learning. In B. Kappler Mikk & I. Steglitz (Eds.) *Learning across cultures: Locally and globally* (3rd ed., pp. 109-138). NAFSA: Association of International Educators; Stylus Publishing.

Ke, Y., Wang, S., Chan, A. P. C., & Lam, P. T. I. (2010). Preferred risk allocation in China's public-private partnership (PPP) projects. *International Journal of Project Management, 28*(5), 482–492. https://doi.org/10.1016/j.ijproman.2009.08.007

Kolb, D. A. (1984). *Experiential learning: Experience as the source of learning and development*. Prentice Hall.

Pan, S. (2011). Education abroad, human capital development, and national competitiveness: China's brain gain strategies, *Frontiers of Education in China, 6*(1), 106–138. http://dx.doi.org/10.1007/s11516-011-0124-4

U.S. Department of State. (2023, June 30). China international travel information. https://travel.state.gov/content/travel/en/international-travel/International-Travel-Country-Information-Pages/China.html

Visbal, O. (2009). *The erosion of stereotypes through intercultural exchange programs: Testing Pettigrew's contact theory*. [Doctoral Dissertation, Hamburg University]. State and University Library Hamburg Carl von Ossietzsky.

Weimer, M. (2013). *Learner-centered Teaching: Five key changes to practice* (2nd ed.). Jossey-Bass.

APPENDICES

Appendix 12.1: Sample Reading List of Assigned Articles

Brimm, L. (2016). What the best cross-cultural managers have in common. *Harvard Business Review*. https://hbr.org/2016/06/what-the-best-cross-cultural-managers-have-in-common

Ghemawat, P. (2017). Globalization in the age of Trump. *Harvard Business Review*. https://hbr.org/2017/07/globalization-in-the-age-of-trump

Govindarajan, V., & Bagia, G. (2017). What U.S. CEOs can learn from GM's India failure. *Harvard Business Review*. https://hbr.org/2017/06/what-u-s-ceos-can-learn-from-gms-india-failure

Hofstede, G. (1993). Cultural constraints in management theories. *Academy of Management Executive, 7*(1), 81–94. https://doi.org/10.5465/ame.1993.9409142061

Khanna, T. (2014). Contextual intelligence. *Harvard Business Review*. https://hbr.org/2014/09/contextual-intelligence

Khanna, T., & Palepu, K. G. (2006). Emerging giants: Building world-class companies in developing countries. *Harvard Business Review*. https://hbr.org/2006/10/emerging-giants-building-world-class-companies-in-developing-countries

Kumar, N., & Puranam, P. (2011). Have you reconstructed for global success? *Harvard Business Review*. https://hbr.org/2011/10/have-you-restructured-for-global-success

Meyer, E. (2017). Being the boss in Brussels, Boston, and Beijing. *Harvard Business Review*. https://hbr.org/2017/07/being-the-boss-in-brussels-boston-and-beijing

Neeley, T. (2017). How to successfully work across countries, languages, and cultures. *Harvard Business Review*. https://hbr.org/2017/08/how-to-successfully-work-across-countries-languages-and-cultures

Neeley, T., & Kaplan, R. S. (2014). What is your language strategy? *Harvard Business Review*. https://hbr.org/2014/09/whats-your-language-strategy

Ohmae, K. (1989). Managing in a borderless world. *Harvard Business Review*. https://hbr.org/1989/05/managing-in-a-borderless-world

Porter, M. (1990). Competitive advantage of nations. *Harvard Business Review*. https://hbr.org/1990/03/the-competitive-advantage-of-nations

Porter, M. (1998). Cluster and the new economics of competition. *Harvard Business Review*. https://hbr.org/1998/11/clusters-and-the-new-economics-of-competition

Prahlad, C. K., & Lieberthal, K. (2003). The end of corporate imperialism. *Harvard Business Review*. https://hbr.org/2003/08/the-end-of-corporate-imperialism

Appendix 12.2: Typical Travel Itinerary for Study Abroad in China

Dates	Topics/Activities	Comments
Tuesday May 14	Course introduction and lecture on trade theories	Pre-departure
Wednesday May 15	Lecture on environmental challenge of IB. CAGE Framework	Pre-departure
Thursday May 16	Understanding the role of culture	Pre-departure
Sunday May 19	Travel to Shanghai	
Monday May 20	Arrive in Shanghai	Free time and dinner. Please note that when you have free time, be sure to pair up and do not venture out on your own!
Tuesday May 21	Lecture and Volkswagen plant visit	Lecture plant manager (wear comfortable shoes).
Wednesday May 22	Visit to financial district, role of port of Shanghai in East West trade	Lunch with company executives
Thursday May 23	Travel to Hangzhou Normal University	Travel by bus, meet HZNU students upon arrival, stay in dormitory on campus

Dates	Topics/ Activities	Comments
Friday May 24	Formal welcome to HZNU, lecture on digital economy in China (Chinese professor), visit to Alibaba headquarters	Lunch with HZNU students Cultural activity with HZNU students hosting
Saturday May 25	Morning: Tour of Hefang Street market Afternoon: Visit to Westlake	Visit to cultural centers and lecture by Chinese guide.
Sunday May 26	Reading assignments Meet with Chinese students	Free time in Hangzhou
Monday May 27	Morning: Class lecture Afternoon: Visit to New Retail Concept in China, Hema retail store	Not a time to shop!
Tuesday May 28	Morning: Class lecture, including Chinese professor as guest lecturer. Afternoon: Visit to the student innovation incubator lab. Evening: Chinese cultural experience (calligraphy and tea ceremony).	Dinner in the evening with Chinese colleagues
Wednesday May 29	Leave for Beijing	Take bus to train station and then take 6-hour bullet train ride to Beijing.
Wednesday May 29	Arrive in Beijing Short cultural lecture by Chinese host.	Hotel stay Dinner together
Thursday May 30	Visit to the Great Wall Visit to Summer Palace	Next two days we will be in very crowded places. Stay together and pair up.
Friday May 31	Visit to Tiananmen Square Visit to Forbidden City	
Friday May 31	Morning: Debriefing at Hotel Afternoon: Departure starts	Send email when you get back to alert safe arrival.

Chapter 13

Experiential Learning in London: Evaluation of Study Abroad Learning for Criminal Justice Students

Lee Miller Wade

Note: Section II includes Chapters 4-14. These chapters use a standardized template to discuss the details of their respective study abroad programs and reference Deardorff's (2012) framework for intercultural competencies. The use of this template and the intercultural competencies framework are described in the Section II introduction. All courses in this section (except for Chapter 6) were taught through Middle Tennessee State University (MTSU), a mid-sized state school located in Murfreesboro, Tennessee (USA).

The short-term study abroad course *Criminal Justice in London* (CJA 493) aims to broaden students' understanding of the criminal justice system. The unique feature of this program is the comparative analysis approach of the British and U.S. criminal justice systems. Carefully selected activities and assignments provide students with opportunities to interpret, analyze, and reflect on topics such as policing, courts, and correction systems in both countries. Since 2017, this is an annual program available for all MTSU students. The program runs during the May semester for two weeks. On average, eight students attend each year.

THEORETICAL FOUNDATIONS

As with many education abroad programs, the foundation and outcomes of this course involve increasing intercultural competency, strengthening a foundational knowledge of a specified topic, and allowing the students to grow as individuals through their own experiences. Therefore, this course has a theoretical foundation in the constructivist approach, which is a more experiential, student-centered approach. In other words, the course is facilitated by the instructor more than lecture format teaching (Tangney, 2014). The course also utilizes the integrative approach, which allows students to interact with the outside world, a foundational element of this course (Tangney, 2014). Living, studying, and traveling in another country, experiencing that country's culture, and learning can theoretically have a lasting impact on a person for the rest of their life. These experiential learning foundations lead us toward the goal of opening the mind of the students and applying the knowledge they have gained to make them better global citizens.

COURSE DESCRIPTION

The purpose of the London, England, Criminal Justice Study Abroad program is to broaden students' understanding of the criminal justice system. The U.S. criminal justice system was based on the English Common Law system, particularly in the organization of police and courts in larger cities throughout the 1800s that existed throughout large cities in Britain. This program exposes students to the policing and court systems in the United Kingdom (U.K.), providing them with an experience by which they can compare policing and courts in the U.S. Students are given readings from the text *World Criminal Justice Systems: A Comparative Survey* (Terrill, 2015) to familiarize themselves with how the U.K. approaches common problems found in the U.S. like personal and property crime, police-community relations, and judicial fairness. The readings were selected from this text due to the format, which compares international criminal justice systems directly with the U.S. criminal justice system. Lectures by criminal justice faculty provide an overview of comparative criminal justice systems between the U.K. and the U.S. The study abroad experience itself includes daily visits to criminal justice institutions (New Scotland Yard, Old Bailey, Inns of Court, Royal Court, etc.) and other historical references (Tower of London) with an end-of-day debriefing discussion about what was learned and how it compared to the U.S. criminal justice system.

Course Learning Outcomes

The course learning outcomes are as follows:

a. Develop knowledge based upon experiential learning and apply theoretical concepts towards solving practical problems within the student's discipline.
b. Create a connection between experiences and disciplinary knowledge towards critical examination of issues related to their discipline.
c. Increase student growth toward serving their communities from experience and theoretical concepts.
d. Compare and contrast the criminal justice systems of the United States and the United Kingdom.
e. Critically analyze the role of criminal justice system officials in both law enforcement and the core components of each system, including policies, legal issues, and impact on the community.

COURSE HISTORY

The course preparation began in 2016 with financial assistance from the Vice Provost of International Affairs at MTSU. Working with a retired London Metropolitan Police Detective Inspector as a guide and co-instructor, we visited and lectured at landmarks related to the U.K.'s criminal justice system. These were planned as destinations for historical context and experiential learning for students. Recruitment began an academic year before the summer semester. Criminal Justice undergraduate and graduate students comprised the first cohort, and during subsequent years this did not change. Approximately eight students on average participated in the program until 2020 when the program was paused for three years due to the COVID-19 pandemic.

COURSE LOGISTICS

This study abroad program is a 3-credit hour course listed as *International Criminal Justice* (CJA 4930) in our curriculum that takes place over two weeks. Students may select the course as part of their general, upper-division electives, and it also is an option in the Homeland Security concentration of our undergraduate degree program. The in-class instruction for the first week involves three lectures, over three hours each, at MTSU, and there are lectures as part of our itinerary in London (see Appendix 13.1 for program itinerary details). There is no pre-requisite for the course, and it is open to all majors and minors as an opportunity to compare the U.S. and U.K. criminal justice systems.

PRE-PROGRAM ACTIVITIES

Prior to departure to London, there are three daily lectures (3-hour segments) covering the basics of the government structure and laws in the United Kingdom. The lectures also cover the comparison and history of policing, courts, corrections, and juvenile justice. Students are then assigned readings that illustrate the contrasting issues in each of these components of the criminal justice system. Additional lectures are provided during the time in London depending on the availability of the instructor during our program.

A few days before departure, students are asked to evaluate readings from our online course platform. These readings cover controversial items regarding juvenile gang crime, policing in the U.K. with or without guns, and English court proceedings. These readings help reinforce some of the concepts in the pre-departure lectures, but they also prepare students for some of the information they will receive abroad in London. Moreover, the students begin, at this point, to select a topic for the final project, where they will eventually compare a criminal justice concept of components between the two systems.

CLASS ACTIVITIES & INTERCULTURAL COMPETENCIES

Content Lectures with Intercultural Competencies

Government Lecture and Parliament Tour

To reinforce the U.K. government structure lecture that occurred prior to departure to London, the students attend a lecture with a London-based political science professor. This is further reinforced when students visit the U.K. Parliament located in Westminster to learn more about the legislative branch and citizen participation in elections. In this activity, the students get their first glimpse into the organization of the court structure in the U.K. The lecture specifically contrasts the branches of government in the U.K. and the U.S. and discusses the electorate. In this lecture, students learn the key differences in legislative processes, criminal offense statutes, and fundamental rights established by the law. In addition to the government structure, students visit Parliament Square for a tour of monuments and areas inside buildings of the U.K. Parliament. Students are guided through the House of Commons and House of Lords while learning the historical importance of Parliament to the U.K. government structure. In addition, students are instructed on how bills become laws, how citizens contact their members of Parliament, and how often elections occur in the U.K.

London Metropolitan Police Lecture and Museum Visit

The students attend a few lectures from police constables and detective inspectors at the Supreme Court of the United Kingdom, which is also located in Westminster, London. The lectures provide students with the background and basics of police operations in London and the U.K. Criminal laws are the same throughout the U.K., so students can make inferences about the enforcement of laws in other parts of the country.

The first lecture is focused on how a London Metropolitan patrol shift operates throughout each of London's boroughs. This lecture has a question-and-answer session focused on student interest, and students often ask direct questions that can contribute to their final project. For example, if a student were to do their final project on the differences between police officers being armed in the U.K. versus the U.S., they would ask those questions about gun policies, gun crime, and gun violence.

The second lecture is focused on how investigations of crime unfold and some of the procedures of gathering evidence that are conducted by detective inspectors. For instance, students are introduced to how London and the London Metropolitan Police use surveillance video facial recognition to solve most crimes throughout their jurisdiction. This lecture is also followed by a question-and-answer session for students to discuss criminal investigations and comparisons with U.S. police investigations.

The City of London Police Museum visit is usually scheduled in tandem with the police lectures or with the Old Bailey visit. The City of London is a smaller territory inside Metropolitan London. Both the City of London and Metropolitan London have their own police force. The City of London polices the central financial district only and the Metropolitan London Police Force (also known as Scotland Yard) is responsible for the greater London region. This is a walkthrough museum where students begin with the inception of modern policing from Sir Robert Peel in 1829 to the present day. Students can see the various uniforms, equipment, and historical events throughout London's policing history. The museum features hands-on activities that connect to the law enforcement lectures and coursework in our program. For example, students can view the original crime scene photos from Jack the Ripper murders in 1888 and can practice using surveillance video and facial recognition software.

These activities connect to course outcomes, with four outcomes comparing the core components of the U.K. system with the U.S. system. The law enforcement component of the U.K. system has both similarities and differences with the U.S. system. Thus, by observing the history and current functions of the law enforcement component of the criminal justice system in London, the students can make these connections. These in-country lectures indicated the efficacy of the integrative approach for students by allowing the classroom to intersect with the experiences of being in a foreign country. A summary of intercultural competencies related to the learning objectives is listed in Table 13.1.

Table 13.1: Intercultural Competencies for Content Lectures

Knowledge	Skills	Attitudes
• Content knowledge • Culture-specific knowledge • Academic content knowledge	• Observing and applying • Listen, observe, interpret	• Open minded • Adaptability • Stepping outside the comfort zone

Visits to Scenes of Crime with Intercultural Competencies

Jack The Ripper

Usually scheduled near in timing to the police museum activity is the Jack the Ripper activity, which includes a night-time tour of all murder scene locations from 1888. This activity begins in the City of London and moves towards the Whitechapel District near the East End of London. A tour guide provides a chilling account of the details of each murder as recorded in history intermingled with theories of who Jack the Ripper could have been and why he was never caught by the police. Through this context, students are introduced to the serial killer classification system used by both the London Metropolitan Police and the Federal Bureau of Investigation (FBI) in the U.S. Due to the historical nature of these serial crimes, students are further connected to the culture and history of London in 1888, and how its conditions led to criminogenic factors as well as the documentation of the first serial killer.

Soho Gang Activity

Much like the Jack the Ripper activity, this tour throughout the Soho District of London highlights how organized crime developed in both Central and East London. The students are led to various locations in Soho that featured feuds between gangs in the 20th century. While stopping at these locations, students are told the history of how the gangs interacted and how it relates to the criminal justice system in London.

The activities in this part of the program have focused more on the constructivist approach to education abroad learning. The constructive approach focuses on more hands-on tasks, student-centered learning, and building on past knowledge of content knowledge of the discipline (Deardorff, 2012). A summary table of intercultural competencies related to the learning objectives is listed in Table 13.2.

Table 13.2: Intercultural Competencies for Visits to Scene of Crime

Knowledge	Skills	Attitudes
• Culture-specific knowledge • Academic content knowledge	• Problem solving • Analyze, evaluate, and relate	• Open-minded, empathy, and curiosity. • Flexibility and adaptability

Lecture and Tours of Court Systems with Intercultural Competencies

Inns of Court

Students who have legal aspirations often enjoy this tour and lecture on the origins of lawyers, or "solicitors" and "barristers," as they are referred to in England. The lecture covers the history and organization of the different *Inns*, which began in Temple Church, and are now professional associations for barristers. The lecture also discusses the requirements of becoming a lawyer in England and Wales, the differences in education with U.S. schools, and then concludes with a question-and-answer session for students.

Royal Courts of Justice

Due to its proximity, students travel up Fleet Street toward the Strand to visit the Royal Courts of Justice, which is in a Victorian-styled building. The Royal Courts of Justice serve as the appellate courts for both criminal and civil cases. The students are allowed to sit in on an appellate court hearing. This is significant because students can note the differences between appellate court hearings in the U.S. and England, but they can also note the differences in procedures of hearings after watching a trial or preliminary hearing in an English criminal court at the Old Bailey.

Old Bailey Courthouse

During the excursion, students will observe a criminal proceeding at the Old Bailey courthouse in London. This experience will introduce the students to common law procedures shown in the British system that are both similar (adversarial system) and dissimilar (wigs and court dress for barristers). In past excursions, students have observed both pre-trial proceedings and an actual murder trial. Students were able to see the procedural questioning of witnesses and the accused, see legal arguments over the admissibility of evidence, and see the decorum of the courtroom. For example, jury trials are more heavily used in U.K. proceedings, and court members refer to the female and male judges as *Lady* or *Lord*. Moreover, the court buildings are built in a Baroque architectural style compared to court buildings in the United States.

These activities connect to course outcomes related to comparing the core components of the English and Welsh system with the U.S. system. The court component of the English system has both similarities and dissimilarities with the U.S. system, and by observing the history and current functions of the court component in London, the students can make these connections. Instead of evaluating the differences between the U.K. and U.S., English and Welsh court systems are evaluated, which is due to the differences in court proceedings, such as the Scottish court system being influenced by historical French legal doctrine. Historically, lawyers were trained in France and brought over civil doctrine towards more codification of laws within Scotland. The integrative approach of learning in the actual, historical settings where courts began encourages students to take what they have learned and apply it in the U.S. A summary table of intercultural competencies related to the learning objectives is listed in Table 13.3.

Table 13.3: Intercultural Competencies for Lectures and Tours of Court Systems

Knowledge	Skills	Attitudes
• Culture-specific knowledge • Academic content knowledge	• Problem-solving • Analyze, evaluate, and relate	• Open-minded, empathy, and curiosity • Flexibility and adaptability

Visits to Correction Facilities with Intercultural Competencies

Tower of London

The Tower of London was used for various purposes by the English monarchy for about 1,000 years, but it was heavily used for punishment and incarceration. There were hundreds of individuals either incarcerated or executed during the operation of this castle located in central London. In the 1500s, the Tower of London was used as a prison for those who were considered by the crown to be a threat to England. At Tower Hill, adjacent to the castle, there were hundreds of individuals executed through the following methods: beheadings, firing squad, drawn, quartered, and hanged. Students are allowed to interact with yeoman warders at the Tower and ask questions concerning punishment and the history of the castle (Terrill, 2015).

Clink Museum

Located in Southwark District, students can visit the Clink Museum, which was primarily a debtor's prison throughout a period of several hundred years. Students are allowed to walk through as the Museum shows the punishment and conditions of prison life from the 12th- 18th centuries.

These activities connect to course outcomes related to comparing the core components of the U.K. criminal justice system with the U.S. system. The corrections component of the U.K. system has both similarities and dissimilarities with the U.S. system, and by observing the history and current functions of the corrections component of the criminal justice system in London, students can make these connections.

Like the court-related excursions and learning outcomes, these learning environments are part of the integrative approach of learning in the actual, historical settings of how punishment and incarceration were used so they can apply what they have learned to critically analyze policies in the U.S. A summary table of intercultural competencies related to the learning objectives is listed in Table 13.4.

Table 13.4: Intercultural Competencies for Visits to Correction Facilities

Knowledge	Skills	Attitudes
• Culture-specific knowledge • Academic content knowledge	• Problem-solving • Analyze, evaluate, and relate	• Open-minded, empathy, and curiosity. • Flexibility and adaptability

Cultural Student Tasks with Intercultural Competencies

Students are given a week-long pass for public transportation on the underground transport for London (commonly known as "the Tube"). This helps students become familiar with how to use public transportation, travel on their own throughout London, and learn about the boroughs throughout the Metropolitan area. Many students from the U.S. are unfamiliar with a comprehensive public transportation network and requiring the students to use "the Tube" opens their eyes to this facet of metropolitan life in London.

Other locations for students to visit are for historical, religious, and artistic emphasis. For religious or historical context, students are asked to visit St. Paul's Cathedral and Westminster Abbey. For artistic culture, the National Gallery and Tate Modern are also highly encouraged. In addition, students are often encouraged to visit the many other museums, communities, and parks throughout Greater London. These cultural explorations lead to a valuable experience in developing self-awareness, taking risks, and opening their minds to the diverse culture of London, England.

To further stimulate intercultural competencies, the faculty leaders invite students to attend dinners or meetings at various pubs in central London (because MTSU has a zero-tolerance policy regarding alcohol, attendance at pubs in London was held in adjacent, private meeting rooms). These meetings usually involve interactions with locals and tourists from other parts of Great Britain or Europe. Students often get into debates about political, cultural, and social issues that are similar or different from the locals' perspectives. The intercultural competencies strengthened by these activities are the students' awareness of others outside of their home country and state, their awareness of themselves in comparison to others in the U.K.; and their individual development of skills to adapt to the culture of the U.K., relate to their citizenry, and expand their own perspectives of living in another country (Deardorff, 2006). A summary table of intercultural competencies related to the learning objectives is listed in Table 13.5.

Table 13.5: Intercultural Competencies for Cultural Tasks

Knowledge	Skills	Attitudes
• Cultural self-awareness and understanding others' worldviews • Culture-specific knowledge	• Problem-solving • Teamwork • Communication skills • Listen, observe, and interpret	• Patience and respect • Curiosity and discovery • Risk-taking • Stepping outside the comfort zone

POST PROGRAM AND FUTURE CLASS ACTIVITIES

Future class activities will involve a possible extended program and a trip to Edinburgh, Scotland. The National Museum of Scotland has many historical displays, and one exhibit of interest is the "punishment" displays. This is where students could see the replicas and artifacts associated with methods of punishment used by churches and societies. In addition to the museum, students could visit Edinburgh Castle located just up the Royal Mile. The Castle was used as a military outpost primarily, but it also has a small museum depicting the incarceration of American prisoners during the American Revolutionary War. Finally, also found on the Royal Mile, is the High Court of Justiciary, which is similar to the U.S. Supreme Court, but it hears criminal cases. As mentioned previously, there are some differences in the court system of Scotland versus England, and having a distinct perspective could benefit students in their understanding of criminal justice in Scotland. By extending the program to include Scotland, students could learn the historical and political influence of other countries on the formation of government systems by learning this distinct perspective.

EVALUATION AND ASSIGNMENTS

The following summarizes the course evaluation of students and their corresponding assignments.

Participation/Behavior (formative)	50%
Reading essay questions/Discussion Board (formative)	20%
Final Assignment (summative)	30%
Total	100%

- Participation: The expectation is that students are fully engaged in all aspects of the class and travel. Each student is expected to represent the University in a positive manner at each location during the trip and program while in London.
- Reading essays: Students create responses for three essay questions assessing their understanding of the readings.

- Final Assignment: A presentation focusing on a specific aspect of comparative criminal justice including academic resources and experiential findings. Refer to Appendix 13.2 for the final project guidelines and overall course expectations.

Student Assignments

Final Assignment

At the conclusion of the program, students will present a comparison of one component of the criminal justice system (courts, law enforcement, corrections, etc.) and how learning from the U.K.'s system could improve the U.S. criminal justice system. This assignment is to be presented to the class from the perspective of the student and their experiences. They are also asked to tie their experiences to a future and potential occupation in the criminal justice system. According to Bennett et al. (2000), creating assignments that emphasize cross-cultural skills in critical analysis enhances the individual and makes them more marketable. These assignments are connected to the student learning outcomes associated with critical thinking and analyzing the criminal justice system from different perspectives to enhance their future role as possible practitioners.

Reading Essays

Prior to departure to London, students are assigned articles on critical issues in the U.K. criminal justice system. At the conclusion of the trip to London, students are to write essays on the articles that summarize the main points of the critical issues but also include their reactions after learning more about the criminal justice system abroad. These essays usually show some reflection and synthesis of learned experiences or concepts from either lectures or activities. The students have cited experiences both in the U.S. and U.K. systems in past essays.

Reflective Discussion

The reflective discussion board associated with our course is essential for both student feedback and to illustrate the knowledge gained by students. Students reply to each other on the discussion board to report their insights on what they have learned. Many of the students reported the program increased their intercultural competencies as follows: they opened their minds, stepped outside their comfort zone (e.g., flying in an airplane to another country), increased their knowledge of other cultures, and enhanced their understanding of other countries.

A summary table of intercultural competencies related to the learning objectives for all assignments is listed in Table 13.6.

Table 13.6: Intercultural Competencies for Student Assignments

Knowledge	Skills	Attitudes
• Cultural self-awareness • Understanding others' worldviews • Culture-specific knowledge • Academic content knowledge	• Creative thinking and problem solving • Leadership, articulation, and teamwork • Interpret, analyze, evaluate, and relate	• Withholding judgment • Empathy, curiosity, and discovery • Stepping outside the comfort zone

STUDENT FEEDBACK

Approximately eight students each year evaluated the course program as extremely high in a five-point Likert scale in final evaluations for the instructor and course. This evaluation occurs in the final discussion board posts of the course and through a series of concluding remarks during the final presentation. Most of the detailed qualitative feedback on the program came from the reflective discussion that occurred at the end of the course. When the students were asked what events impacted them the most, they responded as follows: Approximately two-thirds of the students mentioned that cultural excursions impacted them the most, with lectures by law enforcement second, and the Tower of London ranking third. Most of the responses were varied in terms of what interested them, what they would like to see again, and how the experiences helped them. For example, a few students stated they would definitely travel to another country again, and most said they would have liked more time to have cultural excursions to increase intercultural competencies. In all, the students indicated in their reflections the course and experiences positively influenced their lives. Additionally, for many students, this is their first time out of the United States or their first time on an airplane. Both experiences are important and impactful, as they have stated in post-course evaluations.

CAVEATS AND REFLECTIONS

There are both challenges and strengths of the course. One challenge is recruiting students to step outside their comfort zone and travel to another country. Through mass emailing, study abroad fairs, and advertising, only an average of eight students take this course each year. A second challenge is ensuring that students are prepared each day for traveling throughout London. Due to jet lag or other sleep deprivation issues, students struggled to be alert while traveling or during lectures. A third challenge is condensing all the lectures and activities into one week. Because traveling to and staying in London is expensive, the trip abroad must be limited to one week. This makes scheduling a challenge for students to experience the basics of what they need to learn coupled with personal time to explore the culture of London. Some solutions to the recruitment challenges have been to market to individual students more, such as providing additional access to scholarship funds and partnering with another department's program. The other challenges involve logistics and planning, such as the length of the program being one-week long. If the instructors were to expand the program, the expansion could ameliorate other issues stated, but a longer program would create more challenges regarding recruitment, costs, and course length. In other words, a longer program is more expensive, which would restrict student affordability, and the course is limited to the two-week summer Maymester period at MTSU.

Despite the challenges, there are strengths to this program, and as such, I would be reluctant to alter the components of the course too much. First, students can travel abroad (for most, the first time in their lives) to a foreign country without needing to learn a new language or have a translator. Second, the course satisfies an elective in the Emergency Management/Homeland Security concentration of the Criminal Justice Administration undergraduate degree program. Furthermore, federal employers often ask if students have study abroad experience, and students from the program can increase their marketability. Third, based on feedback from the students, the course and experiences gleaned from it have positively impacted the students in two ways. Firstly, students can learn to look outside their country for solutions to problems related to the criminal justice system, both in graduate work and working in the criminal justice system. Secondly, students have increased their worldviews and perspectives on life and in learning about other cultures.

In summary, this course was created to provide students with many opportunities and to make students better global citizens. When creating the course, the Department of Criminal Justice Administration and its faculty realized an *instructional gap* in our Homeland Security concentration curriculum. Put simply, some of our graduates were hired as U.S. Customs and Border Protection officers/agents, yet they never had the opportunity to study abroad. Moreover, a Homeland Security agent should have some experience with other cultures and/or countries to better serve others. As such, our faculty created this program to fill this gap.

As our study abroad students complete this program and experience other cultures, even one as close to their own culture as the U.K., intercultural competencies and skills are reinforced. This will allow our graduates to increase their knowledge of the world, critically analyze policies and practices in the criminal justice system, and open their minds to further education abroad opportunities or connections in the future.

REFERENCES

Bennett, R., Aston, A., & Colquhoun, T. (2000). Cross-cultural training: A critical step in ensuring the success of international assignments. *Human Resource Management, 39*(2-3), 239–250. https://doi.org/10.1002/1099-050X(200022/23)39:2/3<239::AID-HRM12>3.0.CO;2-J

Deardorff, D. (2006). Identification and assessment of intercultural competence. *Journal of Students in International Education, 10*(3), 241–266. https://doi.org/10.1177/1028315306287002

Deardorff, D. K. (2012). Framework: Intercultural competence model. In K. Berardo & D. K. Deardorff (Eds.), *Building cultural competence: Innovative activities and models* (pp. 45-52). Stylus Publishing.

Tangney, S. (2014). Student-centered learning: A humanist perspective. *Teaching in Higher Education, 19*(3), 266–275. https://doi.org/10.1080/13562517.2013.860099

Terrill, R. J. (2015). *World criminal justice systems: A comparative survey* (9th ed.). Taylor & Francis. https://doi.org/10.4324/9781315624389

APPENDICES

Appendix 13.1: Program Itinerary

Day	Activity
1	Fly to Great Britain from Nashville
2	Walking tour of London; Clink Museum
3	Morning site seeing tour of London and visits to the Inns of Court and Royal Courts of Justice; Soho Gang Lecture
4	Old Bailey visits and Whitechapel (Jack the Ripper) tour; Police Museum
5	Supreme Court of U.K. and discussion with Metropolitan Police Officers
6	Tower of London; Cultural Excursions
7	Walking tour of Parliament and Buckingham Palace; Second talk with Metropolitan Police Officer
8	Travel to Nashville

Appendix 13.2: Final Project Guidelines, Course Schedule, and Expectations

Final Assignment

A presentation focusing on a specific aspect of comparative criminal justice including academic resources and experiential findings must include answers to the following five questions.

1. Describe the issue you focused on?
2. How is it approached/addressed in the U.S. and the U.K.?
3. How would you change the way it is approached/addressed in the U.S.? What obstacles might you encounter as you try to implement this change in the U.S.?
4. What did you learn on the trip that you can apply to your response?
5. How did this trip impact you – what did you find yourself focusing on as you experienced the different excursions? What are two things you will take back with you that has impacted either your life as a student, as a future practitioner/academic, or a general citizen of the U.S.?

Course Schedule

Date	Topics/Assignments	Delivery Method
Mon, May 13th	Lecture – Comparing the U.K. and the US; Discuss Readings; Logistics discussion	PDF documents emailed to students
Tues, May 14th	Work on preliminary information for project/Flex Day	PDF documents emailed to students
Sun., May 15th-22nd	London	
Fri., May 24th to Thur., May 31st	Complete presentation projects Discussion Board: One significant thing you got from the trip (Personal or Educational); how did this experience contribute to your education and/or career goals?	
May 31st	Presentations turned in to online course site Discussion Board respond to classmates	Online course site for presentations & Discussion Board

Communication Guidelines and Expectations

Class Expectations

- Attend class each day, arrive on time, and to stay the entire class period. If you have a situation in which you must arrive late or leave early, you need to speak with one of us.
- Attend all excursions in London; always spend time with a classmate – never go out alone; be back and rested so you do not miss anything.
- Be mindful of the behavioral expectations of the professors.
- Read the assigned material.
- Complete assignments by their deadlines.
- When you arrive in class, please turn off your phone OR turn it on vibrate and place it outside of your sight line. Do not "play on" your phone in any manner (texting, scrolling through Facebook, tweeting, etc.).

Expectations While Travelling

- Attend all tours and assigned activities
- Be respectful of everyone
- Keep up!
- Be responsible for yourself
- Budget properly

Chapter 14

Covering the Anniversary of D-Day in France: A Journalism Study Abroad Experience

Christine C. Eschenfelder

Note: Section II includes Chapters 4-14. These chapters use a standardized template to discuss the details of their respective study abroad programs and reference Deardorff's (2012) framework for intercultural competencies. The use of this template and the intercultural competencies framework are described in the Section II introduction. All courses in this section (except for Chapter 6) were taught through Middle Tennessee State University (MTSU), a mid-sized state school located in Murfreesboro, Tennessee (USA).

Journalism Special Topics: Covering the 75th Anniversary of D-Day was a course that took place in May and June of 2019. There was an in-country, study abroad component of the course occurring from May 21-29, 2019. This was the first course of its kind specific to the School of Journalism and Strategic Media (SOJSM) at MTSU. It was created specifically with the idea to allow student journalists to cover this historic event from England and France. The unique aspect of the course was to take journalism students from our university to England and France to cover the 75th anniversary of D-Day. The program was designed to retrace the steps of Allied troops who fought for freedom on June 6, 1944. The in-country portion of the class began in London (England), proceeded with a stop in Normandy (France), and concluded in Paris (France). Seven undergraduate students from MTSU took part in the course. The demographics of the students were five females and two males: four white students, two African American students, and one Asian student. One student identified as nontraditional.

THEORETICAL FOUNDATIONS

Inspired by Strange and Gibson (2017), a combination of two learning theories informed the framework for this course: Kolb's Experiential Learning Theory and Mezirow's Transformative Learning Theory. Strange and Gibson (2017) explain that Kolb's Experiential Learning Theory "provides direction as to how we can develop the type of action-oriented experience that is likely to induce transformation" (p. 88). Kolb and Kolb (2017) write that experiential learning creates a unique relationship between the teacher and the student, as both get to experience the subject matter. In the case of this study abroad program, I was actively learning in-country along with my students while also coaching and modeling. Experiential learning is the foundation of study abroad courses because, "using the cycle of learning, all participants receive information through concrete experience of the subject matter and transform it through reflection and conceptualization and then transform it again by acting to change the world" (Kolb & Kolb, 2017, p. 16). Kolb's cycle of learning consists of concrete experience, reflection, abstract thinking, and acting on what has been learned.

In Transformative Learning Theory, Mezirow (1978) suggested that reflecting on one's experiences can lead to a perspective transformation. These theories informed the desired learning outcomes for the course, and it was planned using a backward design. Harvey (2017) explains that backward design "simply means beginning with the end in mind…it is fundamental to designing significant, transformative intercultural learning" (p. 111).

COURSE DESCRIPTION

The theme of the course was a unique opportunity for student journalists to cover the 75th Anniversary of D-Day, the invasion of the beaches at Normandy in France by Allied troops during World War II. At the time, France was occupied by Nazi Germany. The D-Day invasion was an Allied victory and began the campaign to liberate France from Nazi Germany's occupation. Covering the event and learning more about it was achieved through visiting London, Normandy, and Paris. The objectives of the course were to provide journalism students an opportunity to experience newsgathering and life skills in other countries, create original media content for a news special, and follow industry standards for ethics and professionalism. Specific competencies included opportunities to learn, practice, explore, and apply journalism techniques. Students created original journalistic work about the anniversary of France's liberation from Nazi Germany in 1944 as well as general travel reporting on England and France. The students' original work became part of the special coverage of the anniversary by MTSU Student Media which was published and broadcast by the student media property "Middle Tennessee News" (Middle Tennessee News, 2019).

No textbooks were required as all the students enrolled had previously completed the required prerequisites in other courses. Students were encouraged to read and view materials about the D-Day invasion's history and basic French conversational language and etiquette abroad. Some of the films suggested included the award-winning film *Saving Private Ryan* (1998) directed by Steven Spielberg (Spielberg, 1998) and the television mini-series *Band of Brothers* (2001), with an emphasis on season one, episode two (Orloff & Loncraine, 2001). The Library of Congress has an expansive website with multimedia archival content (Library of Congress, n.d.), as does the Imperial War Museum (Imperial War Museums, n.d.). Travel author Rick Steves has excellent websites with information on England and France (Rick Steves' Europe, n.d.). The countries also have informative websites for foreign travelers (Explore France, n.d.; Visit Britain, n.d.). Language apps such as Babbel and Google Translate were suggested for those with limited French language skills.

While in-country, students used smartphones, cameras, and audio recorders to take photos, shoot videos, record audio, and conduct interviews relating to the D-Day anniversary. Upon return to the MTSU campus, the remainder of the summer session focused on writing and editing the stories. All the content created in-country was put together for a special multimedia website and television program that aired on the actual anniversary date of June 6, 2019.

Course Learning Outcomes

The learning outcomes for this course were similar to other journalism courses but additionally included outcomes related to the intercultural competency goals of the course. The learning outcomes for this course were:

a. Create and present original, professional quality media content for multiple platforms.
b. Demonstrate critical and creative thinking as well as problem-solving skills through work in the field and production of original media content.
c. Cultivate writing and storytelling craftsmanship.
d. Demonstrate knowledge of journalism in practice while following industry standards for ethics and professionalism.
e. Develop cultural self-awareness as well as an understanding of the diversity of peoples and cultures in a global society.
f. Students will step outside of their comfort zone in order to discover new cultures and worldviews.
g. Demonstrate general knowledge of World War II and the D-Day Invasion through story pitches, writing, and final original media content.

COURSE HISTORY

As a journalism instructor and former professional broadcast journalist, the idea for this study abroad experience was inspired in 2018. I was aware that the following year, 2019, would be the upcoming 75th anniversary of the World War II D-Day invasion. D-Day refers to June 6, 1944, when Allied forces consisting primarily of the United States, British, and Canadian troops launched the largest amphibious invasion in history. The Allied landings on the beaches of Normandy began the campaign to liberate Paris from Nazi occupation.

As I had covered many United States veterans' stories as a professional journalist, I believed this could be a rewarding and once-in-a-lifetime experience for a group of advanced and engaged journalism students. It would give students a unique opportunity to use the skills they had acquired in classes to date to collect stories in the field from an unfamiliar location. I also wanted to provide more study abroad opportunities for my journalism students at MTSU as none were currently being offered in the school. Further, I have personally traveled internationally many times and am aware of the transformative learning that travel provides.

The itinerary I drafted for student coverage of the D-Day anniversary was very detailed, so I thought it would be best to work with a third-party provider instead of doing all the planning and bookings myself, as it would require travel to multiple countries and locations. I contacted a third-party study abroad provider that had an existing itinerary for a World War II and Liberation of Paris tour. The company was one of the existing approved providers for MTSU education abroad programs.

The pre-designed itinerary the company offered was very much like the trip I had in mind. My correspondence with the company began in July 2018. I agreed to the terms for the trip with the third-party provider and submitted the study abroad class for approval in August 2018. It was approved by the MTSU School of Journalism and Strategic Media (SOJSM), and the College of Media and Entertainment that August and received final approval from the Office of International Education in September 2018. Upon approval, I began contacting journalism students about the class. The method of contact was within my own classes, other journalism classes, emails, university-wide study abroad fairs, and the MTSU Office of International Affairs. Seven students had successfully registered for the course by the February 2019 deadline. This deadline was set by the third-party provider to finalize airline, hotel, and other reservations.

While this study abroad course covered the one-time event of the 75th anniversary of D-Day, the class has since been continued but with changes to content and destinations. It is incumbent upon the journalism instructor to think proactively and consider or anticipate world events and travel opportunities well in advance of the next study abroad course. For example, I planned a study abroad trip to Paris in 2022 with the topic of "Paris Off the Beaten Path" as a travel reporting special for those traveling again after the COVID-19 pandemic. A study abroad trip which will run in the summer of 2023 will take place in England and Scotland as changes are anticipated following the death of Queen Elizabeth II and the beginning of the era of King Charles III.

COURSE LOGISTICS

Students in the class earned three credit hours. As a 4000-level course, primarily junior- or senior-level, all students enrolled were journalism majors who had already taken the pre-requisite classes. These prerequisites included foundational courses that developed skills in media writing, interviewing and reporting techniques, photography, audio recording, videography, and editing for video and audio. It was necessary to have at least a basic acquisition of these skills as they would be necessary in the field. When broadcast journalists are in the field, they must often work very quickly and under various environmental conditions including challenges with light, ambient sound, and lack of power outlets or internet connection. They are also usually under a strict time deadline. Broadcast journalists are tasked with shooting video at a location or collecting audio and finding people to interview on camera or via an audio recording. Many will also take photos to accompany their stories and post them to social media before, during, and/or after their story collection. Thus, there is not much time in a scenario like our coverage of the D-Day anniversary to do much teaching of basics in the field. As the instructor I did, of course, supervise, make suggestions, and provide guidance and assistance throughout the trip, but basic knowledge of equipment function and journalism methods was essential.

PRE-PROGRAM ACTIVITIES

Several pre-departure orientations took place on the MTSU campus, each lasting approximately one to three hours. During those sessions, we discussed the requirements of the class, rules for conduct, and emergency procedures. As this was a journalism class, students were required to gather journalistic content in various forms including photos, audio, and video. They were required to create content specifically for social media and post to social media frequently from England and France. Students were also required to edit their work for publication in student media outlets upon their return to the United States. In addition, students needed to conduct background research on World War II, the D-Day invasion, and other historic events and people surrounding the anniversary. As this special report was targeted at viewers in the Tennessee area, students were also required to locate veterans or others with special connections to D-Day to localize coverage.

A few days before departure, the class met on the MTSU campus for approximately two hours during which I disseminated equipment for student use in-country. The MTSU College of Media and Entertainment and the SOJSM offer free rentals of professional quality gear for student use. This gear is purchased primarily with student course fees. Journalism students enrolled in classes requiring the use of cameras, microphones, and other newsgathering equipment for completion of projects have access to this gear during fall, spring, and summer semesters through an online checkout system.

For this study abroad trip, my students used several types of gear including the Canon 80D, which is a digital single-lens reflex camera or DSLR camera. This camera shoots still photos and video and is quite user-friendly, dependable, and easy to carry in the field. A few students were given Sony 100 video cameras to use in-country. These are professional-quality video cameras. Students using the Sony 100 cameras were issued tripods to use with the camera. Professional-quality lavalier microphones, which are small clip-on microphones, were distributed along with headphones to monitor audio. The MTSU SOJSM also purchased several additional items, especially for use in study abroad classes including travel adapters. I answered any questions students had about gear and reminded them of proper care and use of the equipment. I also made sure they all had or planned to purchase SD cards on which to record media. We went over final packing suggestions and the plans to meet at the Nashville International Airport.

Most of the camera gear can be safely packed in checked or carry-on baggage provided it is wrapped carefully in some protective material or padding. Lithium-ion batteries must be packed in carry-on luggage as noted by the Federal Aviation Administration. The gear does take up some additional space in luggage which students and faculty should be aware of ahead of time. Faculty could elect to transport video cameras and tripods in professional hard-sided camera cases such as Pelican brand cases. This would require extra checked baggage and the resulting extra baggage fees. Some faculty may choose to incorporate mobile journalism methods in-country requiring smaller gear such as smartphones, small tablets, and smaller tripods for these devices as well as the complementary microphones. On a subsequent study abroad trip to Paris in 2022, we utilized camera-friendly padded backpacks for the transport of camera gear. The backpacks were used as carry-ons during flights and in the field while in-country.

CLASS ACTIVITIES & INTERCULTURAL COMPETENCIES

We departed Nashville, Tennessee on May 21, 2019, and arrived in London on May 22, 2019. For some students, this was their first experience with international travel, which in itself was transformative. The process, from getting the passport to deplaning in a foreign country and finally returning home, gives students confidence that their world has no boundaries. It creates a sense of agency and self-confidence.

We met our trip guide at the London Heathrow Airport who introduced us to another group of students that would be accompanying us on our adventure. The third-party provider paired our MTSU group with a study abroad group from a different university. These students were not journalism students, which offered an opportunity for multidisciplinary interaction. My students ended up engaging the others in some reporting and photography lessons which were very rewarding to watch as an instructor. The students from the other school and their faculty leaders shared transportation with us, accompanied us on all the tours, and stayed in the same hotels. While the class was in-country, I supervised, coached, and mentored my students in the field as they took still photos, shot video, conducted interviews, and did on-camera work to be used later for the television special, which aired on the MTSU student media property Middle Tennessee News (Middle Tennessee News, 2019).

While in London, the group took a walking tour of the city, including a visit to the Imperial War Museum. The students told me that the exhibits at the museum made an impression on them and sparked further curiosity and story ideas. These exhibits told the story of World War II primarily from the United Kingdom's perspective. Getting a chance to view events from a global perspective was a transformative moment. We were also given a crash course on how to navigate the London Underground, or "the Tube" from a London native. This provided an excellent opportunity to get my students out of their comfort zone, creating both a robust transformative and experiential learning opportunity. It was transformative in that public transportation in unfamiliar cities can be a bit disorienting, but students rose to the challenge. It was also experiential in nature as they had the concrete experience of navigating London's public transportation, and the resulting reflective observation occurred when students completed their social media posts about the experience. This is a transformative experience because MTSU's student population primarily consists of commuters who drive their own vehicles to and from campus and are not accustomed to public transportation (U.S. News & World Report, 2023).

That evening, all the students on the trip attended a fish and chips dinner in London. This also created transformative and experiential learning moments. Not only was it an opportunity for the MTSU students to get to know the student group from the other university, but it also helped them become more comfortable with their own peers from MTSU. Shared meals can often help groups bond. Dining together encourages conversation and allows for the shared cultural experience of new foods and environments (Deardorff, 2012). They also had the experience of tasting an authentic British meal and reflecting on it on social media. Not being from the generation of digital natives, I am always interested in how so many young people take photos of their food and share those photos on social media. This is one of the reasons I have come to require the use of social media in my study abroad class because it provides a quick and easy way to reflect on culture and act on concrete experiences which can be shared easily and is a skill most students have already obtained.

As students shared hotel rooms, it was important to provide moments early in the trip for them to become better acquainted, thus more comfortable in their temporary living arrangements. On this trip, the third-party company arranged for all the students to be assigned to shared rooms based on biological gender, with MTSU students rooming with students of the same gender from the other university. Faculty and older students were given single rooms. The next day, the group took a WWII-themed guided tour of London which included a visit to the Cabinet War Rooms where Prime Minister Churchill and the Allied Commanders planned the Allied war effort. Students were engaged with the locations and took many photos and videos. I observed a growing sense of self-awareness among the students. Perhaps they were quite keen to take in as much of London as possible as this was our last night in the city. They had already overcome some of the challenges of being in foreign surroundings, but we were still in a country that speaks English as the primary language.

On Friday, May 24, the group departed London for Caen. We traveled by ferry across the English Channel to the Normandy region of France, the same route used by Allied naval forces. Students said the ferry ride was quite enjoyable as many of them had never used this form of transportation. It was amusing as there was also a group of very rambunctious French secondary school students aboard the ferry. This provided a unique opportunity to observe a different aspect of French culture. The time aboard the ferry also provided yet another chance for students to form bonds over lunch and shared experiences.

On Saturday, May 25, 2019, the group toured the D-Day beaches of Normandy with an expert local guide. We boarded a tour bus, and the guide provided a history lesson on the D-Day invasion and the significance of the sights we were about to see. The timing of the trip, just days before the actual 75th anniversary, was beneficial. Many tourists had come to the area for the anniversary, providing ample opportunities for interviews and b-roll, which is video used when creating television news-style stories. Students gathered many photos, videos, and interviews at Pointe du Hoc. This is a promontory with 110-foot cliffs located between the Utah and Omaha Beaches and is the location of the World War II Pointe du Hoc American Ranger Monument.

The stops at Omaha Beach and the Normandy American Cemetery and Memorial had a profound effect on everyone. My students took many photos and videos on Omaha Beach. This was also the location where many of them recorded themselves on the beach for use in their video stories and social media. They were very respectful of the solemnity of this location, however, and handled themselves accordingly. Knowing we would be visiting this site, several students brought small glass bottles in which they collected a bit of sand.

At the Normandy American Cemetery, the sight of so many white crosses in lines along the green grass gave everyone pause. Again, all were respectful of the somberness of this location. In just a few days, the United States President would be here at the cemetery to attend the anniversary ceremony along with thousands of other visitors. During our tour, students were able to see workers busy erecting stages and setting up seating for the ceremony. The tour that day also included a visit to the Caen Memorial and Arromanches. The post-experience reflections and creation of journalistic content with media collected this day demonstrated the transformative effect of this part of the itinerary. Students wrote with much candor and emotion about how moved they became while touring the sites and talking with people at various locations. They also took great care in selecting the best photos, video, and audio for their stories which showed the respect they had for the content.

On Sunday, May 26, 2019, the group boarded a bus and traveled via Rouen to Paris, with a brief tour of the Rouen. Students had the opportunity to attend a Catholic Mass at the stunning gothic Rouen Cathedral and walk along the historic streets. About two hours later, the scenery changed dramatically. We had arrived at the final stop of our adventure, Paris. There was quite a bit of excitement when the students woke from a short nap to see the Parisian skyline. After checking in to the hotel, we embarked on a walking tour of the Latin Quarter. Unfortunately, just weeks before our arrival, the Notre Dame Cathedral was engulfed by a massive fire. We were only able to view the 12th-century Gothic landmark from afar, but seeing the beautiful cathedral was a memorable moment. Later that day, we boarded a boat for a breathtaking tour of the Seine River where we once again were treated to a view of Notre Dame and many other Parisian landmarks including the Louvre. Students took many photos and videos from the boat.

The following day was dedicated to a tour of Paris with sites including Place de la Concorde, the Champs-Élysées, Arc de Triomphe, and a glimpse of the exterior of the Eiffel Tower and Hôtel des Invalides. We were aboard a tour bus with a guide who provided details about each location. We were able to get off the bus for the Arc de Triomphe and walk for just a few minutes on arguably the most famous street in the world, Champs-Élysées. While there, the group announced to me and the tour guide that they needed to use the bathrooms. Our French guide told us that the only way to accomplish this considering our location next to the Arc de Triomphe with our bus driver waiting was to pop into a nearby café and order a coffee at the standing counter. Upon drinking our coffee, the establishment would allow us to use the bathrooms, so that is exactly what we did. It was a wonderful way to experience the culture and adapt to an unfamiliar situation.

Our day took a much more somber note as we toured the Shoah Holocaust Memorial and Museum in Paris. I do not recall the group taking many photos at this location. We were all so full of emotion and empathy. The exhibitions that tell the stories and describe the horrors of the extermination of nearly six million Jews gave us all a chance to reflect on the past and the atrocities of war.

As we returned to the streets of Paris, we shifted our focus once again to gaining some intercultural competency skills, such as developing confidence and independence via the public transportation system (Deardorff, 2012). With Paris Metro tickets in hand, the group was forced to navigate the trains back to our hotel. While we would encounter a few Metro mishaps during our stay in Paris, I believe those encounters are among the most salient learning experiences. Students were also becoming somewhat more confident in their basic conversational French language skills. The language apps came in quite handy. I noticed the students were all venturing out on their own to do some shopping and tasting of new foods. They were acting on the new information and skills acquired in the last few days. It was rewarding as a teacher to see their courage and excitement.

The following day, Tuesday, May 28, 2019, was our last full day in Paris. It was a free day for the group. Some chose to tour Versailles, attend a tennis match at the French Open, do some shopping, or visit some museums. That evening, we all gathered in the Latin Quarter for a farewell dinner at a quaint French bistro. The following morning, we checked out of our hotel and the bus took us to Charles de Gaulle airport for our flight home (See Appendix 14.1 for a tabular program itinerary).

Task: Public Transportation

While not related to developing journalism skills, using public transportation in both England and France was one of the most important lessons in developing intercultural competency, which has been defined as "a set of cognitive, affective, and behavioral skills and characteristics that support effective and appropriate interaction in a variety of cultural contexts" (Bennett, 2008, p. 97). One of the most important benefits of study abroad is gaining an understanding of the world and different cultures.

As Deardorff (2012) notes, "attitude is a fundamental starting point" (p. 255). Attitudes change when students are curious, as well as when they must step out of their comfort zones and learn to adapt in a foreign place. Most of my students do not use public transportation on a regular basis. MTSU is in a suburban area without a robust public transportation system. This made it a bit more difficult for them to navigate the London Underground and Paris Metro, but they were quite successful, save for a few mistakes here and there. I often allowed the students to take the lead on navigation. It became a wonderful display of teamwork and a rewarding challenge when we arrived at the right stop.

It was also a chance for the students to watch people on board the trains. When they became curious and started to observe the other passengers they noticed the manner, dress, and actions of the British and French commuters. It became apparent that the French were much quieter and more reserved than our effervescent American group. British and French passengers also appeared very well-dressed. At times, our group stood before a map at a station apparently looking quite lost. Several times, locals in London and Paris offered us assistance. This was welcomed by the students who remarked on what was an unexpected kindness shown by strangers. See Appendix 14.2 for the guidelines on this task. As noted in Table 14.1, specific knowledge, skills, and attitudes were acquired or developed by students using public transportation while abroad. On the surface, public transportation may appear to be useful only for budgetary reasons or quicker travel around a busy city such as London or Paris, but there are numerous benefits for students.

Table 14.1: Intercultural Competencies for Public Transportation Task

Knowledge	Skills	Attitudes
<ul><li>Culture-specific knowledge (navigating public transportation)</li><li>Cultural self-awareness</li></ul>	<ul><li>Problem-solving</li><li>Teamwork</li><li>Technology skills</li><li>Analyze</li><li>Observe</li></ul>	<ul><li>Confidence</li><li>Flexibility</li><li>Discovery</li><li>Patience</li><li>Willingness to go out of comfort zone</li><li>Resilience</li><li>Risk-taking</li></ul>

Task: Experiencing Local Cuisine

Attitudes again played a role in developing intercultural competencies when the students enthusiastically sampled unfamiliar foods with an open mind. Eating out in England and France was a different experience, especially in France when the language was harder to navigate. Food is entwined with culture. Smells and tastes elicit memories and remind us of home or meaningful experiences. The difference in food domestically can vary, but once in another country, new tastes can be exciting and a bonding experience. Many travel memories revolve around food and dining, and this trip was no different. It is no coincidence that the third-party provider included intentional dining experiences, a welcome dinner, lunches during day trips, and a lovely farewell meal. Breakfast was included at all the hotels where we stayed during the trip: one hotel in London, one in Normandy, and one in Paris. The food offerings at breakfast were very different in all three locations.

As a faculty member, each morning was a rewarding experience as I observed and interacted with the students over breakfast. Many of them had questions about my soft-boiled egg in Normandy as they had not seen an egg prepared in that manner. In London, we were treated to several types of sausage. It was something of an adventure to figure out what type of sausages they were and how they tasted. My students were also of the generation which enjoys photographing their food and posting pictures to social media. As a result, I saw many trip photos that featured delicious, or otherwise remarkable, dishes as the subject.

If I did not dine with the students for a particular meal, I often asked them about their adventures in gastronomy that day. I was delighted that they all seemed to take risks and order something unfamiliar. In France, those with limited language skills sometimes ended up with a dish they had not intended to order but savored the experience if not so much the taste. We joked about avoiding the American fast food chain McDonald's while in England and France, but I will admit that the taste of home was enjoyed a few times by my students and their teacher. We even compared the taste of a French cheeseburger to its American counterpart. Many of the students remarked that "everything tastes better in Paris." See Appendix 14.2 for the guidelines on this task. Table 14.2 identifies some of the knowledge, skills, and attitudes that can be learned or developed by experiencing local cuisine. Unfamiliar foods and dining experiences have many potential learning opportunities for students abroad.

Table 14.2: Intercultural Competencies for Experiencing Local Cuisine Task

Knowledge	Skills	Attitudes
• Cultural understanding • Cultural self-awareness	• Evaluate • Observe • Communication • Relate	• Stepping outside of comfort zone • Respect • Flexibility • Open-minded • Risk-taking

Assignment: Pre-Production Research

The first assignment for this course involved a good amount of pre-departure research. The topics for research included general cultural knowledge about England and France but emphasized knowledge of World War II and D-Day, as coverage of the 75th Anniversary of D-Day was the purpose and focus of our trip. This knowledge was essential. Journalists must always conduct research for the stories they are covering. In the case of the anniversary of D-Day, the journalism students could not ask informed questions without this general knowledge. Further, they also needed information on local ties to the D-Day anniversary in order to tell stories relevant to our local angle of the event.

Deardorff (2012) points out that among the four developmental stages created by the American Council on International Intercultural Education is general knowledge of history and world events. This assignment facilitated at least some acquisition of that general knowledge, which was enough information in order to carry out journalism practices. However, I observed that this newly acquired knowledge also led to empathy and respect in their understanding of the differences in the way United States citizens experienced World War II compared with the citizens of England and France. Deardorff (2012) notes that the first stage of development is openness to other cultures, values, and attitudes and "that the first stage was most important to all global learners" (p. 256). I found that the research assignment aided in the students' openness to aspects of the cultures they were about to experience. See Appendix 14.3 for the guidelines on this task.

Research into locations and culture before traveling to a different country can make travel much more rewarding as it helps the traveler better understand and appreciate context. For journalism students, this was an essential task; journalists research stories beforehand in order to get information and context. Table 14.3 identifies the knowledge, skills, and attitudes developed by students by doing pre-production research for this study abroad course.

Table 14.3: Intercultural Competencies for Pre-Production Research Assignment

Knowledge	Skills	Attitudes
- General knowledge of England and France and World War II - Understanding others' worldviews	- Technology - Analyze - Interpret - Teamwork	- Curiosity - Empathy - Discovery

Activity: Story Gathering in the Field

All students in the course were required to gather and create original media content from the field while in-country for the television and online special. This required them to carry out tasks such as taking photographs, conducting interviews, and collecting audio while in England and France. Through their journalistic work, they were interacting with locals and communicating with people who often did not speak the same language. I found that the students naturally divided themselves into teams and tended to work in those teams throughout the trip. There was an odd number of students in the group. One of my students teamed up with a student from the other university group. This worked out very well as they shared similar personalities and interests. My journalism student even taught the other student a bit about photography and social media. The teams that self-selected their own team members seemed to develop from prior familiarity on campus.

As I observed the teams in the field, I was pleased with their enthusiasm for the topics we were covering and their interaction with people in various locations. One example took place at the Caen Memorial. One of the student teams noticed a young French boy dressed in an American military uniform. They were naturally curious and approached his parents. The family spoke French and not much English. One of our travel companions who was fluent in French was able to interpret and my students conducted a touching interview about the young boy who was dressed in the uniform to honor the role of the American soldiers who helped liberate France. My students demonstrated curiosity, observational skills, flexibility, and adaptability and left that interview with a new sense of understanding others' worldviews. See Appendix 14.4 for the guidelines on this task. Competencies gained by students during the story gathering activities are outlined below in Table 14.4.

Table 14.4: Intercultural Competencies for Story Gathering Activity

Knowledge	Skills	Attitudes
• Journalistic field methods • Multimedia story gathering • Cultural understanding • Understanding others' worldviews	• Observation • Teamwork • Technology • Listen • Relate • Communication • Creative thinking	• Flexibility • Adaptability • Patience • Respect • Curiosity • Discovery

Activity: Travel Journals

Students in the class were required to complete several social media posts and travel journal posts during and after the trip. Many of the travel journals were done as video or photo slide show posts. Some students submitted these individually, but one self-appointed team of young women enjoyed doing their video posts together. I was impressed with the professional quality of all the students' work but also with the detail and candor of the content. The most salient intercultural competencies revealed in these travel journals included the level of cultural self-awareness, open-mindedness, and discovery.

The prompt for these social media posts and travel journals was quite simple. Take us along with you on an adventure or reflect on something you experienced, observed, or felt. The submissions varied from euphoria at the top of the Eiffel Tower to reverence while standing on the sands of Omaha Beach. Each student allowed themselves to be open and vulnerable and truly feel the weight or joy of the moment. I believe this freedom of expression and openness to the surroundings came in part from the freedom of the activity; there was no time pressure or tedious rubric. Some students are not comfortable with ambiguity, so I was delighted at how cheerfully this group embraced this activity. I think this is yet another activity that demonstrates this group's level of intercultural competency. It goes back to attitude as a fundamental aspect of and for success. See Appendix 14.5 for the guidelines on this task. Specific knowledge, skills, and attitudes cultivated through the travel journal activity are detailed in Table 14.5. These competencies also align with course objectives.

Table 14.5: Intercultural Competencies for Travel Journal Activity

Knowledge	Skills	Attitudes
• Cultural Self-awareness • Cultural understanding	• Creative thinking • Articulation • Evaluate • Technology • Interpret	• Curiosity • Open-minded • Discovery • Risk-taking • Flexibility

Assignment: Media Content and Post-Production

This essential assignment required students to edit together the media they collected in-country upon their return to the U.S. These included photo slideshows, audio pieces, and television news packages as well as recording on-camera presentations for the television special. There was a great deal of reflection in this assignment. In the excitement of being in the moment, we may not fully appreciate the profound composition of a photo we have taken or the beauty of the play of light in another. During an interview we recorded, we may have heard the words spoken by the subject but not noticed the subtleties in their body language or facial expressions. Upon reviewing our photos and other media, I noticed the students almost reliving the moments and discovering things in their work they had not noticed or fully appreciated at the time. Their sincere appreciation and affection for the people and places we encountered was evident as well as their journalism and technology skills. They had all made wonderful discoveries, even though at times it was challenging to work under a deadline in unfamiliar surroundings. The television special and website they were working on also gave them a chance to share their adventures with the world, which was very motivating. See Appendix 14.4 for the guidelines on this task. Post-production tasks offer opportunities for the development of specific knowledge as well as numerous skills and attitudes as noted in Table 14.6.

Table 14.6: Intercultural Competencies for Post-production Assignments

Knowledge	Skills	Attitudes
• Academic content knowledge • Cultural understanding • Cultural self-awareness	• Creative thinking • Teamwork • Leadership • Technology • Interpret • Analyze • Evaluate • Listen • Communication skills	• Curiosity • Discovery • Risk-taking • Tolerance for ambiguity • Patience • Resilience • Flexibility

POST-PROGRAM AND FUTURE CLASS ACTIVITIES

Upon return to the U.S., we gathered again on campus to write and edit stories. The time spent on post-production varied among the students depending on the medium (video, audio, etc.), but was approximately 15 to 20 hours. Once all the media was completed, a colleague and I worked with students to create the website and television special. Two students from the class served as presenters for the television special. Those two students recorded introductions to various stories on the MTSU campus at the Veteran's Memorial. One of the other students also recorded an on-camera introduction to a story he completed for the special. These on-camera recordings took about three to four hours. Once everything had been completed, the website and tv special went live.

Before we resumed work on campus, I gave myself and my students a couple of days to rest and unpack. A few days later, we gathered again on campus to review all the media we collected, then to write and edit stories and other content. There was much laughter and reminiscing. Students also returned the equipment they borrowed for the trip.

Future Class Activity Ideas

This course was conducted in 2019 and was so successful that I had already launched another study abroad class for the summer of 2020, but the COVID-19 pandemic created challenges that did not allow for this to take place. I incorporated lessons learned from the 2019 trip into future trips, including a study abroad trip I led to Paris in 2022. I again used a third-party provider, but I asked for more free time for students to explore on their own or just enjoy some downtime as well as more time for student journalists to gather media at various locations. I also dedicated myself to spending more leisure time with the students. This allows me to make more observations and enjoy more interactions with them over meals and other diversions. I find these casual moments are when I observe the students stepping out of their comfort zone and showing their resilience and cultural self-awareness.

EVALUATIONS AND ASSIGNMENTS

The grading criteria for the course was as follows:

Original Content and Stories	65%
Social Media and Travel Journals	35%

When evaluating all submissions, I looked for indicators of intercultural competencies but did not specifically measure those competencies for evaluation. I did, however, include evidence of competencies in my feedback to students. Much of my evaluation related to the quality of journalistic skills and practice. Original content and stories were summative in nature as they were heavily weighted and demonstrated student proficiency in storytelling and production skills. Sample rubrics were provided to students based on the format of their media content. The rubric for the Newswriting was evaluated on organization, lead and writing, objectivity and accuracy, AP Style conventions, and headline writing. Scores ranged from a 1 for inadequate work to a 6 for excellent work with specific benchmarks and indicators for each numeric score. The Broadcast Story assignment rubric was also scored on a range of points, from 1 for inadequate work and up to 4 for excellent work. Specific benchmarks and indicators were also described in each point range. Broadcast story criteria included organization, story topic, video, videography, editing, lighting, audio, writing, and performance. The social media and travel journals were formative as they helped students take ownership of the experience and reflect on the process.

STUDENT FEEDBACK

Students offered positive verbal feedback on the trip. No written feedback was submitted. One of the students on this 2019 trip had already registered for a similar trip I was planning to lead in 2020; however, that trip was canceled due to the COVID-19 pandemic. That same student used materials from the study abroad trip for their undergraduate honors thesis which was outstanding and very well-received. Students were also delighted with the results of our website and television special. They swept state and regional awards, including the Tennessee Associated Press student awards, with judges for one contest calling the website "a multimedia masterpiece." This was a great source of pride and accomplishment for the students.

CAVEATS AND REFLECTIONS

This course was an outstanding experience for both myself as the instructor and I believe for the students as well. The strengths include the unique opportunity to help students develop intercultural competencies through careful planning of the activities, assignments, tasks, and itinerary. Utilizing a backward course design that begins with the desired outcomes yields a course that offers robust intercultural engagement. Another strength specific to my discipline is giving journalism students first-hand experience working in the field under often challenging circumstances. This strength can also be a challenge as it relates to the use of the third-party provider. The itinerary used in this trip had been created by the provider and as such was not customized for either journalism students or my specific requests as faculty. While much of the itinerary was ideal, the time allotted for stops in various locations often did not allow my students much time to conduct interviews or gather photos and videos.

Further, our MTSU group was paired with a study abroad group from a different university. These students were not journalism students. They accompanied us on the tour bus and on all the tours. Fortunately, the faculty and students from the other university were very accommodating and even assisted us with some of the story gathering and photography. However, my group often caused a delay in the schedule because we requested a few extra minutes at various locations to gather media.

This course plays an important role in the overall mission of my school, college, and university as we seek to provide the most robust experiential and engaged learning opportunities possible. Students come to us seeking theory and practice. Classes such as this and other study abroad classes campus-wide offer students that chance. However, a significant challenge in offering study abroad classes at MTSU is the ability of some students to afford the cost of these courses. The MTSU Office of International Affairs does offer generous scholarships but some students still remark to me that they would love to go on a study abroad class but do not have the means. Another challenge related to cost is duration. Of course, a longer in-country experience means a higher cost. Strange and Gibson (2017) found that a short-term study abroad trip can be as transformative as a semester or year-long experience if the duration is longer than 18 days. I increased the length of my subsequent 2022 Paris study abroad trip to two weeks, but the result was a higher cost and lower enrollment. It is my goal to plan future trips of two-to-three-weeks in length which will require great attention to the budget to keep the program as affordable as possible.

Some of the benefits of offering this course with the inclusion of intercultural competencies are that it allows students to be actively engaged in and be aware of their growth as citizens of the world. As they are aware of the markers of intercultural competency, students will be more cognizant as these skills develop.

REFERENCES

Bennett, J. M. (2008). Transformative training: Designing programs for culture learning. In M. A. Moodian (Ed.), *Contemporary leadership and intercultural competence: Understanding and utilizing cultural diversity to build successful organizations* (pp. 95-110). Sage Publishing.

Deardorff, D. K. (2012). Framework: Intercultural competence model. In K. Berardo & D. K. Deardorff (Eds.), *Building cultural competence: Innovative activities and models* (pp. 45-52). Stylus Publishing.

Explore France. (n.d.). https://www.france.fr/en

Fink, L. D. (2013). *Creating significant learning experiences: An integrated approach to designing college courses* (2nd ed.). Jossey-Bass.

Harvey, T. A. (2017). Design and pedagogy for transformative intercultural learning. In B. Kappler Mikk & I. Steglitz (Eds.), *Learning across cultures: Locally and globally* (3rd ed., pp. 109-138). NAFSA: Association of International Educators/Stylus.

Imperial War Museums. (n.d.). https://www.iwm.org.uk/

Kolb, A. Y., & Kolb, D. A. (2017). Experiential learning theory as a guide for experiential educators in higher education. *Experiential Learning & Teaching in Higher Education (ELTHE): A Journal for Engaged Educators, 1*(1), 7–44. https://nsuworks.nova.edu/elthe/vol1/iss1/7

Library of Congress. (n.d.). https://www.loc.gov/

Mezirow, J. (1978). Perspective transformation. *Adult Education Quarterly, 28*, 100-110. http://dx.doi.org/10.1177/074171367802800202

Mezirow, J. (1991). Transformative dimensions of adult learning. Jossey-Bass.

Middle Tennessee News. (2019). *75th Anniversary of D-Day*. https://www.middletennesseenews.net/special-report-d-day

Orloff, J. [Writer], & Loncraine, R. [Director]. (2001, September 9). Day of days (Season 1, Episode 2) [TV series episode]. In S. Spielberg & T. Hanks (Executive Producers), *Band of brothers*. Playtone; DreamWorks Television; HBO Entertainment; British Broadcasting Corporation.

Rick Steves' Europe. (n.d.). https://www.ricksteves.com/

Spielberg, S. (Director). (1998). *Saving Private Ryan* [Film]. Amblin Entertainment; Mutual Film Company.

Strange, H., & Gibson, H. J. (2017). An investigation of experiential and transformative learning in study abroad programs. *Frontiers: The Interdisciplinary Journal of Study Abroad, 29*(1), 85–100. https://doi.org/10.36366/frontiers.v29i1.387

U.S. News & World Report. (2023). *Middle Tennessee State University student life*. https://www.usnews.com/best-colleges/middle-tennessee-state-university-3510/student-life

Visit Britain. (n.d.). https://www.visitbritain.com/en

Wiggins, G. J., & McTighe, J. (2005). *Understanding by design* (2nd ed.). Pearson.

APPENDICES

Appendix 14.1: Program Itinerary

Date	Activity
May 13-20, 2019	Pre-departure activities on campus
May 21, 2019	Depart Nashville airport
May 22, 2019	Arrive London airport (Heathrow): Take a walking tour of London including Strand, Trafalgar Square, Leicester Square, and Covent Garden. Visit the Imperial War Museum, enjoy a fish and chips dinner in London, and check in at hotel
May 23, 2019	Take a WWII-themed guided tour of London including the Cabinet War Rooms in which Prime Minister Churchill and the Allied Commanders planned the Allied war effort
May 24, 2019	Caen, Normandy Region: Check out of London hotel then travel by ferry from Portsmouth to the Normandy region of France along the same route used by Allied naval forces
May 25, 2019	Normandy Region: Tour the D-Day beaches of Normandy with an expert local guide. Visit the Caen Memorial, Pointe du Hoc, Normandy American Cemetery and Memorial, and Arromanches
May 26, 2019	Caen, Rouen, Paris: Travel via Rouen to Paris, tour Rouen with Tour Director and visit the Rouen Cathedral; ride on bus to Paris with walking tour stops in the Latin Quarter and Notre Dame; cruise on the Seine River and check into hotel
May 27, 2019	Paris: bus tour with sights including Place de la Concorde, Champs-Élysées, Arc de Triomphe, Eiffel Tower, visit the Shoah Holocaust memorial and museum
May 28, 2019	Open day for storytelling in Paris; farewell dinner in Paris
May 29-30, 2019	Depart for Nashville from Paris (De Gaulle)/Arrive in Nashville
June 3-5, 2019	Finalize writing, editing, recording special

Appendix 14.2: Public Transportation and Experiencing Local Cuisine Task Guidelines

Some tickets and passes for public transportation were provided in the program cost. Students were given a brief introduction on how to navigate the Underground and Metro and were encouraged to use public transportation as often as possible in order to achieve some measure of intercultural competency. Eating in restaurants with local cuisine was encouraged by faculty and the tour guides. There were no specific guidelines noted in the syllabus for these two tasks, as these were meant to be organic experiences, but these skills were clearly communicated in the syllabus as a course outcome.

Appendix 14.3: Pre-Production Research Assignment Guidelines

To understand the historical and cultural impact of the locations on this trip itinerary, it was essential to conduct pre-departure research on World War II, D-Day, local ties to D-Day and World War II, and cultural information on England and France. Using suggested sources of materials for research, students were instructed to prepare a general body of knowledge as an aid in-country. Students were directed to sample materials provided in the course description. There were no additional articulated guidelines in the syllabus. I did have discussions with the students to gauge their amount of preparation. Tour guides also provided background information in-country.

Appendix 14.4: Story Gathering in the Field Activity and Completion of Media Content and Post-Production Assignment Guidelines

This activity and assignment are connected as is the case in journalistic practice. As the class consisted of journalism students, they already were aware of how to conduct themselves in the field to gather media content.

Students will complete original media content primarily in-country, which will be published and/or broadcast on student media properties as part of this course. Content may be created for several platforms including video, audio, and photojournalism. Students will identify several topics and angles of interest before departure and during the in-country experience. After considering several topics and angles, students will decide on the focus of their stories. Some stories may present themselves in the field, so students should be observant and prepared to cover stories on the spot. In many cases, you will research your topic, collecting sources for your background research. If at all possible, try to make a local connection in order to localize your topic through local individuals and organizations within the local area that can address the issue in Middle Tennessee (such as local World War II veterans). Do not be afraid to approach people in-country, even if there is a language barrier.

Students will capture original photos, audio, and video as well as interviews and natural sound. The visuals and interviews should be original work. When capturing video, use a tripod to make the images as steady and clear as possible. Photos with audio and natural sound are very engaging. Students may also create graphics to help visually tell portions of the story such as maps, data charts, photos with text, quotes, or compelling statistics.

Audio stories must include visuals so there isn't just a black screen visible while the audio is playing. Photo essays must have captions or student-created slideshows with audio narration. Television broadcast packages must have professional quality video, natural sound, interviews with excellent audio, and preferably a reporter stand-up. These will also need to be written, tracked, and edited. Running time for audio and television stories will vary, but most will run approximately 1:30-3:30 minutes. Please see the rubrics for the specific standards.

Appendix 14.5: Travel Journals Activity Guidelines

Students will complete several social media posts and multimedia travel journals during the in-country portion of the class. For these assignments, students will reflect on in-country experiences utilizing various media platforms. Students will be tasked with showcasing how they have internalized and experienced the world around them. Print-focused submissions are approximately 700 words, double-spaced, in Times New Roman 12-point font with one-inch margins. Indent the paragraphs. You will be judged on the clarity of your writing, the coherence of your thoughts, and how well you communicate your personal reflections. All submissions, including social media posts, must include professional-quality photos or videos. Please present yourself in a professional manner. Refrain from profanity. Prompts include showing us a location, event, or other cultural experience and telling us your reactions. How did it make you feel? How did it taste? What emotions were you feeling? How did those around you appear or act? What surprised you? What were you not expecting? How can you describe what this is like to those who have never experienced it? What are the smells? What are the sounds? How has this changed your thinking?

Section III
Moving Forward in Short-Term, Faculty-Led Study Abroad Programs

Chapter 15

Conclusion

Seok Jeng Jane Lim and Priya Ananth

> *A nation's culture resides in the hearts and in the soul of its people.*
>
> —Mahatma Gandhi—

This famous quote by Gandhi (Mahatma Gandhi Quotes, n.d.) captures the essence of our discussion on describing intercultural engagement as associated with short-term, faculty-led study abroad programs across multiple disciplines. Through the chapters in this book, we have seen that intercultural engagement begins with intercultural thinking and an intercultural mindset. Without simultaneous changes in learners' attitudes and mindsets, no amount of content knowledge can make a significant difference in the learning process. If a nation's culture indeed resides in the hearts and in the souls of its people, then it becomes critically important to incorporate elements of intercultural engagement directly aligning with the development of intercultural competencies, such as inclusion, withholding judgment, and empathy (AAC&U, 2009), into the course curriculum and pedagogical practices in study abroad programs. It is our hope that this edited volume has been able to provide ideas and multiple perspectives to achieve that very purpose.

Throughout this book, we have seen that intercultural engagement is relevant to all disciplines. We summarize the main points from the preceding 11 chapters to provide readers with a space to start their own process of visualizing and (re)constructing an interculturally-engaging course curriculum for a faculty-led study abroad program.

SUMMARY OF CHAPTERS

The 11 case studies of short-term, faculty-led study abroad programs, presented in Section II of the book, are summarized and organized into the following four sub-sections:

- Theoretical Foundations
- Intercultural Competencies in Class Activities, Tasks, and Assignments
- Student Feedback
- Caveats and Reflections

Theoretical Foundations

Table 15.1 shows the theoretical foundations used by each faculty leader in Section II.

Table 15.1: Summary of Theoretical Foundations

Program Name	Discipline	Theoretical Foundations
Administering Early Childhood Program in Singapore	Education	Global citizenship scale, experiential learning theory
MTSU in Japan	Liberal Arts	Experiential, thematic-based, backward design approach
USF Japan: Culture, History, and Society	Liberal Arts	Constructivist, experiential learning theory, collaborative
MTSU Summer in Normandy	Liberal Arts	Experiential learning theory, VARK modalities, ACTFL OPI
Cuba in the 21st Century	Liberal Arts	Imaginative geographies, experiential learning, place-based education
MTSU in Scotland	Liberal Arts	Experiential learning, place-based education, thematic approach
The History of Western Art Music in Vienna	Liberal Arts	Experiential, reflective, collaborative, integrative, transformative learning theory
International Management: Globalization in China	Business	Experiential learning theory
Criminal Justice in London	Behavioral and Health Sciences	Constructivist, experiential learning theory, integrative approach
International Agriculture (in Argentina)	Basic and Applied Sciences	Experiential learning theory, integrative approach
Journalism Special Topics: Covering the 75th Anniversary of D-Day (in France)	Media and Entertainment	Transformative learning theory, experiential learning theory

From Table 15.1, the majority of the faculty leaders used Kolb's experiential learning theory as the theoretical foundations for their curriculum. The constructivist, integrative, and transformative learning theories were the second most frequently used pedagogical theories across the chapters. Other theories and approaches, such as the backward design approach, thematic approach, and place-based approach were used less frequently. Refer to Chapter 3 of this volume for descriptions about the various learning theories.

Intercultural Competencies in Class Activities, Tasks, and Assignments

The items listed are not an exhaustive list of class activities, tasks, and assignments used in study abroad programs. However, they are the ones most frequently used in the programs introduced in this book. For the purposes of the current discussion, nine categories of the most frequently used class activities, tasks, and assignments designed and implemented for facilitating intercultural competencies in our faculty-led programs are presented in Figure 15.2.

Table 15.2: Frequency of Use of Intercultural Competency in Class Activities

Class activities	Frequency of use
Assignments (pre, during, post)	17
Site Visits (schools/museums/concerts)	16
Navigating/Getting to Know the Place and Transportation	10
Cultural/Place-based Learning Lessons and Recreation Activities	5
Local Cuisine – Preparation & Dining out/Dining with Locals	5
Service Learning and Partnership with Locals	4
Lectures/Seminars	4
Homestay	2
Grocery Shopping	2

Assignments

Of the nine categories under discussion, "assignments" is the one in which all faculty leaders integrated intercultural competencies. These assignments were administered in three stages: before, during, and after the program, as tabulated in Table 15.3. Table 15.4 lists the top three intercultural competencies emphasized in these assignments.

Table 15.3: Summary of Assignment Types

Pre-Program	During the Program	Post Program
• Expectation essay • Pre-production research • In-flight letter	• Class presentation during school visit • Site assessment form • Daily journal/photo reflection • Travel journal	• Postproduction assignment • Final group presentation • Reflection essay • Final assignment

Table 15.4: Top Three Intercultural Competencies in Assignments

Knowledge	Skills	Attitudes
• Content knowledge • Self-awareness • Understanding different worldviews	• Communication • Teamwork • Creative thinking and problem-solving	• Curiosity • Stepping outside comfort zone • Empathy

As seen in Tables 15.3 and 15.4, the intercultural competencies embedded in assignments help in shaping global citizens who can work with others through teamwork and express a sense of curiosity to research and develop life-long learning. In addition, the course content knowledge provides opportunities for the students to learn beyond the classroom settings by connecting what is in the textbook to what is out in the world.

Site Visits (Schools/Museums/Concerts)

All the programs included site visits in their daily itinerary. Varying depending on the discipline, these visits consisted of school visits, museums, concerts, court systems, battlefields, and research centers, to name a few. Table 15.5 identifies the main intercultural competencies experienced during site visits.

Table 15.5: Top Three Intercultural Competencies in Site Visits

Knowledge	Skills	Attitudes
• Academic content • Culture-specific knowledge • Cultural self-awareness and understanding	• Observation & interpretation • Analysis • Problem-solving	• Open-minded • Flexibility & adaptability • Respect

By carefully selecting appropriate destinations for site visits, faculty leaders can encourage the students to focus on their observation and analytical skills. These experiences provide students with opportunities to practice open-mindedness and respect when interacting with people from other cultures.

Navigating and Getting to Know the Places and Transportation

Although traveling to places was not one of the graded assessments in study abroad courses, students exhibited skills such as communication and teamwork by navigating from one destination to another. Some faculty leaders were more intentional in assigning navigation activities, such as scavenger hunts and allowing the students to explore the location (Johnston, Chapter 11), while others allowed the students to map out the route to their destination (Ananth,

Chapter 5). Many of the students had never experienced public transportation in the United States and suddenly having to rely on it during study abroad was an eye-opening experience for many of them (e.g., Lim & Reed, Chapter 4; Chaney, Chapter 7; Graham, Chapter 9). Table 15.6 highlights the most common intercultural competencies in navigation tasks.

Table 15.6: Top Three Intercultural Competencies in Navigation Tasks

Knowledge	Skills	Attitudes
• Geographic awareness • Culture-specific knowledge • Self-awareness	• Planning and navigating • Communication • Teamwork and problem solving	• Risk taking • Stepping outside one's comfort zone • Adaptability

These navigation tasks allow students the opportunity to develop attitudes such as risk-taking and adaptability by using the local language to communicate and navigate in the foreign country. Using skills such as planning, navigating, and problem-solving in real life situations allows students to expand their capacities and help to increase their geographic awareness. In addition, traveling in a group ensures students' safety and accountability to each other as required in the majority of the study abroad courses. Finally, as students adapt to navigating abroad, unanticipated issues arise which allow the group to brainstorm and generate alternative solutions.

Cultural and Place-Based Learning and Recreation Activities

Some faculty leaders organized specific cultural activities such as playing the Taiko drum in Japan, experiencing farm activities in Cuba, or mountain hiking in Argentina. These cultural and place-based activities were assigned to immerse the students to experience the country's unique features and help to promote the intercultural competencies displayed in Table 15.7.

Table 15.7: Top Three Intercultural Competencies in Place-Based Activities

Knowledge	Skills	Attitudes
• Understanding others' worldviews • Historical awareness • Cultural self-awareness	• Observation • Communication • Collaboration	• Stepping outside one's comfort zone • Open-mindedness • Respect and empathy

While learning about tobacco cultivation and cigar production in Viñales (Chaney, Chapter 7) or learning from professional Taiko performers in Tokyo (Nozu, Chapter 6) students have the opportunity to observe, communicate, and work collaboratively. They learn to step outside their comfort zones developing empathy and respect for a different worldview by comparing them with their own cultures.

Local Cuisine and People – Preparation and Dining Out

Enjoying the local cuisine was integrated into the itinerary of the study abroad courses in various ways. For example, through cooking lessons in Vienna, dining out with locals in London and Normandy, or simply independently dining out in France and Singapore, students were able to authentically immerse themselves in an important aspect of everyday life. These intercultural competencies are listed in Table 15.8. Organizing special occasions to enjoy the local traditional cuisine can become opportunities for students to develop tolerance and adaptability towards food as well as important practical skills of observation and communication.

Table 15.8: Top Three Intercultural Competencies in Local Cuisine and Dining Out Experiences

Knowledge	Skills	Attitudes
• Culture-specific knowledge • Cultural self-awareness • Understanding others' worldviews	• Communication • Listen; observe; relate • Problem solving	• Stepping outside one's comfort zone • Risk taking • Adaptability

Service Learning and Partnerships with Local People

Several faculty leaders organized service outreach activities for students to work with the local community during their study abroad. For example, in Cuba, students had the opportunity to volunteer and help in school restoration; in Japan and Singapore, students partnered with locals to teach in public schools; and in China, co-curricular activities such as soccer and dumpling-making were assigned to students to build lasting relationships with the local citizens. These intercultural competencies skills are listed in Table 15.9. Working alongside Chinese students in China (Sokoya, Chapter 12) or teaching an elementary school in Japan (Ananth, Chapter 5) students are provided with the opportunity to cultivate language and communication skills, while also advancing patience, respect, and empathy for the people around them.

Table 15.9: Top Three Intercultural Competencies in Service Learning with Locals

Knowledge	Skills	Attitudes
• Culture-specific knowledge • Cultural self-awareness • Content knowledge	• Communication • Teamwork • Listen, observe, relate	• Respect • Withholding judgement • Empathy

Lectures and Seminars

Of the nine most frequently used class activities, tasks, and assignments, lectures and seminars ranked the lowest for integration of intercultural competencies. That is because lectures and seminars primarily target learning content knowledge and do not generally focus on developing particular skills and attitudes. From the chapters, we learned that by conducting lectures and seminars outside of the classroom, students can potentially develop skills such as professionalism and attitudes such as open-mindedness as indicated in Table 15.10.

Table 15.10: Top Intercultural Competencies in Lectures and Seminars

Knowledge	Skills	Attitudes
• Academic content knowledge • Culture-specific knowledge	• Listen; observe; evaluate and interpret • Emerging professionalism • Critical thinking and reflection	• Stepping outside one's comfort zone • Open-mindedness

Homestays

Two of the study abroad programs in this volume incorporated homestays, Cuba and Normandy. Staying with host families allowed students to participate in an immersive local experience. The homestay provided students with an opportunity to perceive how local citizens live their everyday lives. The intercultural competencies observed are listed in Table 15.11.

Table 15.11 Top Intercultural Competencies in Homestay Experiences

Knowledge	Skills	Attitudes
• Cultural self-awareness • Understanding others' worldviews • Culture-specific knowledge	• Listen; observe; evaluate and interpret • Communication	• Withholding judgement • Adaptability • Respect

Through daily French immersion in France (Goldberg, Chapter 8) or Spanish in Cuba (Chaney, Chapter 7), homestay programs provide a unique opportunity for students to acquire skills such as communication and interpretation. They can also help in developing attitudes such as withholding judgment and adaptability to foreign cultures and different ways of life as students learn to use non-verbal and verbal strategies to overcome barriers.

Grocery Shopping

The final category is grocery shopping. Some programs, such as the *International Agriculture in Argentina* program, incorporated grocery shopping with scavenger hunt activities, encouraging learning about local food and produce. Another, the *Administering Early Childhood Education* program in Singapore, used it as a first stop for students to stock up on essential items needed for the duration of the course. The intercultural competencies students exhibited are listed in Table 15.12.

Table 15.12: Top Intercultural Competencies in the Grocery Shopping Task

Knowledge	Skills	Attitudes
• Food custom awareness • Global knowledge	• Communication • Problem solving • Teamwork	• Discovery • Tolerating and engaging ambiguity • Respect

Learning to use local currency in Singapore (Lim & Reed, Chapter 4) or purchasing unfamiliar food items as part of the scavenger hunt in Argentina (Johnston, Chapter 11) can be helpful for students to learn to engage with ambiguity in daily life. In the process, students are provided the opportunity to problem-solve and communicate in culturally appropriate ways through negotiating skills in their daily contact with vendors in local markets.

In higher education, it is important to align the findings on the most commonly integrated intercultural competencies in class activities, tasks, and assignments with the student learning outcome articulated in the General Education (Gen Ed) program. The Gen Ed program at any academic institution provides the foundation for the academic standards of that institution. The Gen Ed curriculum at Middle Tennessee State University (MTSU) uses the VALUE rubric developed by the American Association of Colleges and Universities (AAC&U) as the assessment tool for measuring the stated descriptors of intercultural understanding (AAC&U, 2009). The revised 2024 Gen Ed curriculum at MTSU places special emphasis on the achievement of intercultural competencies as one of its cornerstone objectives and articulates the relevant learning outcome as follows:

> "Students will demonstrate intercultural understanding by building knowledge, self-awareness, and conceptions of global and intercultural perspectives, values, systems, and attitudes." (MTSU General Education, n.d.)

Further, the term "intercultural understanding" is explained using descriptors such as cultural self-awareness, knowledge of diverse cultural frameworks, verbal and non-verbal communication, empathy, curiosity, and openness. We have established that the intercultural competencies in the areas of knowledge, skills, and attitudes that our faculty leaders incorporated into their class activities, tasks, and assignments align well with one of the key student learning outcomes in the Gen Ed curriculum as stated earlier. Although formal assessment of intercultural competencies is outside the scope of this volume, we recognize that this is an area for future research.

Student Feedback

Student feedback also demonstrates how intercultural competencies were gained by the students who participated in our faculty-led programs. This data was extracted from the self-reported student feedback sections from each of the chapters in Section II. Table 15.13 lists the knowledge, skills, and attitudes as reported by the students in their feedback.

Table 15.13: Summary of Key Competencies as Self-Reported by Students

Knowledge	Skills	Attitudes
• Cultural self-awareness • Intercultural sensitivity • Awareness of others • Culture-specific knowledge • Academic content knowledge	• Self-assessment • Stress management • Reflection • Decision making • Language skills • Comparing and analyzing • Observing differences • Communication • Teamwork • Technology skills • Listen • Interpret • Evaluation skills	• Confidence • Adaptability • Stepping outside the comfort zone • Open minded • Empathy • Appreciating others • Humility • Determination • Taking risks • Respectful • Curiosity • Flexibility • Tolerance for ambiguity • Discovery

Since a formal assessment for the acquisition of these competencies was not conducted, it is difficult to know conclusively whether there was an increase in student competency as compared to before the program, or if these competencies were retained by them after the program. For this reason, it is critical that faculty leaders conduct pre- and post-assessments to measure gains in intercultural competencies as a study abroad outcome. This is an area for future research.

Caveats and Reflections

We now turn our focus to the voices of the faculty leaders featured in this book. These faculty leaders took the time to pause and reflect on strengths, challenges, and future strategies as they relate to their respective programs. We believe that more work needs to be done to ensure that not only students, but also the faculty, have gained intercultural competencies and are strategic in incorporating this aspect into the syllabus.

Strengths

From Section II (Chapters 4-14), three major strengths emerged overall: program effectiveness, course learning outcomes, and employability of students. In terms of program effectiveness, all the faculty leaders indicated that the program goals had been met. This is important as all faculty need to ensure that the syllabus goals are met regardless of whether the program is conducted in person, online, or as a study abroad. Ensuring that all the academic goals are met in addition to the reported gains in intercultural competencies by the students through study abroad is indeed remarkable.

The second strength observed by the faculty leaders was the students' reflections highlighting gains regarding intercultural competencies as a study abroad achievement. Students who participated in the study abroad programs not only took a leap of faith by enrolling in a program outside their comfort zone and in unfamiliar territory, but many also indicated that the study abroad experience changed their worldviews and perspectives in life. Several of these students were first-generation college students and experienced their first overseas travel through the program. Other students, such as those studying Journalism, experienced working with the locals and gained firsthand knowledge of interviewing on foreign soil. Students representing language-specific programs, such as French and Japanese, showed improvements in their foreign language proficiency as a result of their study abroad participation.

The faculty leaders identified the third strength as how the study abroad experience places the students in an advantageous position in their future careers. For example, intercultural engagement is considered one of the most important criteria that employers seek in their prospective employees. Being able to work with a diverse workforce and being a team player will help to enhance the overall mission of any prospective career choice.

Challenges

There are undoubtedly numerous challenges to overcome when conducting study abroad programs. Most of the challenges that the faculty leaders reflected upon pertain to the pre-departure administrative details of the program. Generally, most faculty strength resides in their content knowledge, yet when leading a study abroad program, they also become responsible for marketing and student recruitment. If the number of enrolled students falls below the minimum threshold, the class is likely to be canceled. Next, the high program cost is usually a major deterring factor for students. Thus, new faculty leaders must remain mindful of their time and effort commitments that are necessary in setting up new programs as students might drop out of the program due to the cost involved, which then causes enrollment to fall below the minimum threshold. Additionally, finding the appropriate contacts and logistical support in the countries of study becomes crucial for the course program to succeed. Sourcing for the appropriate provider can become an additional challenge for faculty leaders preparing programs. Using a third-party provider can alleviate the logistical burden to a certain extent, but outsourcing to outside providers often limits the time allocated to delivering the content knowledge that the faculty leader might desire. In addition, travel restrictions and approved destinations by regulatory agencies can pose additional challenges for faculty leaders.

Another challenge, as reflected upon by the faculty leaders, relates to the experiences of the students when they are abroad. Traveling to a new country in a different time zone is already difficult, and having to adjust to jet lag and study at the same time can be physically draining for students. Faculty leaders must consider innovative ways to keep the students focused on tasks amidst the fatigue and time constraints of completing the required syllabus content in a short-term study abroad as is expected for the full semester course. Finally, some faculty described the lack of meeting times and assessment measures prior to the study abroad as additional layers to the overall challenges of the program.

Future Strategies

As described by the faculty, implementing a study abroad is not an easy process. From pre- to post-program, faculty leaders work on course conception, seek approval from the university, market the course, recruit students, plan logistics, collaborate with overseas partners, chaperone students abroad, execute the program, and debrief at the program's end.

In Chapter 8, Goldberg provided a list of practical suggestions that she deemed successful after 14 years of taking students to France. In addition, several faculty members decided that in the future they would include more rigorous pre-departure meetings with students either in person or online to ensure a smoother transition during the course abroad. All faculty leaders described the importance of intentionally including intercultural competencies throughout the course assignments. This is an important dimension to develop in the future. For the post-program stage, maintaining documentation of the student reflections is also important. In addition, designing and collaborating on a multidisciplinary study abroad program can assist in recruiting more students which can help ensure the minimum number of class enrollment is achieved. Finally, sharing the workload in collaborative programs proved to be an insightful suggestion.

RECOMMENDATIONS FROM THE EDITORS

The following are recommendations to consider when designing an interculturally engaging faculty-led study abroad program. Faculty leaders and administrators who are interested in incorporating the ideas and multiple perspectives offered in this edited volume can help maximize the benefits for their students by focusing on intercultural competencies. The following recommendations can help with such goals.

Recommendation 1

At the most fundamental level, intentional integration of intercultural competence is a key ingredient in building a study abroad course syllabus. These competencies should not only be integral to the curricular and co-curricular activities but also to the extra-curricular activities conducted beyond the classroom. It is also a key element that should be clearly articulated in the vision, mission statement, and strategic planning by the administrators. An example of a strategic plan articulated in "Strategic Goals 2021-2026" by the MTSU Office of International Affairs reads as follows:

> "We will be a community leader in internationalization by facilitating programming that supports international competency, inclusion, acceptance, tolerance, and empathy."
> (MTSU Impact Report, 2022, p. 3)

Following through with clear articulation, universities commit to a straightforward prioritization with respect to faculty training, faculty support for conferences and workshops, and expansion for events and programs at the local level. These additional resources necessitate intentional allocation of funding for such endeavors.

Recommendation 2

For students, all three aspects of intercultural competence, content knowledge, skills, and attitudes, become indispensable for productive engagement in their college lives as well as in their local community. Further, acquiring intercultural competence reveals as a transferable asset for better employment prospects both domestically and internationally. For example, competencies such as flexibility, risk-taking, foreign language skills, and budgeting that may have been developed during study abroad can be directly applied at the place of employment both in-country and abroad. It is crucial to effectively articulate these competencies on job application materials. See Appendix 15.1 for key terms/phrases to articulate intercultural competencies in students' resumes.

Recommendation 3

Intercultural competence is a universal concept and is relevant to all disciplines. Arasaratnam (2014) reflects that there is not enough interdisciplinary research work being done in this area. There is a need for faculty scholars and leaders to look beyond their disciplines and create multiple perspectives on intercultural competence development. The collaborative efforts of faculty from across disciplines lead to collective wisdom which then becomes a common resource. This edited book is one example of such a cross-disciplinary collaborative effort, though more effort is needed in this area.

Recommendation 4

Emerging as another area requiring attention is employing appropriate assessment measures to gauge the acquisition and retention of students' intercultural competencies. It is critical that faculty leaders evaluate intercultural competencies in assignments and include it in the grading criteria. As a first step, the grading criteria for the course must include formative and summative assessments that directly target intercultural competency skills and attitudes. Some examples of effective assignments could be reflections, papers, photos, videos, and electronic portfolios showcasing some of these assignments as evidence. Students' self and peer evaluations could also be an important component besides the faculty leaders' evaluations. In addition to the direct measures mentioned above, indirect assessment tasks such as pre- and post-program surveys and interviews could target strategic questions representing intercultural competencies. All the direct and indirect measures can offer multiple perspectives to illustrate the growth and change in students across time relating to knowledge, skills, and attitudes.

Recommendation 5

Another recommendation relating to the previous point is the importance of showing a connection between assessment results and the learning outcomes that were set up at the beginning of the course. Frequently, assessments selectively monitor only content knowledge. By the time the assessment results are generated, assessment fatigue sets in and the crucial step of linking the results with the course objectives and learning outcomes set at the beginning of the course may inadvertently be forgotten. The advice here is to remember to link the assessment results with the initial course objectives sooner than later. In doing this, the fruits of conducting multi-perspective assessments can be invested back into the cycle to reap better results next time.

Recommendation 6

It would be beneficial for faculty leaders and administrators involved with study abroad courses to familiarize themselves with current, prevalent theoretical foundations and conceptual models of intercultural competence. This is not only important for the purpose of aligning course curricula with reliable research-based pedagogies, but also to raise awareness regarding what is current and helpful in the field. By participating in study abroad conferences and workshops, faculty leaders can stay updated with effective pedagogies and outcome-based practices. For those interested, exploring the World Council on Intercultural and Global Competence (https://iccglobal.org) may be a good place to start.

Recommendation 7

Finally, consider becoming an advocate for raising awareness regarding the value of intercultural competencies for all courses—study abroad, online, or in the classroom. It may be as simple as talking with the higher administration about including clearly articulated goals on the development of intercultural competencies in the strategic planning documents and policies. Another step may be inviting colleagues from multiple disciplines to a brown bag lunch and initiating a discussion on this topic. A small step is to introduce the concept of intercultural competence in your classes and spend time with students to define, identify, and prioritize the components of knowledge, skills, and attitudes. Then, systematically design and assess the activities, tasks, and assignments in the course curriculum.

FINAL THOUGHTS

As we conclude this chapter as well as the edited volume, we want to express our hope that the ideas and perspectives on the curricular design and implementation of study abroad programs that integrate intercultural competence presented here will be a useful resource for anyone interested in leading or administering a short-term, faculty-led study abroad program. In this final chapter, key findings within nine categories of the most-used class activities, tasks, and assignments to facilitate intercultural competencies as well as the reflective voices from the 11 case study chapters of Section II were highlighted. We also offered recommendations with additional resources to readers who wish to incorporate these ideas and perspectives into their own study abroad course curricula. In the end, the long view focuses on the overall advancement of the individual learner with a keen eye on sustaining growth of their intercultural and global competencies. In the words of Dr. LaNitra Berger, President and Chair of Board of Directors of 2022 NAFSA (Association of International Educators), "Addressing global challenges requires us to possess both tangible skills and the ability to sit with and interpret complexity and ambiguity in our work" (Berger, as cited in White et al., 2022). In other words, our future college graduates can be fully prepared to face global challenges only when they acquire both tangible content knowledge as well as intangible intercultural competencies.

REFERENCES

Arasaratnam, L. A. (2014). Ten years of research in intercultural communication competence (2003-2013): A retrospective. *Journal of Intercultural Communication, 35*. https://immi.se/oldwebsite/nr35/arasaratnam.html

Association of American Colleges and Universities (AAC&U). (2009). *Value rubric*. Retrieved from https://www.aacu.org/initiatives/value-initiative/value-rubrics

Mahatma Gandhi quotes. (n.d.). *BrainyQuote*. Retrieved August 4, 2023, from https://www.brainyquote.com/quotes/mahatma_gandhi_160857

Middle Tennessee State University Office of International Affairs (2022). *Annual impact report 2021-2022*. Retrieved from https://issuu.com/mtsumag/docs/mtsu_ia_annual_report_2021-22.

Middle Tennessee State University (n.d.). *General education*. Retrieved from https://www.mtsu.edu/gen_ed/.

SUNY COIL (n.d.) *Student guide*. https://slcny.libguides.com/sunycoil/benefits

White, C. D., LaFleur, D., & Hartman, J. N. (2022, May 25). *International education professional competencies for 2022 and beyond* [PowerPoint slides]. NAFSA. https://www.nafsa.org/sites/default/files/media/document/IE-Competency-AC22-5-25.pdf

World Council on Intercultural and Global Competence (n.d.) *Homepage*. https://iccglobal.org/

APPENDICES

Appendix 15.1: Articulating International Experiences Handout

(The contents of this handout were adapted from the SUNY COIL Student Guide website with permission.)

Articulating International Experiences on Your Resume: Some Key Phrases to Keep in Mind

Below are some thought-provoking phrases to help you articulate international experiences on your resume. Combine these ideas with your personal experiences to develop unique, individualized points for your own resume.

- **Learned about other cultures:**
    - Adapted to foreign cultures and ways of life
    - Incorporated local customs into my daily routines
    - Overcame societal differences to promote cultural understanding
    - Gained a greater appreciation for diversity and culture

- **Learned through Interaction with Others**
    - Developed negotiation skills through daily contact with vendors in local markets

- Developed a better understanding of foreign cultures within their own unique contexts

- **Developed Language and Communication Skills**
    - Cultivated language and communication skills through contact with people from around the world.
    - Encouraged open communication between locals and foreigners
    - Learned to use non-verbal and verbal communication to overcome communication and language barriers
- **Flexibility and Risk-Taking**
    - Learned how to adapt to unanticipated situations and improvise new plans due to periodic travel mishaps and unexpected events
    - Modified my way of life to maximize exposure and opportunities for learning among foreign cultures
- **Responsibility, Planning, and Budgeting**
    - Developed creative solutions to maximize travel experience on a limited budget
    - Budgeted months of world travel on $ (insert amount)

About the Authors

Alphabetical order by last name

Priya Ananth is a Professor of Japanese in the Department of World Languages, Literatures, and Cultures at Middle Tennessee State University. She earned her Ph.D. in East Asian Languages and Literatures from The Ohio State University. Her teaching and research focus on issues related to applied Japanese linguistics, Japanese second language acquisition, Japanese pedagogy, and study abroad. She has successfully led short-term study abroad programs in Japan.

James Chaney is an Associate Professor in the Department of Global Studies and Human Geography at Middle Tennessee State University. His research focuses on Latin America, immigration, and ethnic geographies. He has conducted extensive fieldwork in Latin America and regularly leads study abroad programs in the region.

Christine C. Eschenfelder joined MTSU's School of Journalism and Strategic Media in Fall 2015. She received her Ph.D. in Mass Communication from the University of Florida. She also has professional experience working in television news. Her research focuses on broadcast journalism education, newsroom diversity, and women in broadcasting.

Rehab (Rubie) Ghazal is the Associate Vice Provost for International Affairs. She is a skilled Global Educator with experience in student engagement, corporate partnerships, and program evaluation and accreditation. Her research and work focuses on promoting cultural understanding in educational settings and developing the professional skills of English as Second Language (ESL) teachers and administrators.

Nancy Sloan Goldberg taught French language and literature for 32 years at Middle Tennessee State University (MTSU). She created the *Summer Abroad in Normandy* program and served as a member of the MTSU Education Abroad Committee. Goldberg, a respected scholar, is the author of two books and twenty articles on French novels and poetry of World War I.

Stacey Graham is a Research Professor at the Center for Historic Preservation at Middle Tennessee State University. She teaches courses in the History Department, including graduate courses in the Public History program. She received her M.A. and Ph.D. from the University of California, Los Angeles.

Tony V. Johnston has taught courses abroad for 23 of his 28-year higher education career. He has taught seven different courses abroad, all designed for and adapted to the study abroad environment. He advocates and pursues collaborative and interdisciplinary teaching abroad and has taught alongside faculty members from five other departments at MTSU.

Seok Jeng Jane Lim is an Associate Professor in the Early Childhood Education program at Middle Tennessee State University in Murfreesboro, Tennessee, USA. Her research interests include study abroad, professional development, and the issue of bullying among underrepresented populations, specifically refugee children.

Joseph E. Morgan has a primary research focus on the dramatic music, theory, and aesthetics of Germany in the early 19th century. His secondary topic of interest is popular music and culture. He currently serves as a tenured Associate Professor in the School of Music at Middle Tennessee State University.

Mako Nozu is a Senior Instructor of Japanese at the University of South Florida. She is the Japanese section head in the Department of World Languages. She teaches the beginning Japanese and Japanese calligraphy courses. She is interested in task-based language teaching and implements tasks in her lesson plans.

Jason Lee Pettigrew completed his Ph.D. at the University of Tennessee in Knoxville. He is an Associate Professor of Spanish at Middle Tennessee State University, where he teaches a variety of courses on the Spanish language and Latin American literature. His research interests primarily lie in contemporary Latin American poetry. While in graduate school, he developed an interest in study abroad after accompanying a group of students to Spain.

Karen Nourse Reed, Ph.D., is an Associate Professor at Middle Tennessee State University where she works at the James E. Walker Library. She began her career at MTSU in 2013, serving as the Education Librarian, before transitioning into the role of Research & Data Librarian in 2022.

Sesan Kim Sokoya is a Professor of Management at Middle Tennessee State University and serves as the Associate Dean for Graduate and Executive Education. He has lectured in colleges and universities in the United States and abroad. Kim Sokoya has been very active in international education at MTSU and has led study abroad trips for MTSU students to many countries in the past 20 years.

Robert Summers serves as the Vice Provost for International Affairs overseeing the Center for Asian Studies; the Center for Chinese Music and Culture; Education Abroad; International Admissions and Recruitment; and International Student and Scholar Services. He is a trained linguist and faculty member in the Department of World Languages, Literatures, and Cultures.

Lee Miller Wade, Ph.D., has over 20 years of experience in the criminal justice system. Currently, Dr. Wade is the interim Associate Dean of the College of Behavioral and Health Sciences and former chair of Criminal Justice Administration at Middle Tennessee State University.

Press Acknowledgements

Generous support has been provided by the following individuals and organizations:

External Reviewers
Keshia Abraham
Karen McBride

Assistants to the Editors
William "Wesley" Birdwell
Tabitha Brown

Proofreaders
Ginelle Baskin
Emma Sullivan

Consultant
Angel Peterson

Middle Tennessee State University

Operations and financial support from Walker Library include:
Jayme Brunson, Administration
Kathleen Schmand, Dean

Consultations and operational support from:
College of Business
Contract Office
MTSU Institutional Review Board
Office of the University Counsel

Index

active learning, 8, 11, 32-33, 113-114
administering early childhood program, 8, 57-58, 60-61, 71-72, 75, 246
agribusiness, 181, 190
American Association of Colleges and Universities (AAC&U), 14, 44, 48, 50, 245, 252, 258
American Council on the Teaching of Foreign Languages (ACTFL), 129-130, 133, 139, 141, 143, 147, 246
appropriate assessment measures, 256
Austria, 5, 8, 16, 173-174, 178
Argentina, 5, 9, 179, 182-186, 189-190, 193-194, 246, 249, 251-252
backward design, 46, 51, 77-78, 224, 246
barrister, 214
broadcast journalism(ist), 225-226, 261
camera, 224, 226-228, 235-236
campus internationalization, 30, 44-45, 48
caveats and reflections, 56, 70, 89, 106, 124, 140, 161, 177, 190, 204, 219, 237, 245, 253
Center for Historic Preservation (CHP), 149, 151, 162-163, 261
China, 5, 9, 60, 63, 73, 108, 169, 195-207, 246, 250
co-curricular activities, 9, 14, 195-196, 201-203, 250, 255
collaborative
    approach, 95-96, 98, 167, 170
    learning, 46, 48, 51, 168, 170, 177
Common European Framework of Reference for Languages (CEFR), 129-130, 141
community organization, 21
constructivism, 30-31, 41, 108
    constructivist approach, 30, 95, 98, 209, 213
correction(s), 9, 209, 211, 215-216, 218
court(s), 9, 172, 209-212, 214-218, 221, 248
COVID, 1-3, 8, 16, 22, 33, 60, 79, 97, 138, 153, 161, 182, 204, 211, 226, 236-237
criminal justice system, 9, 209-213, 215, 218, 220, 262
cross-cultural awareness, *see* cultural awareness
Cuba, 5, 8, 113-128, 246, 249-251
cultural
    awareness, 8, 13, 34, 40, 42, 45, 57, 96, 122, 174, 182-183, 203
    sites, 8, 63, 201
culture shock, 20, 45, 187
curriculum
    design, 7, 30, 46, 140
    development, 14, 20, 51, 89
Developmental Model of Intercultural Sensitivity (DMIS), 35-36, 38, 40-42, 48
early childhood education, 59, 61, 68-69, 72, 75, 251, 261
education diplomacy, 57, 71
England, 9, 156, 210, 214-217, 223-224, 226-227, 231-233, 241
    see also United Kingdom (U.K.)
English Common Law, 210
environment of international management, 199
essential competency, 169
evaluation, 7, 11, 18, 20, 22-23, 38-39, 45, 56, 67, 72, 78, 87, 104-106, 116, 122-123, 130, 138-139, 159, 161, 176, 184, 188-189, 197, 203, 209, 217, 219, 237, 253, 256, 261
experiential
    activities, 79, 89, 114
    learning, 8, 15, 31-32, 44, 50, 71, 89, 95-96, 99, 103, 107, 125, 129-130, 141, 149, 154, 167, 169, 182, 191, 195, 205, 209-211, 223-224, 228, 239, 246
    theory, 31-32, 41, 51, 58, 63, 77-78, 81, 223, 239, 246

faculty-led program, 1, 4, 6-9, 11, 15-16, 18, 24-26, 29, 43, 48, 50, 55, 57, 60, 70, 77, 79, 89, 113, 115, 124-125, 140, 150, 163, 167, 195, 209, 238, 245, 247, 253-255, 257, 261
faculty-led short-term study abroad (FLSTSA), *see* faculty-led program
faculty-led signature program, *see* faculty-led program
faculty-led study abroad, *see* faculty-led program
financial aid, 14, 21, 26, 107, 132
foreign
    culture, 132, 151, 251, 258-259
    language, 43, 49, 79, 89, 129, 140, 147, 254, 256
formative assessment, 11, 87, 98, 104, 122-123, 159, 176, 189
France, 5, 9, 16, 129-131, 133-136, 139, 142, 144-145, 147, 215, 223-224, 227, 229, 231-234, 238, 240-241, 246, 250-251, 255
French immersion program, 129
general education (gen ed) program, 15, 252, 258
geography(ies), 8, 17, 68, 75, 78, 113-116, 121, 123-126, 155, 180, 246, 261
geopolitics, 115, 121
geopolitical, 114-117, 123-124, 150
global
    citizens, 25, 44-45, 107, 210, 220, 248
    citizenship, 57-58, 69, 71, 246
guest lecture, 81, 90, 188, 193, 198-199, 204, 207
high-impact practices, 44
historic preservation, 8, 149-151, 154-155, 160-163, 165-166, 261
history of education abroad, 13
Homeland Security, 211, 220
homestay, 8, 115-118, 123, 130-132, 134-135, 137, 140, 147, 247, 251
imaginative geography(ies), 113-114, 121, 123-125, 246
immersion assumption, 39, 41
incarceration, 215-217
incubator, 198, 200, 207
inquiry-based learning, 47
integrative approach *see* integrative learning
integrative learning, 168, 177, 209, 212, 215-216, 246
intensity factors in intercultural experiences, 40
intentional integration, 255
intercultural
    awareness, *see* cultural awareness
    curriculum, 11
    engagement, 1, 4, 9, 65, 237, 245, 254
    learning, 10-11, 20, 33, 39-45, 49-50, 52, 77, 107, 155, 163, 205, 224, 238
    mindset, 36, 245
    workshops, 41, 50
Intercultural Communicative Competence Model, 34, 49
intercultural competence (definition of), 11
Intercultural Development Continuum, 35-36
Intercultural Development Inventory (IDI), 37, 41, 49-50
interdisciplinary, 6, 24-25, 47, 50-51, 116, 163, 177, 239, 256, 261
international agriculture, 9, 179, 182, 190-191, 194, 246, 251
international trade theories, 196, 199
internationalization, 10, 13-15, 18, 21, 23, 25, 30, 34-35, 43-45, 48-49, 52, 71, 79, 162, 255
Japan, 5, 8, 51, 77-93, 95-101, 103-104, 106-111, 246, 249-250, 254, 261-262
journalism, 9, 223-228, 231, 233-235, 237-238, 241, 246, 254, 261
language proficiency assessment, 133
law enforcement, 210, 212, 218-219
lawyer, 214-215
learning trip, 95-99, 101, 103-104
leisure, 63, 78, 81, 84, 90, 120, 188, 236
    see also recreation
logistics, 7, 19, 55, 61, 79-80, 98, 116, 132, 153, 169, 180-182, 190, 197, 211, 219, 222, 226, 255
material culture, 150-151, 154, 159, 162, 165
misconceptions, 114-115, 124

multicultural awareness, *see* cultural awareness
multinational corporations (MNCs), 9, 190, 196-201, 204
multiple disciplines, 4, 6, 29, 245, 257
museum, 63, 73, 80-81, 84, 90, 93, 108-109, 114, 126-127, 131, 134, 138, 142-146, 150, 154-156, 158-161, 163, 165, 170, 173-175, 183, 212-213, 215-217, 221, 224, 228, 230, 238, 240, 247-248
National Association of Schools of Music (NASM), 169, 177
national competitiveness, 199-200, 205
newsgathering, 9, 224, 227
Normandy, 8, 129, 131, 133, 140, 142-146, 223-225, 229, 232, 240, 246, 250-251, 261
Oral Proficiency Interview (OPI), 133, 139, 141
organized crime, 213
Parliament, 165, 211-212, 221
pedagogical strategy(ies), 36-37, 47
performance-based learning, 46, 48
place-based learning, 8, 113-114, 116-117, 120-121, 150, 154, 247, 249
political science, 8, 113, 116, 124, 211
post-program, 8, 18, 23, 26, 56, 66, 86, 89, 103, 121-122, 138, 158, 166, 176, 187, 202, 236, 255-256
pre-departure orientation, 19-20, 26, 132, 197, 226
pre-program, 61, 63, 66-67, 80, 98, 116, 132-133, 154, 169-170, 181, 197, 211, 226, 247
preschool(s), 8, 58-59, 63-64, 67, 75
prison, 215, 217
problem-based learning, 46-47, 50-51
Process Model of Intercultural Competence, 34-35, 39-40
project-based learning, 46-47
public history, 151, 153, 162-163, 261
public-private partnership, 198, 200-201, 205
public transportation, 12, 65, 92, 99, 106, 118, 126, 131, 138, 156-157, 171, 203, 216, 28, 230-231, 240, 249

recreation, 183, 185-188, 193, 247, 249
    see also leisure
reflection-based learning, 46-47, 49
Scotland, 5, 8, 149-154, 156, 158, 161-166, 210, 212, 215, 217, 226, 246
    see also United Kingdom (U.K.)
self-reflection, 33, 38-39, 175-176
service learning, 8, 11, 24, 48, 113-114, 117, 119, 122-123, 125, 127, 130, 137, 142, 154, 247, 250
short-term faculty-led study abroad programs, *see faculty-led program*
short-term study abroad, *see faculty-led program*
Singapore, 5, 7-8, 24, 57-70, 72-73, 75, 246, 250, 252
social media, 81, 87, 89, 226-229, 232, 234, 237, 242
solicitor, *see* lawyer
student engagement, 10-11, 129, 261
student
    feedback, 7, 23, 56, 69, 86, 88, 105, 123, 139, 161, 189, 203-204, 218-219, 237, 245, 252
    health, 20, 22
    learning outcomes (SLOs), 43-44, 218, 252
    media, 224, 227-228, 241
    partnerships, 86
summative assessment, 11, 67, 87, 104, 122, 159, 176, 189, 256
textbook, 46, 62, 78, 96, 168, 180, 196, 224, 248
theater, 81, 183
thematic-based learning, 46, 77, 246
transformational learning theory, 32-33
travel reporting, 224, 226
UNESCO (United Nations Educational, Scientific and Cultural Organisation) World Heritage Site, 149-151, 164
United Kingdom (U.K.),
    For specific member countries, see England and Scotland
University of South Florida (USF) Japan, 8, 95, 97-99, 102-103, 105, 107, 246, 262
VALUE rubric, 44, 48, 252, 258
VARK modalities, 130, 246

volunteer(ing, s), 84-85, 114, 119, 122-123, 152, 250
World Council on Intercultural and Global Competence, 257-258
world food supply, 181

www.ingramcontent.com/pod-product-compliance
Lightning Source LLC
Chambersburg PA
CBHW082037230426
43670CB00016B/2683